United States—Comanche Relations
The Reservation Years

William T. Hagan

D1160818

University of Oklahoma Press : Norman and London

To Charlotte
by any name a great companion on the trail

Library of Congress Cataloging-in-Publication Data

Hagan, William Thomas.
United States–Comanche relations : the reservation years /
William T. Hagan.
p. cm.
Reprint. Originally published: New Haven : Yale University
Press, 1976.
Includes bibliographical references.
ISBN 0-8061-2275-7
1. Comanche Indians—Government relations. 2. Comanche
Indians—Reservations. 3. Indians of North America—
Government relations—1869–1934. I. Title.
E99.C85H26 1990   89-29029
323.1′1974073—dc20   CIP

Copyright © 1976 by Yale University. New edition copyright
© 1990 by the University of Oklahoma Press, Norman, Pub-
lishing Division of the University. All rights reserved. Manu-
factured in the U.S.A. First printing.

Contents

Illustrations

Preface to the Paperback Edition

Since this study of the Comanches was first published in 1976 it has remained the most frequently cited source of information on these people during their reservation period. Some additional work has been done on particular phases of Comanche life; for example, Robert John Stahl's "Farming among the Kiowa, Comanche, Kiowa Apache, and Wichita" (Ph.D. dissertation, University of Oklahoma, 1978). Quanah Parker continues to attract writers, the most recent evidence being H. Glenn Jordan and Peter MacDonald, Jr.'s "Quanah Parker: Patriot or Opportunist," in *Indian Leaders* (Oklahoma Historical Society, 1979), and my own "Quanah Parker," in R. David Edmunds's *American Indian Leaders* (University of Nebraska Press, 1980). Quanah and his mother, Cynthia Parker, were recognized by pop culture in three comic books published in 1977 and 1978. What is even more remarkable is that the Texas State Historical Society has made these available in paperback, slightly censored, in Jack Jackson's *Comanche Moon* (Rip Off Press, Inc., 1979). On the more serious side, two studies of missionary activity, Bruce David Forbes's "John Jasper Methvin: Methodist 'Missionary to the Western Tribes,'" in Clyde A. Milner II and Floyd A. O'Neil's *Churchmen and the Western Indians, 1820–1920* (University of Oklahoma Press, 1985), and Rebecca Herring's "Their Work Was Never Done: Women Missionaries on the Kiowa-Comanche Reservation," in *Chronicles of Oklahoma* 64 (1986): 68–83, tell us relatively little about the Comanches and much about the problems of the missionaries.

What is missing is an attempt to do for the Comanches what Loretta Fowler has done for the Arapahos: tell the story from the Indian viewpoint and bring it into the modern period. One of my colleagues, Morris Foster, may meet this need.

A study of the Comanches since 1907 would trace the tribe's further deterioration as they continued to lose land, as intermarriage with whites and members of other tribes increased, and as tribal unity—never a strong point of the Comanches—was further weakened by factionalism. The nadir for the Comanches must have come during the depression years of the 1930s, when many Indians were forced to leave the vicinity of the old reservation and seek employment wherever they could find it. World War II accelerated the process as job opportunities multiplied in the defense industry and Comanches joined the burgeoning ranks of war workers. Young Comanches entered military service in large numbers, many of them as volunteers, which was appropriate for a people that still cherished their warrior past. Today the focal point of the Comanche Tribal Complex is a monument that lists the names of about 350 veterans, with another 200 to be added, testifying to the contributions that Comanches have made to the armed forces of the United States, contributions out of all proportion to their small population.

The post–World War II period was a difficult time for Comanches as defense plants closed production lines and the armed forces sharply reduced their numbers. Those Comanches drifting back to what has been the reservation area fell into the old pattern of living from hand to mouth, working at odd jobs and looking to more affluent kinsmen for help, while depending upon the government's inadequate medical and education support.

The federal government's termination policy of the 1950s did not inspire much apprehension among the Comanches, because they and the Kiowas and Apaches, with whom they have been linked since the Treaty of Medicine Lodge of 1867, were not judged to be ready to have their ties to the government severed. But the concern the policy aroused generally among American Indians helped set the stage for the Indian activism of the 1960s and 1970s, to which the Comanches did respond.

Equally important for the Comanches and other tribes was the final disposition of most of their claims against the government and the payment of some large judgments by the United States. In the 1970s the Indian Claims Commission found in favor of the Kiowas, Comanches, and Apaches in three suits with awards totaling over $40 million. When combined with the federal funds available to Indians through the programs launched by President Lyndon B. Johnson's War on Poverty, the result was significant improvement in the living conditions of the Comanches.

In the same period the Comanches underwent an important political change. Indian nationalism was a growing force among American Indians, and it was manifested among the Comanches by their decision to secede from the Kiowa-Comanche-Apache Intertribal Business Committee, which had served as their government under the provisions of the Oklahoma Indian Welfare Act of 1936. Although still linked with the Kiowas and Apaches by a committee limited strictly to business, which administers jointly held land and business enterprises, the Comanches today enjoy their own tribal government, which operates out of a bustling tribal complex just off Interstate 44 near Fort Sill, Oklahoma. Like a hundred other tribes, they have discovered that bingo can provide them some income. In addition, they are about to embark on joint ventures with the Kiowas and Apaches, including a water park and a factory manufacturing gloves, and they are investigating the possibility of opening a living Comanche village and cultural learning center as a tourist attraction.

To someone becoming reacquainted with the Comanches after the passage of nearly fifteen years, the biggest change is in their mood. I concluded my study in 1975 with the observation that the Indians were handicapped by their close ties with and dependence on the federal government. To a lesser extent this is still the case; however, there are today among the Comanches a confidence and newfound energies that bode well for their future.

One thing has not changed and that is their pride in their rich heritage as Comanches. Following the initial publication of this book several Comanches contacted me seeking additional information about members of their families. It was a pleasure to be able to assist in this fashion, and it is to be hoped that the new edition will find increased readership among the Comanches and stimulate further interest in their history, family and tribal.

WILLIAM T. HAGAN

University of Oklahoma

Preface to the First Edition

To trace the ordeal of the Comanches in the reservation years is to get a feeling for what United States policy meant for all Indians, and particularly for Plains Indians. The era opened in the 1860s with the negotiation of treaties with the Plains tribes, treaties designed to open the region to white travelers and settlers by locating these nomadic tribesmen on reservations. It is highly unlikely that most of the Indians the United States regarded as bound by the terms of these documents actually understood them. Indeed, some bands had not even been represented at the negotiations. Recognition in recent years that the treaties were manifestly unfair has led the Indian Claims Commission to make substantial awards to the Indians involved. The Comanches and two other tribes party to the same treaties have been awarded judgments totaling about $37 million.

About a decade elapsed before the Plains Indians had been forced to accept residence on the reservations established by the treaties. During the next quarter of a century the government would attempt to transform these hunters and warriors into farmers and stockmen. It quickly became apparent that most of the reservations were not well adapted for agriculture. Nevertheless, the goal of government policy did not change—the Indians should become self-sufficient on homesteads equivalent to those of settlers in regions with heavier rainfall. Concurrently, the Indians were subjected to a program designed to effect cultural change. Their cherished values and life-style under constant attack, unable to subsist themselves, and only begrudgingly supported by the government, Indians suffered terribly.

The period closed around the turn of the century with

most of the reservations, including that of the Comanches, being broken up by allotment in severalty. This was to have been the last step in an acculturation program that would have prepared the Indians for integration into American society with all the rights and responsibilities of citizens. What actually occurred between 1867 and 1906 was to transform the Comanches from a proud and fiercely independent people into apathetic wards of the United States.

To understand United States Indian policy in the late nineteenth century one must trace it from its origins in the Indian Office and Congress to its actual impact on specific tribes. Throughout this period policy was made in Washington as though Indians were a homogeneous group. To implement general policies, identical circulars were dispatched from Washington to about sixty agencies containing Indian populations in a wide range of geographical settings and of social and economic development. A single agent, as did the one for the Comanches, might preside over the destinies of nearly a dozen different tribes on two separate but contiguous reservations. The Indians the agent administered ranged from a small group of Delawares, who had been in contact with the whites for three centuries, to the Comanches, who had only recently been forced to give up nomadic lives as hunters and warriors.

The Comanche experience even differed somewhat from that of the Kiowas and Kiowa-Apaches, the two tribes party to the same treaties as the Comanches and sharing the same reservation with them. However, these Indians were so closely related in the reservation period that it is sometimes difficult, if not impossible, to separate the Comanche story from that of the Kiowas and the Kiowa-Apaches.

A close examination of the Comanche ordeal at the hands of the United States reveals the many forces shaping the government's Indian policy and affecting its implementation in the post-Civil War era. Members of Congress differed in their approach to Comanche affairs depending upon the interests of their constituents, who might be Texas cattlemen searching for pastures for expanding herds or Kansas farmers eager for homesteads to be carved from reservations. The constituents might be Massachusetts and Pennsylvania reformers working for what they regarded as the best interests of the Indians by opposing railroad executives eager to run lines across Indian land and able to command support in several state delegations.

On the Comanche reservation the agent attempting to implement the policies finally arrived at in Washington would have to contend with a sometimes overlapping set of special interest groups: cattlemen, missionaries, army officers stationed at Fort Sill, intermarried whites, licensed traders, and land-hungry settlers who had managed to infiltrate the reservation. The result was a complex set of relationships constantly in flux as the groups combined and divided to further their own interests. The Indians contributed their own brand of debilitating factionalism, which played into the hands of their exploiters.

During the reservation period the agent was not only the key individual in implementing the policies conceived in Washington, he also originated most of the documentation upon which the historian must depend in attempting to reconstruct the relations between the United States and the Indians. Unfortunately, the Indian side of the story is much more difficult to recapture. Documentation in the usual sense is almost nonexistent, and Comanche family traditions suffer from the same distortions that family pride and present concerns inflict on white oral history.

In attempting to reconstruct the relations between the United States and the Comanches I have become indebted to many people and institutions. The Research Foundation of State University of New York assisted me with grants at critical stages. The staffs of a number of libraries and man-uscript repositories have been uniformly courteous and helpful, among them the Fort Worth Federal Records Center, the Haverford College Library, the Historical Society of Pennsylvania, the National Anthropological Archives, the Gilcrease Institute, and the Panhandle Plains Historical Society. Of particular assistance have been John P. Saulitis, whose warmth and hospitality help set the tone for Reed Library of the State University College at Fredonia, Robert M. Kvasnicka of the National Archives, Rella Looney and Martha Royce Blaine of the Oklahoma Historical Society, Gillett Griswold of the Fort Sill Museum, and Jack D. Haley of the University of Oklahoma Library.

Other individuals have aided my research in a variety of ways. Wanada Parker Page, Ed Cox, Aubry C. Birdsong, and Sarah Pohocsucut kindly consented to reminisce about the old days. James Eschiti, Jr., helped me in my attempt to unravel the enigma of his grandfather's names. Floyd A. O'Neil assisted me in acquiring scarce materials. Herbert Woesner, who had moved Quanah's house to Eagle Park, near Cache, Oklahoma, personally conducted me through it. Ronnie C. Tyler, Jerrold E. Levy, Donald J. Berthrong, and Eugene G. O'Quinn graciously shared their own research findings with me. William Grissom, superintendent, and Bernhard Reichert, tribal operations officer, both of the Anadarko Area Office of the Bureau of Indian Affairs, took time from busy schedules to answer questions. My colleague Douglas Shepard provided bibliographical assistance unstintingly. Sarah E. Hagan transcribed notes with uncanny accuracy. Mary Notaro did her usual excellent typing job. Last but not least, Charlotte Nix Hagan assisted in all stages of the research and writing.

Some of the material in this book appeared previously in the *Pacific Historical Review* (August 1971), and in John G. Clark, ed., *The Frontier Challenge* (Lawrence: University Press of Kansas, 1971).

1. The Road to Medicine Lodge

In the fall of 1867 several thousand Indians of the south plains gathered on Medicine Lodge Creek in southern Kansas to negotiate with representatives of the United States. One treaty that resulted would be the framework for the relations between the Comanches and the federal government in the reservation period. For the United States the negotiations had been a response to an increasingly complex problem of Indian–white relations.

By 1850 the lure of gold in California and good farmland in Oregon were drawing thousands of Americans across the plains. The white travelers occupied water holes, cut timber in the river bottoms, and killed game in an area that seemed to them virtually unoccupied. Nevertheless it was claimed, and by people to whom warfare was a normal condition. With few exceptions, all adult males of the Plains tribes were warriors until old age deprived them of the vigor required for the strenuous life. It was unrealistic to expect that these virile people would permit strangers to invade and occupy their country, or resist the impulse to add to their status as warriors by counting coup on the intruders. The Civil War did not slow the western movement of Americans and by 1866 there were frightening prospects of a general war on the plains.

Efforts to open a new road into the Montana mining country had produced several clashes and one, the Fetterman Massacre, had shocked many easterners into recognizing the grim possibilities implicit in large-scale fighting with the Plains Indians. Newspaper columns and official reports to Congress regaled readers with the gory details of the stripped and terribly mutilated bodies of Fetterman and the men who followed him out of Fort Phil Kearny

1

and into a Sioux ambush on the Bozeman Trail, December 21, 1866.

Letters from the fort in the following weeks emphasized the gravity of the situation. The fort's commanding officer had made preparations to blow it up, together with its garrison and their dependents, if the Indians broke through the defenses. "We are fighting a foe that is the devil" was one message from the terror-ridden little fort as snow and bitter cold enveloped it and Indian signals were seen on surrounding hills.[1]

The snow and cold eventually drove the Indians from Fort Phil Kearny to their winter lodgings, but as the snow melted the following spring and their ponies began to fatten on the new grass, the warriors became active again. By June 1867 reports of attacks and anticipated attacks were streaming into Washington. It was hard to separate the real from the imagined, although Kansas governor Samuel J. Crawford was difficult to ignore. Claiming the Indians had killed over 500 people in Kansas since July 1, 1866, the governor vowed:

> I cannot and will not allow a band of irresponsible, un-
> civilized, blood-thirsty fiends to invade the State,
> murder our citizens, stop the work on our most im-
> portant railroads, and completely blockade the routes
> of travel to other States and Territories.[2]

The governor grossly exaggerated Kansas casualties. Nevertheless, construction on some sections of the Union Pacific Railroad, in which the government had a heavy financial investment, was virtually at a standstill and stagecoach lines had stopped running on portions of the plains. Nor were the prospects good for the United States Army to force the Indians into submission.

Campaigning against Plains Indians was a very arduous and frustrating task. In trying to bring these elusive fighters to account more military reputations were lost than made. In the late 1860s there were still large areas of the southern plains unmapped, and cavalry columns pushing into these areas not only had to carry grain for their mounts but also worry about the location of the next water hole.

Seldom were cavalry able to run down warriors on the open plains. Each warrior usually would have more than one mount and his equipment would be much lighter than that of the cavalrymen. Switching from mount to mount, the Indians with ease could outdistance the stronger but heavily burdened cavalry horses. If the pursuit grew too hot the party would gradually break down. Warriors slipped away, where the terrain offered opportunities, until the army column would find itself with rations practically gone and pursuing only one or two members of the original party.

Even entire Indian camps of several hundred people were difficult to surround in the spring and summer, when the grass was high and the Indian ponies in good condition. On a half hour's notice (on the open plains this was seldom lacking) an Indian camp could be struck. Lodges and equipment would be loaded on packhorses and travois, and the entire village headed away from the point of danger with the warriors prepared to fight a rearguard action. And these people knew in what direction the next water hole lay and where the terrain could complicate the task of the pursuer.

Even identifying the Indians who committed the hostile act posed real problems. It was very seldom that an entire tribe was hostile. However, even the most peacefully disposed Comanche band might spawn a war party. Whites by the thousands were intruding on Indian land, and all it took was a few young Indians motivated by desire for revenge, hope of loot, or the need to establish their reputations as fighters in a warrior society. Such a party could leave a camp in the shadow of their agency, strike a wagon train or isolated ranch 200 miles away, and be back with their scalps and plunder before officials were aware of their absence. The identity of the perpetrators probably never would be determined. Many of the whites attacked had never seen an Indian before, or if they had it was one of the shabby and demoralized native Americans whom the frontier had bypassed. They bore little resemblance to the painted horsemen streaming feathers and brandishing lances and bows who seemed to spring from nowhere. Unable to tell a Mescalero Apache from a Penetethka Comanche, or either from a Southern Cheyenne, the stunned white survivors rarely could identify their attackers. If by some chance a trail were picked up it probably ended in a camp of generally friendly Indians.

The only offensive action by the army on the southern plains in the spring of 1867 had revealed how conventional forces led by a conventional general could only add to the government's problems. General Winfield Scott Hancock had burned a village abandoned by Cheyennes who had been stampeded by his approach. Hancock's destruction of their property may have intimidated some of the Indians; it probably further antagonized and provoked the warriors to another round of raids.

General Hancock's operation and the Fetterman Massacre were among the matters considered by the members of Congress as they wrestled with the Indian problem in 1867. Many points of view were represented. Those stressing negotiation rather than military force prevailed. Reasons of humanity were cited to support negotiations, but the need for economy and the sheer difficulty of plains warfare were equally persuasive. The cost of killing an Indian was estimated at $1 million[3] by a senator who set the cost of one day's campaigning on the plains at $125,000 to $250,000.[4] Offered in evidence was the statement of a commanding officer of a western post that the Comanches were "the finest skirmishers" he had ever seen and that they could mobilize 7,000 well-mounted warriors.[5] He grossly exaggerated Comanche numbers, but the $5.26 per bushel he cited for corn delivered to his post was accurate and helped convince the members of Congress that troop operations on the plains were almost prohibitively expensive.

The reports of two groups who had visited the West helped set the stage for negotiations. In January 1867 a joint congressional committee appointed nearly two years earlier to investigate the causes of Indian warfare finally submitted its report. The committee laid much of the blame at the door of aggressive whites who ignored Indian boundaries "in their eager search for gold or fertile . . . land."[6] It estimated that to use force to end Indian resistance would require at least 10,000 soldiers, produce a war lasting as much as three years, and cost more than $30 million.[7]

The second group had just returned from an investigation of conditions in the West and was made up of members selected by the General of the Army and by the Secretary of the Interior. Their report agreed on the desirability of negotiations. Some on this commission went so far as to suggest that Indian hostilities had been exaggerated by those who stood to profit by increased army operations—the contractors, freighters, and railroaders.[8]

The opinion of Commissioner of Indian Affairs Nathaniel G. Taylor also was sought. The commissioner had only recently taken office and the views he expressed in July 1867 resembled closely those of his predecessor, Lewis V. Bogy. Bogy had seen the alternatives as "total and speedy destruction of the Indians" or their concentration on reservations to clear more land for the whites.[9] Commissioner Taylor saw the alternatives just as clearly: "Swift extermination by the sword, and famine, or preservation by gradual concentration . . . and civilization." The last was to be achieved by

> consolidating them . . . on large reservations, from which all whites except government employees shall be excluded, and educating them intellectually and morally, and training them in the arts of civilizations, so as to render them . . . self-supporting, and at the proper time to clothe them with the rights and immunities of citizenship.[10]

Taylor subscribed to a theory similar to that of pioneer anthropologist Lewis Henry Morgan that although Indians were at a less advanced state than whites, they could and would evolve from the hunting stage through the pastoral to agriculture. Commissioner Taylor would soon have an opportunity to implement his views in negotiations with the Plains tribes.

Senator John B. Henderson of Missouri brought matters to a head by introducing a bill "to establish peace with certain hostile tribes." He and friendly colleagues supported the proposal with arguments well developed in debates on Indian policy over a year and a half. The senator pointed out that the $150,000 being asked for the actual negotiations would be "less than one day's cost of the present war,"[11] and quoted General William T. Sherman on the inability of 3,000 soldiers to cope with 50 warriors.[12] The debate in the Senate was relatively brief and the bill precipitated even less discussion in the House. The majority of the members of Congress had convinced themselves that negotiations should be attempted, although the minority succeeded in amending the bill to provide that if negotiations failed the president could enlist 4,000 mounted volunteers "for the suppression of Indian hostilities" (*Statutes at Large,* 15 St. 17).

Conspicuously muted in the discussions of the bill were references to procedures for handling the Indians once they had been concentrated on reservations. Congress was seeking only a way to open the West to more white settlers and their accompanying railroads and stagecoach lines without the tremendous expense of a war that might last years. Apparently the hope was that once on the reservation the Indians would lose their fighting qualities and quietly vegetate as the once mighty Senecas and scores of other tribes had done.

The law that President Andrew Johnson signed on July 20, 1867, created a commission of three generals and four civilians to negotiate settlements with the hostile Indians to remove all just causes of complaint on their part, and at the same time establish security for person and property along the lines of railroad now being constructed to the Pacific, and other thoroughfares of travel to the western Territories, and such as will most likely insure civilization for the Indians and peace and safety for the whites (*Statutes at Large,* 15 St. 17).

To achieve these objectives the Indians were to be persuaded to locate on reservations where they could learn to support themselves by farming and stock raising. Initially the reservations would be large enough to permit the Indians to partially support themselves by hunting. However, as they became more proficient at farming and stock raising the size of the reservations would be gradually reduced, thus providing for the anticipated increased demand of white settlers for land. Ultimately the Indian would be confined to a holding of a few hundred acres, comparable to that of the typical frontier farmer.[13] As the successive purchases of Indian land were made, the proceeds would be applied to the acquisition of livestock and tools for the Indians and to the education of their children, reducing the burden on the American taypayer.

The 1867 law specifically provided that whites generally would be excluded from these reservations and that $300,000 would be made available to support those Indians who chose to separate themselves from the hostiles and seek the protection of the United States. In its final form the law differed from Senator Henderson's original bill principally in that it did not attempt to specify the two areas in which the northern and southern Plains Indians should be concentrated. In general the law reflected the desire of the commissioner of Indian Affairs and the members of Congress to avoid a brutal and expensive Indian war. It remained to be seen whether negotiations could achieve the objective or if the provision of the law authorizing 4,000 volunteers would have to be implemented to subdue the Comanches and their fellow Plains Indians.

While Congress debated the proper policy to pursue toward the Plains Indians, 1,500 miles west of Washington the Comanche bands went their several ways in the spring and summer of 1867. The term *tribe* could not then with any accuracy be applied to the Comanches. At any given time they might be found scattered over a region that stretched from western Oklahoma and the central part of Texas westward to the vicinity of the Rio Grande. They seldom were seen north of the Arkansas, but south to the Mexican border and even beyond it they held sway as the "Lords of the Southern Plains." Others, white or red, entered this region at their peril.[14]

The band was the basic political unit of the Comanche and in 1867 there were said to be at least nine. They were as different as the Penetethka of the Wichita Agency, who already could be classified as reservation Indians, and the Quahadas, who generally ranged farthest west and had no official relations with the United States. Estimates of the number of Comanches varied widely, from as low as 1,800 to over 20,000. The actual figure probably was around 3,000, although no one could be sure. The number of bands and their membership were constantly fluctuating. In contrast to the many Indians who had tightly drawn clan and band lines, the Comanches had no clan structure at all; individual Indians appear to have moved with relative ease from one band to another. Ties of family or friendship and the personality of the band chief helped the individual Indian to determine his band affiliation. The Penetethkas in the tumultuous decades of the 1860s and 1870s seem to have steadily lost restive members to the bands that still roamed the plains.

It was on the southwestern edge of the plains that the Comanches had first seen white men—Spaniards from the settlements along the upper Rio Grande. During the late seventeenth century the Comanches had moved into the area from the north, presumably first acquiring horses at that time and undergoing the same transformation as occurred with other Plains Indians. Horses gave them a mobility that made them more efficient hunters and raiders. As pack animals the horses enabled the Comanches to move camp with greater rapidity while enjoying the luxury of larger tepees and more camp equipment than when their possessions moved on the backs of their women and on travois pulled by their dogs.

The victims of the newly mobile Comanche raiders were the Spanish settlers in New Mexico and Texas. Spanish officials in New Mexico alternately sought to bribe the Comanches to leave them alone or to intimidate the Indians by military action. By the 1780s a truce of sorts had been patched up, and the Spanish even sought the aid of the Comanches against the Apaches.[15] But in the absence of any central authority among the Indians the situation never was very stable. At any given time one Comanche band might be peacefully trading at Pecos Pueblo while a hundred miles away another might be robbing a Pecos hunting party.

Farther east in Texas the Comanches had firmly established their reputation as scourges of the frontier by the time Mexico won its independence in 1821. The Indians periodically swooped down on outlying ranches, driving off their stock, killing the men, and abducting the women and children. These last might be sold to other tribes, or they could remain with their original captors as slaves. Those who survived the difficult transition to Indian life, particularly the young children, might be adopted by Indian families and reared as Comanches.

Mexican independence only weakened the resistance to Comanche raiders because the new government lacked the organization and resources of Spain. But the influx of Americans into the Republic of Texas following the Texas Revolution soon put the Comanches on the defensive. As the Texas settlements pushed into the hunting grounds of the Comanches, the Indians struck back, inflicting much heavier casualties than they suffered. Nevertheless, the white population of Texas grew steadily. Its presence forced the game westward and the Indians had to retreat with it. Thus the settlements served at once as an expanding source of slaves, horses, and other loot for the Comanches and as a relentless force gradually pushing the Indians out of the areas they had occupied in their own expansion.

An incident illustrative of the border warfare occurred on May 9, 1836, at Fort Parker on a tributary of the lower Brazos. Sam Houston's victory over Santa Anna at San Jacinto was only a few days old when a war party of Comanches appeared before the rude stockade housing nine Texas families. Most of the men were off working in the fields. The Indians posed as friends and inquired about a campsite, thus gaining admission to the fort. Once in they killed the men, wounded severely three women, and rode off with two other women and three children. One of the latter, nine-year-old Cynthia Anne Parker, was with the Comanches for the next twenty-four years. Quanah, one of her children by a Comanche father, rose to prominence as a tribal leader after 1875.

North of the Texas settlements the Comanches were facing competition from eastern Indians moved west under the United States removal program, which had been designed to open up Indian lands in the East to white settlement. These emigrant tribes made drastic inroads on the game resources of the area. The Comanches led the resistance to the newcomers and in the process clashed with their patron, the United States. The Americans also were unhappy with Comanche harassment of traders on the Santa Fe Trail, which had opened in the 1820s and commanded the support of a nation looking west.

In 1835 Colonel Henry Dodge persuaded some Comanches and other Plains Indians to return with him to Fort Gibson. The result was the "Treaty with the Comanche and Wichetaw Indians and their associated Bands" of August 24, 1835.[16] Presumably it established "perpetual peace and friendship" among participating Plains Indians, the United States, and those emigrant Indians party to the treaty. It also called for a cessation of hostile acts against travelers on the Santa Fe Trail. To which Comanche bands

Map 1. Military installations mentioned in the text. (Based on Raisz, *Landforms of the United States*, and Prucha, *A Guide to the Military Posts of the United States, 1789–1895*)

Ishacoby (The Wolf) and his fellow signers belonged is not known, but probably they could speak for only a fraction of the total Comanche population, most of whom would have been unaware that the negotiations had taken place.

Certainly this treaty did little to reduce the level of conflect between the whites and the Comanches. However, the pressure of the Texans and the emigrant Indians perhaps did contribute to the southern Plains tribes trying to patch up a common front. South of the Arkansas the Comanches and the Kiowas had enjoyed friendly relations since the 1790s. The third tribe, the Kiowa-Apaches, was too small to challenge the other two and tended to follow their lead. North of the Arkansas the Southern Cheyennes provided comparable leadership for the Arapahos. When the Comanches made a truce with the Southern Cheyennes in 1840, the rather fragile peace between the two most powerful tribes on the southern plains allowed them and their allies to concentrate on resisting the intruders. A young Comanche might still find a fine Cheyenne or Kiowa pony irresistible, but older and wiser heads among the tribes were able to keep these incidents, and the blood-letting that could flow from them, to a minimum.

The truce agreed upon in 1840 came none too soon, for these tribes would need all their strength to cope with new developments in the next decade. First the United States acquired Texas in 1846 and then in 1848 added the Mexican Cession, which included New Mexico and California. Along with the Texans the United States inherited their running war with the Comanches. California's contribution to United States–Comanche relations was to provide the lure for the forty-niners, who would soon be hurrying west.

As other mineral discoveries were made from Montana to Arizona, the wagon and pack trains threading their way through Comanche hunting grounds multiplied. Then stagecoach lines and railroad construction crews made their appearance, to the consternation of the Indians, who never had reconciled themselves to the relatively light traffic of the original Santa Fe traders. The newcomers to the plains brought diseases with them for which the Indians had developed no immunities. Comanche tribal tradition has it that perhaps half their people died of cholera brought to the plains by the forty-niners.[17]

Not all the contacts between the Plains Indians and their neighbors were unpleasant. From New Mexico venturesome groups of Pueblo and Mexican traders, *Comancheros,* found their way to the Comanche camps. The same motivation drew parties from the Five Civilized Tribes and the white settlements to the east. This was a risky business, but the profits could be high. The Comanches needed these traders. The buffalo provided them everything from the raw material for their lodges to the meat that was the basis of their diet. Nevertheless, the Comanches had come to depend upon other items available only from the Comanchero or his eastern counterpart. The hard bread, sugar, and coffee these traders brought to the plains enriched the Comanche diet, and the firearms, kettles, and metal tools simplified the Indian's struggle for existence. The Comanches were nomads, but even the Quahadas had become dependent on trade goods long before they became reservation Indians.[18]

The Penetethka Comanches had been the first to be exposed to the reservation process, which was designed to convert them into facsimiles of white farmers. The annexation agreement between the United States and Texas had provided that Texas would retain its public lands. However, it was understood that the United States would be responsible for the Indian population in the new state.

In May 1846 representatives of the United States, the Penetethka Comanches, and four small Texas tribes met on the Brazos River and negotiated a treaty.[19] To cement the peace the Indians were to receive $10,000 worth of presents, and the services of blacksmiths and teachers. Eight years passed, however, before Texas agreed reluctantly to provide two small reservations for the Indians of Texas who could be persuaded to settle on them. To one of these, a 23,040-acre tract on the Clear Fork of the Brazos, a few hundred Penetethkas were enticed to move in 1855. Land was broken, fences were built, and a school was launched for the Comanche children.

All to no avail. A Comanche male had been reared in a society that honored only two pursuits: hunting and fighting. The presence on the plains of many other Comanche bands was a constant temptation to the Indians of the Clear Fork reservation to slip away and resume the life the Great Spirit had intended for them. Moreover, there was always the possibility that in a region of light rainfall and seering summer heat any crops the Indians could be prevailed upon to plant would not reach maturity. Given these obstacles it is doubtful that the Texas reservation ever had a real chance to work its magic and transform Comanche warriors into peaceful farmers. The local white population did not permit it even that small chance.

Indian raids on the Texas frontier continued throughout this period and Texans suspected that some reservation Comanches were actively involved. Robert S. Neighbors, the supervising agent for Indian Affairs in Texas, was aware that young Penetethka warriors did slip away to the plains to join Comanches who scorned reservation life.[20] His solution was for the government to move as quickly as possible to locate on land acquired from one of the westernmost Five Civilized Tribes the remaining Comanche bands. They were principally the Yamparikas (Root Eaters), Noconies (Wanderers), Quahadas (Antelopes), and Cochetethkas (Buffalo Eaters).

Among those who had been urging a new round of negotiations with the tribes of the southern plains was D. D. Mitchell. His Central Superintendency was responsible for the area roamed by the Comanches, Kiowas, and Kiowa-Apaches. In the fall of 1852 Mitchell advised Washington, as he had done before, that an attempt should be made to get these Indians to conclude a treaty similar to one negotiated in 1851 with the northern Plains Indians at Fort Laramie. Mitchell was pessimistic about their long-range prospects. "Wild and untamable as the animals they pursue" is how he described them. The most he thought possible was to encourage the Comanches and their allies to substitute raising domestic animals for hunting buffalo. "In the course of time," predicted Mitchell, "they will probably become a semi-civilized race—the Gipsies [sic] of this continent."[21]

The assignment to negotiate with the Comanches and associated tribes fell on the capable shoulders of the Indian agent for the Upper Platte and Arkansas, Thomas Fitzpatrick. The former Mountain Man faced a formidable task when he met the assembled Indians at Fort Atkinson in western Kansas in July 1853. The Indians were, to quote Fitzpatrick, "impatient, watchful, jealous, reserved and haughty."[22] The agent respected them "as the most formidable of all those who inhabit the interior of the continent."[23]

The Indians were willing to accept some rights-of-way through their territory and, of course, they had no objections to receiving annual payments of $18,000 in goods from the United States. They only reluctantly agreed to military posts in their territory because the Indians knew the inroads on their timber and game that would result. But the clause they resented most called for them to quit fighting the Mexicans and to return any prisoners they held.

Mexican settlements, including those in the United States as a result of the 1848 cession, were a prime source of loot and captives for the Comanches. Those taken became, as the Indians told Fitzpatrick, "the husbands of their daughters and the mothers of their children."[24] It was thus that the Comanches and their allies maintained their numbers despite a way of life that made warfare a full-time occupation. Nevertheless, the clause banning war with the Mexicans was included in the treaty, which carried the X's of sixteen Comanche, Kiowa, and Kiowa-Apache leaders.

The only change in the treaty made by the Senate was to

specify that, at its discretion, the United States could convert the $18,000 annuity into a fund to help the Indians locate on farms. When their agent explained this to them the following July the Indians were not pleased. A Kiowa chief commented sarcastically that he would be happy to do so and hoped his Great Father would send him some land on which corn could be raised. Shaved Head, a Comanche, subscribed to the same sentiments and the agent was forced to agree that their country was "worthless for agricultural purposes."[25]

The Fort Atkinson Treaty of 1853 did establish a fragile official connection between the United States and the Comanches. There were no further large-scale attacks on the Santa Fe Trail, but other than that the treaty meant little more than that every summer some Indians would meet their agent and collect their annuity. They did not give up their raids on Texas and Mexican settlements, maintaining ingenuously that they had nowhere else to get their horses and mules. Nor would the Comanches and their allies surrender their Mexican captives. The agents were powerless to do more than ask them to cooperate.

Despite this, Washington officials concluded it would be possible to colonize the Comanches and associated tribes on reservations and convert them from hunters and raiders into farmers and stock raisers.[26] In response to this analysis of the situation, Congress in 1857 appropriated $50,000 to make the effort. However, the Comanches assigned to the Upper Arkansas Agency were going to be difficult to persuade, and the United States did not have sufficient troops at its frontier installations to intimidate them. The government did have a site for a reservation. The area between the 98th and 100th meridians, bounded on the north by the Canadian River and on the south by the Red, had been included in the original locations assigned the Choctaws and Chickasaws when they migrated under the removal program. In negotiations with these tribes in 1855 the United States secured the use of the tract, known popularly as the Leased District. If the Comanches and other tribes of the Upper Arkansas Agency could not be prevailed upon to move there in 1859, it might provide the government an out from a very embarrassing predicament with the state of Texas.

The situation on the two reservations set up in Texas in 1855 was critical. Texas outrage at depredations attributed (at least in part) to the reservation Indians, coupled with the white man's greed for Indian land, produced demands for the complete removal of the tribesmen from the state. To cope with Plains raiders in 1857 the governor of Texas was forced to call out state troops. In the spring of 1858 Texas Rangers, accompanied by a party of Wacos, Caddos, and Tonkawas from their reservation on the Brazos, surprised a Comanche village on the Canadian River. That fall a column of United States regulars, again joined by friendly Indians from the Brazos reservation, overran a Comanche village in the Battle of Rush Spring and inflicted many casualties.[27]

The battle could have had the opposite effect of that intended. The Indians had lost their horse herd to the whites, and as a horseless Comanche was unthinkable, they promptly moved to repair the loss. This could only mean at the expense of the settlers, and soon Texans were complaining of a new wave of raids.

Texas complaints got results. Orders came from Washington to move the Indians from the reservations on the Brazos to the Leased District. In July 1859 about 370 Penetethka Comanches, under military escort, headed north. When they crossed Red River, Agent Neighbors wrote his wife: "I have this day crossed all the Indians out of the heathen land of Texas and am now out of the land of the Philistines."[28] Recrossing Red River a few weeks later, Neighbors was killed by a Texan who resented the agent's outspoken denunciation of the murder of an Indian by whites.

Secretary of the Interior Jacob Thompson deplored the murder of Neighbors and the removal of the Indians from the reservations in Texas. He described the latter as aborting a highly successful program designed to make the Indians self-sustaining.[29] At least as far as the Comanches were concerned, this was a considerable exaggeration. The refusal of the Texans to tolerate the reservations had only saved the secretary from having to recognize the failure of this initial effort to civilize Comanches.

The Penetethka Comanches were hardly located on the new reservation before the Civil War was under way. Fort Cobb, the headquarters for the agency, was one of the federal posts abandoned in the face of the Confederate threat. Although it now came under the control of the Confederate States of America, the Wichita Agency, as it was called, had no change in personnel. The agent and other employees, including Horace P. Jones and J. J. Sturm, two men to be associated with Comanche affairs for many years to come, were Confederate sympathizers and retained their positions under the new government.

The few hundred Penetethka Comanches assigned to the Wichita Agency were included in a treaty negotiated in August 1861 by General Albert Pike in behalf of the Confederacy.[30] Pike was interested in keeping these Indians neutral rather than trying to recruit the warriors for use against Union forces. This was about the most that the governments could hope for because the Indians had no reason for a deep attachment to either side. Within a few weeks Penetethkas who had treated with Pike were talking to A. G. Boone, the grandson of the famed Daniel and the United States agent for the Upper Arkansas. The Comanches confided in him their desire to leave the Wichita Agency and Confederate domination.[31]

An attack the following year on the Wichita Agency by Indians from Union-controlled Kansas probably was inspired as much by their dislike of the Tonkawas at the Wichita Agency as by their hostility to the Confederacy. The invaders did sack the agency and for all practical purposes the Confederates ceased to operate there. The Indians removed from the two Texas reservations were left to make their peace with the Union or go it alone.

While Pike was negotiating with the Penetethkas and the affiliated tribes from Texas, he also had drafted a similar treaty with four other Comanche bands. Boone obtained a copy of this from the principal chief of the Yamparikas, who expressed surprise, feigned or otherwise, at learning he had been dealing with enemies of the United States.[32]

In the fall of 1861 Boone made his own agreement with some Kiowas and two Comanche bands for them to surrender some stolen stock and cease their attacks on the Utes and on Colorado citizens.[33] Boone also persuaded some Comanches to scout as far as El Paso, but they failed to detect any Confederate activity.[34] The agent believed it essential to have a delegation of the southern Plains Indians visit Washington, but it did not occur until a year and a half after he had been replaced.

In March 1863 a party that included two Comanche chiefs, Pricked Forehead and Ten Bears, met Lincoln in the White House. They had their photographs taken by one of Matthew Brady's assistants and were loaded with presents including blankets, silver brooches, and gold epaulettes. On a tour of the State Department they had their lands pointed out on a great globe and agreed to a treaty that the United States never ratified. The delegation then made its way to New York City, where it became, unaccountably, a featured attraction for a few days at P. T. Barnum's Museum. These experiences, together with the gift of saddles and horses when they arrived back in Kansas, presumably made them immune to tampering by the Confederates.[35]

As long as Yamparikas, Noconies, Quahadas, and Cochetethkas raided the Texas frontier, they were not likely to enter into sincere negotiations with the Confederacy. Indeed, a new vigor characterized the Comanche plundering of Texans early in the war. The Comancheros took advantage of the relaxed vigilance of officials responsible for overseeing Indian trade and developed a flourishing business in stolen cattle, horses, and mules.

Although by 1863 the level of troop strength in Kansas,

Colorado, and New Mexico was back to, or exceeded pre-1861 levels, the southern Plains Indians were unusually aggressive. Travelers on the Santa Fe Trail reported more and more Indian harassment. It reached a peak in the summer of 1864. The Comanches did not discriminate. While some bands concentrated on the Santa Fe Trail, others provided men for a large war party that in October ravaged the Texas settlements. The latter activity was no concern to the United States, but the interruption of Santa Fe traffic threatened the very existence of the army in New Mexico. To eliminate this danger to his communication lines the commander of United States forces in New Mexico called upon Colonel Kit Carson. Another Mountain Man turned Indian agent, and with the Civil War appointed colonel of a volunteer regiment, Carson struck in November with a column of troops supported by a detachment of Ute Indians, longtime enemies of the Comanches and Kiowas.

A Kiowa village near a Comanche winter encampment on the Canadian River in the Texas Panhandle received the first blow. Carson drove the Kiowas from their tepees and they retreated to the protection of the Comanches. Suddenly the colonel found the roles reversed and himself on the defensive at a place called Adobe Walls. Outnumbered more than two-to-one, Carson might have been overrun had it not been for his two howitzers.[36] The Battle of Adobe Walls did little to convince the Comanches that they should give up their profitable brigandage along the Santa Fe Trail.

In 1865 the Comanches were going their accustomed way, oblivious to the end of the Civil War. War parties continued to harry the Santa Fe Trail and the Texas settlements. In June troops preparing to cross the Arkansas in an effort to punish the raiders were stopped by members of the joint congressional committee appointed a few weeks earlier. Siding with Colonel J. H. Leavenworth, now agent for the Upper Arkansas, who insisted that the great majority of his Indians were peaceful, the committee maintained that an effort to negotiate should precede efforts to punish.[37] The result was treaties with the southern Plains tribes.

The situation was serious in the summer of 1865. The United States wanted badly to achieve by negotiations on the Little Arkansas River with the Comanches, Kiowas, Kiowa-Apaches, Cheyennes, and Arapahos what might otherwise necessitate prolonged and expensive fighting.

After working out terms with the Cheyennes and Arapahos the commissioners turned to the Comanches and Kiowas.[38] These Indians surrendered five prisoners they had been holding, thus demonstrating their good will. For their part the commissioners promised compensation for the prisoners and an additional distribution of blankets, butcher knives, tobacco, and other presents. In this atmosphere the Indians signed a treaty by which the United States assigned them a reservation of about 6,200 square miles, more than half of it in Texas. They also were promised annuities. Moreover, until the Comanches and Kiowas were actually located on this reservation they were free to hunt over the area originally claimed by them south of the Arkansas. Since it is impossible to conceive of Texans agreeing to give up such a large segment of their state to these Indians, the reservation article of the treaty is difficult to explain. It would serve later, nevertheless, to buttress the United States argument that by this treaty the Comanches and Kiowas had given up their claims to all land outside the boundaries of this reservation, an area at least as large as the reservation itself.

Signing the treaty of 1865 for the Comanches were chiefs of five bands. As with all such negotiations, it is impossible to determine how thoroughly aware the Indians were of the import of the treaty. There was no doubt, however, that several hundred Comanches were not even represented at the council on the Little Arkansas and would not be bound by the commitment to perpetual peace and by the ban on Indians camping within ten miles of "main travelled roads."

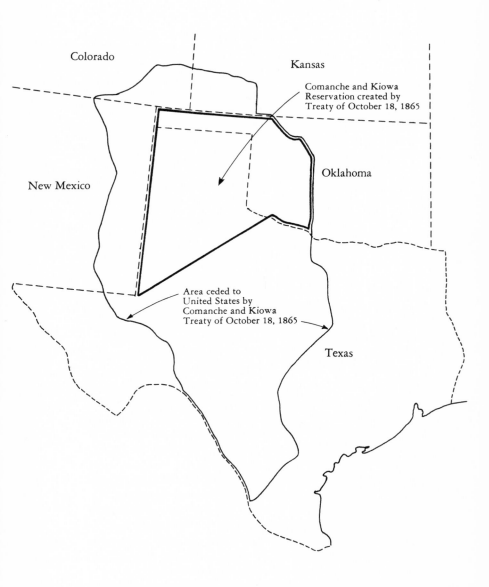

Colorado

Kansas

Comanche and Kiowa
Reservation created by
Treaty of October 18, 1865

New Mexico

Oklahoma

Area ceded to
United States by
Comanche and Kiowa
Treaty of October 18, 1865

Texas

Map 2. Area of the Comanche and Kiowa Treaty with the United States of October 18, 1865. (Adapted from map 57, *18th Annual Report of the Bureau of American Ethnology*, part 2)

Toshaway (Silver Brooch), the principal Penetethka chief, complained about unfulfilled government promises. A veteran of the fiasco on the Brazos reservation, the flight across Red River in 1859, and negotiations in Washington in 1863, Toshaway did not let the commissioners forget it. He reminded them that he had been promised a house and farming equipment that never materialized. Nor, while he had given up white prisoners he held, had the whites reciprocated by releasing Penetethka children they captured at the Battle of Rush Spring.[39]

A treaty that did not bind a significant number of the Comanches, and one whose principal clauses the state of Texas could never be brought to accept, was not likely to provide any lasting peace on the south plains. Nor, although it barred any all-out effort by the army to impose a peace on the Comanches and their allies, did it guarantee the safety of either settlers on the Texas frontier or emigrants on the plains. When less than a month after the treaty Agent Leavenworth estimated that "a large number of the Comanches are anxious to settle down, and become 'a white man,'" he could not have been more wrong.[40]

Throughout 1866 and well into 1867 Agent Leavenworth continued to maintain that his Comanches, as a tribe, were peaceful. Individual warriors might err. And one could always blame the Quahadas, the band on the Staked Plains of western Texas with which the goverment had not established official relations and thus could safely be accused by an agent liable for the activities of other Comanches.

Commissioner of Indian Affairs D. N. Cooley took the same line. In the fall of 1866 he described the Comanches and Kiowas as "peacably disposed," except for "a few outlying bands."[41] The governor of Texas saw it differently. "For the last twelve months, the depredations upon our border have been of the most appalling character," he complained to the commissioner, and demanded that something be done.[42] Every full moon for the past two years, according to an officer in the Texas militia, had seen

Indian war parties on the loose among the settlements.[43] The fullness of a "Comanche moon" was something to be dreaded by Texans in the 1860s.

With the end of the Civil War, officials did take cognizance of the Comanchero trade, which had reached remarkable proportions. Charles Goodnight, a prominent Texan, estimated that he and his fellow ranchers lost 300,000 head of cattle between 1860 and 1867.[44] The superintendent for Indian Affairs for New Mexico Territory reported it filling up with the stolen cattle. So serious did he consider the matter that the superintendent canceled all trade permits for the plains and secured the cooperation of the military in reducing the flow of stolen goods into the territory.[45]

Even Agent Leavenworth indicated recognition of the problem, although he associated it only with the Quahadas. Most of the Comanches and Kiowas, in the agent's opinion, were ready to settle down and become stockmen. In February 1867 he asked the commissioner of Indian Affairs to authorize him to locate a site for their agency within the territory assigned them by the 1865 treaty, and to use part of their annuity fund to buy cattle for the Indians.[46]

The commissioner was more concerned with the growing volume of complaints about whites held captive by the Comanches. He passed on to Agent Leavenworth the secretary of the interior's order that Leavenworth make "a peremptory demand . . . upon the Chiefs of those Indians for the delivery of ... all ... white captives held by them." Moreover, directed the commisioner, the Comanches should be told that no ransom would be paid, and the captives would either be released or "their country will be filled with soldiers and they will be punished severely."[47]

It was not likely that the Indians would surrender the captives without ransom. Selling them back to the government had become a profitable business. During the negotiations on the Little Arkansas in October 1865 the peace

commissioners had "compensated" the Indians for surrender of white captives, and everyone released since that
time had been purchased. The Kiowa release of two white
girls seized in Texas, for example, had cost the United
States $1,026.22 worth of saddles, files, tin cups, tobacco,
and other goods.[48] Furthermore, it was unlikely that the
Indian country would be "filled with soldiers." The
military establishment did not have the numbers to do the
job, and Congress was in no mood to provide them. In
spite of this drawback, General William T. Sherman opposed ransoming a young Texas boy held by the Noconie
Comanches. The general who had taught the South that
war is hell declared: "It is better the Indian race be oblit-
erated, than stolen children be paid for." He proposed
that the Comanches be told to surrender the boy without
ransom, or suffer "war to the death."[49]

By the summer of 1867 Agent Leavenworth reflected
the government's dilemma. He was caught between the
raiding propensities of the Indians for whom he was responsible and the outrage of the white citizens to whom he
ultimately must answer. "I think it hard to punish the innocent for the guilty," said the agent, "but this raiding
into Texas must and shall be stopped."[50]

By July the army was in the field and there was an excellent chance that the innocent would suffer with the guilty.
Ten Bears, the principal Yamparika chief, was heading for
the sanctuary of the Leased District with 250 to 300
lodges of Comanches and Kiowas. This party very possibly
included warriors who had raided recently. Even if it did
not, it stood an excellent chance of being attacked if it
encountered an army column. Should that occur another
massacre could result. The worried Leavenworth decided
to go to Washington, something he was too prone to do, to
present his version of the problem on the south plains. On
the way he met the Peace Commission, which Congress
had created on July 20.

The situation of the Comanches, as their agent turned
back to aid the commissioners, was difficult. The degree

of hostility to the whites varied from band to band. Many
Penetethka Comanches, following the lead of Toshaway,
had been reservation Indians since the days on the Clear
Fork of the Brazos. Other Penetethkas preferred the example of the Quahadas and had scorned reservation life.
These warriors were as active as any other Comanches in
raiding the frontier. Among the Yamparikas a smaller
fraction could be called peaceful, and among the Cochetethkas and Noconies even fewer. The Quahadas, with
their trade needs met by the Comancheros, contained no
element seeking peace with the United States. Despite
the lack of any consensus among the Comanches, and the
complete absence of any tribal political machinery to reflect it if there had been, they were about to be invited
to enter upon another round of negotiations with the
United States.

2. The Treaty of Medicine Lodge

Early in October 1867 one hundred lodges of Comanches gathered on the banks of Medicine Lodge Creek in southern Kansas to meet with members of the Peace Commission. They came at the request of their agent, Colonel Leavenworth, who had been directed by Central Superintendent Thomas Murphy to assemble them there. Leavenworth also had summoned the Kiowas and the Kiowa-Apaches, and the agent for the Southern Cheyennes and the Arapahos had produced delegations of his tribes. By the time the proceedings had ended, over 4,000 Indians would have gathered on Medicine Lodge Creek, and the commissioners would have completed three treaties with the tribesmen.[1]

Although the Comanches were the most numerous of the Indians under his charge, Leavenworth had been able to produce fewer of them than of Kiowas or Kiowa-Apaches. As usual, it is difficult to determine exactly which Comanche bands were represented in the camps on Medicine Lodge. The main Comanche spokesman was Ten Bears, a Yamparika. Toshaway, the Penetethka, was the only other Comanche to speak, although the final treaty was signed by eight others. Of these, only the band affiliations of Howeah (Gap in the Woods) and Iron Mountain, both Yamparikas, and Horse Back, a Noconie, can be determined. It is very likely that three or four Comanche bands, among them certainly the Quahadas, were not included in the negotiations.

The Peace Commission's instructions were clear. By negotiation it was to restore peace on the plains and clear the great highway and railroad routes. If it failed, the law that created the commission provided for a recourse to force. The commissioners had decided early to attempt to

27

concentrate the Indians into two areas and had conferred with the Sioux before moving south to meet with the Comanches and other tribes of their region.

The commissioners did not consider the Indians of the southern plains, with the exception of the Cheyennes, whose activities they saw as a reaction to the senseless Sand Creek Massacre, as dangerous as the tribesmen of the northern plains. Agent Leavenworth described his Indians as "quiet and peacable, so far as relates to the Santa Fe road and the northern frontier." He admitted that "wrongs of great magnitude have been committed on the people of Texas" but insisted that Indians other than the Comanches and Kiowas were responsible.[2] In their final report the commissioners, surprisingly, completely exonerated the Comanches of any hostilities since the treaty on the Little Arkansas in 1865 and held the Kiowas responsible for only one raid in Texas.[3] Obviously the commission was more concerned with the fate of settlers in Colorado and Kansas than with their Texas counterparts.

The members of the Peace Commission were Commissioner of Indian Affairs N. G. Taylor, who was elected president of the commission, John B. Henderson, S. S. Tappan, John B. Sanborn, and Generals William T. Sherman, William H. Harney, and Alfred S. Terry. Henderson was chairman of the Senate Committee on Indian Affairs and author of the bill that had created the commission. Both Tappan and Sanborn had served in the Civil War and, like the three generals, were well acquainted with the plains problems. Sherman was unable to be present for the negotiations with the southern tribes and was replaced on the Peace Commission by one of his subordinates, General C. C. Augur.

Congress had specified that the Plains Indians should be located on reservations and the only task left to the commissioners to determine was where. By the time they reached Medicine Lodge Creek they had decided that the tribes would be placed near the Wichita Agency in the Leased District, which was in the western part of Indian

Territory. The Commissioners proposed to set aside the northern part of the Leased District for the Southern Cheyennes and Arapahos, the southern part for the Comanches and Kiowas.

To call negotiations what went on in the large brush arbor where the commissioners confronted the Indians is to imply a give-and-take that was not present. At an initial meeting it was decided to postpone serious negotiations for four days. The Comanches and Kiowas then met with the white men twice before the treaty was signed. The first day (October 19) Senator Henderson opened the proceedings for the commissioners: "We have come to hear all your complaints and to correct all your wrongs." He concluded his initial statement with a reference to a reservation home for the Indians:

> We are authorized by the Great Father to provide for them comfortable homes upon our richest agricultural lands. We are authorized to build for the Indian schoolhouses and churches, and provide teachers to educate his children. We can furnish him with agricultural implements to work, and domestic cattle, sheep and hogs to stock his farm.[4]

The Kiowas and the Comanches took the lead in responding to the Peace Commission, the Cheyennes choosing to wait until they were joined by representatives from a large group of their tribe forty miles away. The Arapahos and the Kiowa-Apaches were content to play their usual subordinate roles. For the Kiowas, Satanta pled innocent to any charges of hostilities but made it clear that he and his people were not interested in being restricted to reservation life. "All the land south of the Arkansas belongs to the Kiowas and Comanches," said the warrior notorious among the whites as a raider, "and I don't want to give away any of it." Of his view of reservations Satanta left little doubt. "I love to roam over the wide prairie," he stated, "and when I do it, I feel free and happy, but when we settle down, we grow pale and die."[5]

Toshaway reminded these commissioners, as he had others on the Little Arkansas in 1865, that taking the white man's road had not paid off for the Penetethka Comanches. "My young men are a scoff and a by-word among the other nations," he lamented. Recalling earlier promises made to his people, Toshaway delivered a warning: "I shall wait till next spring to see if these things shall be given us, if they are not, I and my young men will return with our wild brothers to live on the prairie."[6]

The second day's proceedings found Ten Bears making the only significant speech for the Indians. The Yamparika Comanche spoke in the same vein as had Satanta the first day. Ten Bears was no stranger to this type of deliberation. He had been at Washington in 1863 and on the Little Arkansas in 1865. Peering through gold spectacles possibly acquired on his trip east in 1863, the old chief spoke eloquently and effectively for his people. In the colorful metaphor of the plains Ten Bears opened by expressing his pleasure at being with the commissioners. "My heart is filled with joy when I see you here, as the brooks fill with water when the snows melt in the spring," he proclaimed, "and I feel glad, as the ponies do when the fresh grass starts at the beginning of the year." After declaring Comanches innocent of all depredations, the white-haired chief attributed recent hostilities to aggressions by the "blue dressed soldiers and the Utes." For campfires, said Ten Bears, the soldiers and the Utes burned Comanche lodges. "Instead of hunting game they killed my braves." So it had been in Texas, but the Comanches had struck back:

> We went out like the buffalo bulls when the cows are attacked. When we found them we killed them, and their scalps hang in our lodges. The Comanches are not weak and blind, like the puppies of a dog when seven sleeps old. They are strong and far-sighted, like grown horses. We took their road and we went on it. The white women cried and our women laughed.

As for the proposal of the reservation, the proud old warrior would have none of it:

> I was born upon the prairie, where the wind blew free and there was nothing to break the light of the sun. I was born where there were no enclosures and where everything drew a free breath. I want to die there and not within walls. . . . If the Texans had kept out of my country there might have been peace. But that which you now say we must live on is too small. The Texans have taken away the places where the grass grew the thickest and the timber was the best. Had we kept that, we might have done the things you ask. But it is too late. The white man has the country which we loved, and we only wish to wander on the prairie until we die. . . .[7]

It was a magnificent statement, but the commissioners were committed to a course of action. Senator Henderson responded that the buffalo were rapidly diminishing and "the Indian must change the road his father trod, or he must suffer, and probably die." And, asserted the senator, "We wish you to live, and we will offer you the way." Referring to the influx of whites, Henderson declared, "Before all the good lands are taken by whites, we wish to set aside a part of them for your exclusive home."

The senator then alluded to a promise the treaty was not to make: "When you become hungry and naked, you can go there and be fed and clothed." The treaty did not provide for rations although the United States did furnish them in varying degrees throughout the life of the reservation. More honest, in terms of the treaty already decided upon by the commissioners, were Senator Henderson's references to services of a blacksmith, a physician, a farmer, and an annual issue of clothing. To facilitate Indian acceptances the senator promised that the Indians would not have to give up hunting buffalo. "You may roam over the broad plains south of the Arkansas river, and hunt the buffalo as you have done in years past, but you must have a place you can call your own," he said. Henderson concluded by locating this place "on the Red River and around the Wichita Mountains" and stating that the treaty would be ready for them to sign the following morning.[8]

At the next day's session the commissioners presented the proposed treaty to the Comanches and Kiowas, article by article. It was basically the same document that would be presented to the other Plains tribes. There seems to have been surprisingly little protest from the Indians. Satanta grumbled briefly about the houses and referred to the decline of the Penetethkas who had taken the white man's road, and then signed. The only Comanche to speak at that point was Toshaway: "I like those houses built, but if they are not completed before next summer, I don't want them."[9]

These comments probably are an index to the Indian understanding of the negotiations and of the treaty process. The only provision in the treaty dealing with Indian houses was an article providing one for Toshaway specifically. That the treaty would be ratified by the Senate in time for the construction of Toshaway's house before the summer of 1868 was very doubtful. Nor is there any evidence that the commissioners discouraged the Penetethka chief from thinking that he could have his house so soon.

The commissioners had something to sell and undoubtedly emphasized the positive features of the treaty, the goods and services promised the Indians. The assurance that the Indians could hunt south of the Arkansas River "so long as the buffalo may range thereon in such numbers as to justify the chase" was undoubtedly a key clause in gaining the acceptance of the Indians.[10] Although for a decade white observers had been predicting the annihilation of the buffalo herds, the Comanches and Kiowas clearly could not conceive of the plains bare of the enormous herds. There had been times recently when they were hard to find, but the following year might see the

Fort Sill Indian School, circa 1871. (Oklahoma Historical Society)

Quirtsquip, 1872. (Smithsonian Institution, National Anthropological Archives)

Asatoyet, 1872. (Smithsonian Institution, National Anthropological Archives)

Cheevers, 1872. (Smithsonian Institution, National Anthropological Archives)

buffalo return in apparently undiminished numbers. The idea that their hunting outside the boundaries of their reservation now would be a privilege, not a right, and capable of revocation was a subtle distinction the Comanches and Kiowas hardly could be expected to grasp given the language barriers. Probably only a handful of Comanches left the council grounds aware that within a year or two they would be expected to give up their roaming and gather on a reservation.

Perhaps even more important in explaining why the Indian leadership trooped forward to make their X's when requested to do so was their anticipation of the distribution of annuities and presents. This had brought them and their followers to Medicine Lodge Creek and it kept them there, some for several weeks. Previous negotiations with the United States had meant little more to the Indians than a distribution of presents, and the promised gifts were uppermost in the minds of the Comanches and Kiowas. During the sessions they had made several references to the pending distribution of goods, and it was lavish by their standards.

Some Comanches already had received one issue of annuity goods from Colonel Leavenworth under the terms of the 1865 treaty.[11] Now they shared in the bonanza at the council grounds. Included were the usual blankets, axes, bolts of cloth, bells, and other trinkets. An unusual item was 3,423 surplus army bugles, nearly enough for every man, woman, and child on Medicine Lodge Creek. Satanta had come to the proceedings with a prized possession, a battered old bugle, strung over his shoulder.[12] Now they were a dreg on the market.

The Comanche warrior fondling a new Colt revolver, and his wives stowing away the calico, sugar, and trinkets, did not comprehend the magnitude of the commitment made in their name by their ten chiefs and headmen who signed the treaty. Its articles can be discussed in two categories according to the mandate the commissioners had received from Congress. First and foremost were, hopefully, measures contributing to a reduction in Indian hostilities and a guarantee of safe passage on the great highways and railroad routes. The treaty with the Comanches and Kiowas provided for war between the parties to cease, punishment of both Indian and white wrongdoers, and the cessation of any opposition by the Indians to construction of railroads outside their reservation. It provided specifically that the Indians would give up capturing white women and children and killing and scalping white men. Aside from closing the new reservation to unauthorized white men, nothing in the treaty dealt with the basic problem, the white men who invaded Comanche and Kiowa territory. Here, as elsewhere, the wording is virtually identical to other treaties negotiated by the commission in 1867 and 1868.

Avoidance of an expensive war and a guarantee of safe passage for the great highways and railroad routes had been the prime objectives of Congress, but the act of July 19, 1867 had also directed the Peace Commission to "insure civilization for the Indians." As a first step the Comanches and Kiowas would be relegated to 3 million acres in the Leased District as their permanent reservation. By the 1865 treaty they had given up, although they probably did not realize it, their claims to at least half the area they had once roamed. Now they had surrendered all but a relatively tiny corner of their once vast domain. Their compensation was in no way commensurate with the value of the land they were surrendering. The Comanches and Kiowas gave up their income under the 1865 treaty and in lieu of it they would receive for thirty years an annuity consisting of one change of clothing per person and $25,000 worth of goods "as from time to time the condition and necessities of the Indians may indicate to be proper." However, there were other financial commitments of a limited nature made by the United States.

To facilitate the civilization process, the treaty committed the United States to provide ten buildings, not to cost more than a total of $28,500, to house employees and key agency functions. The employees would include a physician, carpenter, blacksmith, miller, engineer, and agent. With the exception of the agent, the government had the option to withdraw its support for these positions after ten years and replace it with a lump sum of $10,000 a year to be devoted to education. In addition, for at least twenty years the United States would provide a school and a teacher for every thirty Indian children who would attend. In return, the Indians pledged themselves "to compel their children, male and female, between the ages of six and sixteen years to attend school."

There were other minor financial considerations. To purchase farm tools and seeds, a total of $175 for each head of family would be provided over a period of four years. Overcome by euphoric visions of Indian farmers competing to have the highest grain yield per acre and the best-producing milk cows, the commissioners in a final burst of unrealism promised a $500 fund annually for three years for awards to the ten most successful farmers among the Comanches and Kiowas.

In a separate treaty signed by the Comanches, Kiowas, and Kiowa-Apaches, the latter tribe agreed to settle among the Comanches and Kiowas.[13] The Kiowa-Apaches were to share equally in all the benefits provided by the Comanche and Kiowa treaty, and the annuity of $25,000 was increased to $30,000 to compensate for their addition. The Indians did not seek this accommodation; it was part of the grand design of concentrating the Indians and reducing the number of agencies. In 1865 the Kiowa-Apaches had been lumped with the Cheyennes and Arapahos, but their normal association was with the Kiowas. The Indians accepted this treaty as they had accepted the others. The white chiefs seemed to want it badly and if it would expedite the distribution of the annuities and presents, the Indians were willing to humor the whites.

As the Comanches, Kiowas, and Kiowa-Apaches began to disperse, the remainder of the Cheyennes made their appearance and the commissioners set to work to get their

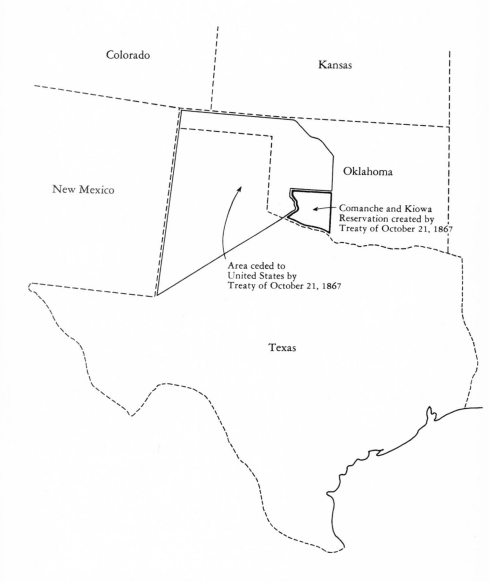

Colorado

Kansas

New Mexico

Oklahoma

Comanche and Kiowa
Reservation created by
Treaty of October 21, 1867

Area ceded to
United States by
Treaty of October 21, 1867

Texas

Map 3. Area of the Comanche and Kiowa Treaty with the United States of October 21, 1867. (Adapted from map 57, *18th Annual Report of the Bureau of American Ethnology,* part 2)

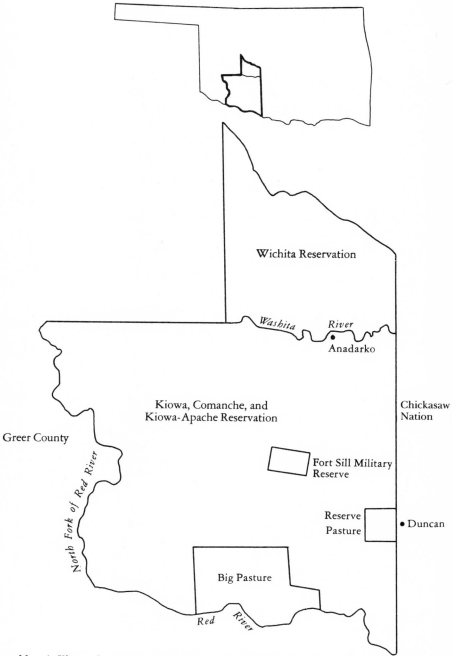

Map 4. Kiowa, Comanche, and Kiowa-Apache Reservation and Wichita Reservation, according to the Treaty of October 21, 1867. (Adapted from map 23, *18th Annual Report of the Bureau of American Ethnology*, part 2)

agreement to a treaty similar to that carrying the X's of Satanta and Ten Bears. Having waited impatiently six days until all the Cheyennes arrived, the commissioners wasted no time in this business. It had taken three days to set the stage for the signing of the Comanche and Kiowa treaty; this one was rushed through in one day.

In their final report to Congress the commissioners were harsh in their criticism of others. Colonel Chivington's troops of Sand Creek Massacre infamy were indicted for engaging in torture, mutilation, and indiscriminate slaughter. The whites were clearly labeled the aggressors in the fighting on the plains and the removal policy that had brought the Five Civilized Tribes and others west was judged "revolting."[14]

That the commissioners themselves had participated in a mockery of true bargaining was not mentioned in the report. They were returning with treaties that would be presented to the Senate as representing the will of the tribes involved, although there was no machinery among the Comanches and the other tribes for registering it and the commissioners knew it. And certainly the 600 or so Comanches present could not commit the four or five times that many other Comanches to residing on a reservation. The only way that the United States would be able to locate these Indians on a reservation and keep them there was by military force. What the treaties did was not to provide the peace on the plains Congress had hoped for but to give the stamp of legitimacy to United States efforts to concentrate the Indians and open the region to white exploitation.

"If we can civilize in 25 years," said the commissioners, "it will be a vast improvement on the operations of the past."[15] But the basic provisions in the treaties with the southern Plains tribes were not new. The midwestern states were littered with the wrecks of small tribes whose treaties with the United States had subjected them to the same reservation process stressing isolation from casual contacts with whites and the introduction of an agency staff designed to educate them in the ways of the white farmer. The government's record in fulfilling the terms of those treaties was miserable. After all, like those dictated on Medicine Lodge Creek, their primary objectives had been to ease the threat to frontier settlers and reduce Indian landholdings, not civilize Indians. Finally, the provisions for teachers, physicians, and farmers implied a people desiring such help. This certainly was not the case with the typical Comanche, who wanted nothing more than to be left alone to pursue the life Ten Bears had described so movingly.

The commissioners were realistic enough to recognize that their only hope lay with the young. "If we attempt to force the older Indians from the chase," read their report, "it will involve us in war." But if peace could be maintained a few years, the buffalo would have disappeared. "In the meantime," the commissioners predicted hopefully, "we will have formed a nucleus of civilization among the young that will restrain the old and furnish them a home and subsistence when the game is gone."[16]

It remained to be seen if a program launched by as specious a document as the Treaty of Medicine Lodge Creek could be effective. More financial support and understanding of the aboriginal population would be required than white men had demonstrated to date. As the commissioners themselves pointed out in their report:

> Members of Congress understand the negro question, and talk learnedly of finance and other problems of political economy, but when the progress of settlement reaches the Indian's home, the only question considered is, "how best to get his lands." When they are obtained, the Indian is lost sight of.[17]

3. The New Era Opens Inauspiciously

The first year under the new treaty saw the United States attempting to settle the Indians on their reservation while the Indians tried to continue life as usual. The Comanches scattered to their winter camps at the conclusion of the deliberations on Medicine Lodge Creek, and the Peace Commission headed east. Agent Leavenworth followed the commissioners and from late November until early January he was in Washington, as usual seeming to prefer jousting with Indian Office bureaucrats to trying to get his elusive charges to hold still for his advice and counsel.

Although the new treaty had yet to be ratified, Leavenworth pressed Commissioner of Indian Affairs Taylor to take the first steps in locating the Comanches and Kiowas in the Leased District and beginning the civilization program. The agent represented his Indians as wishing to launch farming careers, which revealed either Leavenworth's ignorance of the tribes under his jurisdiction or a desire to mislead the commissioner.[1] Only a few Comanches could have made such a request and they would have been among the Penetethkas already assigned to the Wichita Agency in the Leased District. Nevertheless, the agent estimated he would need rations for 1,800 Yamparikas, 700 Cochetethkas, and 600 Noconies. At least he did not include the Quahadas, whose numbers he set at 1,000.[2]

Together with promises of support for farming operations in the spring, Agent Leavenworth secured appointment of a physician, Dr. Edward Palmer, and a clerk, S. T. Walkley. He also selected a site for the agency on Cache Creek in the southeastern part of the Leased District. But in the middle of February Leavenworth finally arrived in the vicinity of Fort Cobb to learn that Indians had threatened freighters with goods designated for Cache Creek and that the wagon train had held up in Eureka Valley east of Fort Cobb. The agent proceeded to set up shop right there and this was to be the site of the Kiowa, Comanche, and Kiowa-Apache Agency until early the following year.

If Agent Leavenworth ever had had any idea that his charges were clamoring for the beginning of their transition from hunters to farmers, the next three months thoroughly disillusioned him. He returned from his extended absence from the plains to learn that the Comanches and Kiowas had been raiding steadily in Texas, and they were to continue to do so during the remainder of Leavenworth's tenure as agent.

It all began very soon after the deliberations on Medicine Lodge Creek. Before the commissioners could get back to Washington with their claims of having pacified the Comanches, two young men of the tribe, sons of Ten Bears and Toshaway no less, had persuaded a dozen of their peers to accompany them on a raid through the Chickasaw Nation and across Red River into Texas.[3]

This was just the beginning. Every band provided warriors for the numerous raids that followed, although most Penetethkas and many Yamparikas abstained. The Comanches, and the Kiowas as well, made no effort to conceal their activities; the young men said that they had never made peace with Texas and were not going to do so now. In December 1868 interpreter Phillip McCusker termed "almost incredible" the Comanche haul of Texas horses and mules for that year.[4] For the moment the Comanchero trade had been broken up and the Indians did not have a market for cattle in New Mexico. However, horses remained a warrior's most important possession and status symbol. By twos and threes, by the dozen and by the hundred, horses from Texas ranches and farms were driven off to swell the herds of proud Comanche warriors. It also was maintained by some that white traders in the vicinity of Fort Cobb were willing to buy horses and mules from the Indians, no questions asked, if the price was right.

The Indians likewise brought back from Texas scalps and prisoners. In May 1868 in a typical operation a war party of Noconies, Yamparikas, and Cochetethkas crossed into the state and struck an outlying farm in Grayson County. They carried off three McElroy children and killed their young uncle. The Comanches also arrived back in the vicinity of their agency with forty Texas horses.

The Comanche and Kiowa depredations south of Red River inspired curiously muffled reaction from the officials responsible for those tribes. In September 1868 Central Superintendent Murphy could say: "So far as I can learn these Indians have committed no depredations since they signed their treaty at Medicine Lodge Creek (excepting a few raids made into Texas)."[5]

Meanwhile, some Texans were making their protests directly to Commissioner of Indian Affairs Taylor. One concerned a raid in Denton County in which eight whites were killed and ten women and children taken captive. Some idea of the ordeal of the parents whose children were carried away was to be found in a letter to Taylor from a man whose teenage daughter had been abducted three years earlier at the same time that his wife had been killed. Writing in the summer of 1868 G. W. Todd passed on a report from an army officer that Todd's daughter Alice was alive and being held by the Kiowas but that Leavenworth could not secure permission to ransom her. "If I had money all the money I would give," pleaded the distraught father, "but money I have not." Describing himself as too poor to leave the area, Todd lamented, "I have been living on the frontier since 1853, and I now curse the day when I commenced it."[6] Todd was to endure months more of terrible anxiety before he learned that his daughter was dead. She had been captured by Comanches, not Kiowas, and they killed her shortly afterward.

The Texan's reference to the prohibition on ransom highlighted a problem in recovering captives. Agents and army officials were constantly being notified of missing white women and children. They might be traced through discrete inquiry by traders visiting Indian camps or by interrogation of band chiefs come to the agencies for rations or annuities. Frequently the search was unsuccessful because, as was the case with Alice Todd, the captive might have been killed. Or the captive might have been traded from one band to another. This would complicate not only physically locating the individual but securing his release.

The government's official policy was no ransom. Had this been followed strictly, few of the white women and children would have been recovered. The Indian viewpoint was simple. The captive was his either by purchase or as a result of his prowess as a warrior. He would not surrender his prize without compensation, and if he were pressured to do so the warrior was known to kill the captive rather than cooperate. Agent Leavenworth in his first encounter with Comanches from the legendary Quahada band was unable to get them to release white children they held because he could not promise them a large ransom. The agent, however, was able to buy the release of the McElroy children from some Cochetethkas, and from Noconies he obtained a girl about twelve years old whom they had "shamefully abused" after killing her mother and baby brother.[7]

In the three months in early 1868 that he was on duty in Eureka Valley, Agent Leavenworth distributed to the Comanches their annuities, plus thousands of dollars worth of rations neither the 1865 nor the 1867 treaty called for. This was an obvious weakness in the treaties and in the civilization program. The treaties with the Comanches, Kiowas, and Kiowa-Apaches did not specify rations for the Indians, although the treaties arranged the next year with Indians of the northern plains did. If the Indians had to hunt to survive they did not have time to plant and care for crops. Without adequate rationing, all the orders from

Washington to keep the Comanches on the reservation would mean nothing, even if the Indians were prepared to give up their nomadic life. Congress never did face up to this problem although it did very grudgingly appropriate funds to supplement what the Indians could obtain by hunting. Since the Comanche treaties did not require this, the United States regarded it as pure charity rather than something to which the Indians were entitled during the transition from hunters to farmers.

From February until November 1868 the ration situation at the Comanche agency was chaotic. Desperately trying to cajole the Indians into attempting farming or at least staying out of Texas, Leavenworth issued what annuity goods he had, permitted the Indians to slaughter cattle brought in as breeding stock to start Indian herds, and bought thousands of dollars worth of rations, on credit, from local traders. This led to official investigations and strident charges of corruption.[8]

The traders did extort exorbitant prices from the frantic agent, but there is no evidence he personally profited. Leavenworth believed he had no alternative. When the party of Quahada Comanches finally called on him after being driven momentarily from the Staked Plains by Navajos, Leavenworth felt he had to satisfy their wish that he "treat them kindly and make their hearts glad." The agent presented twenty-six of the leading Quahadas with uniform coats at $10 each and gave their women over $100 worth of blue cloth. All of this, together with a little tobacco for the Indians, Leavenworth bought on credit from a trader.[9] The agent justified such purchases on the grounds that "Congress would in good faith carry out the promises made to the Indians."[10] His procedures were highly irregular and the government was several years settling his accounts.

By the latter part of May 1868 Leavenworth obviously was discouraged. "My patience with them [the Comanches] and their promises are [sic] exhausted," he informed the commissioner of Indian Affairs.[11] Commissioner Taylor was himself having second thoughts about the situation. In a communication to the secretary of the interior he questioned "inasmuch as the Comanches and Kiowas have acted in bad faith and broken their treaty obligations . . . whether the treaty made with them . . . at Medicine Lodge should be ratified."[12] Taylor still clung, however, to the idea that the Indians should be restricted to a reservation whether or not they wished to be. Meanwhile the Comanches were making memorable Leavenworth's last days as their agent.

The agent had been so alarmed at Indian threats that in late February and again in April he had had cavalry ordered to Eureka Valley. When the Comanches did go on the rampage in May he was defenseless. Warriors, mostly Yamparikas and Quahadas, set out for Texas and en route paid a visit to a trading post near Fort Cobb. From the frightened proprietor they took nearly $5,000 worth of goods, but they left him his scalp. On their return from Texas they burned the headquarters of the Wichita Agency near Fort Cobb and the store they had robbed earlier. By that time Leavenworth had abandoned his post and headed for the safer clime of Washington.

The agent's four-year term was drawing to a close. Discouraged and in ill health he apparently had decided not to seek reappointment. His departure from Eureka Valley perhaps was expedited by a rumor that the Kiowas proposed to kill all the white men in the area. Leavenworth left his clerk, S. T. Walkley, in charge with no orders except to evacuate what equipment and supplies the agency possessed. Walkley loaded those in wagons and sent them off and also abandoned a thirty-two-acre field that had been cleared and planted as a first step in the civilization program. The agent for the Wichitas and affiliated tribes also abandoned his post, and the United States Indian program in the Leased District was a shambles. With impunity, war parties were leaving and returning with scalps, plunder, and captives. Only one clerk, Walkley, remained of the leadership of the two agencies and he was courting the penitentiary by unauthorized purchases of cattle, coffee, sugar, and tobacco in a desperate effort to fill Indian bellies and keep them out of Texas.

Among the whites to flee the valley at this time was the physician whose appointment Leavenworth had recommended. Dr. Edward Palmer had not brought much aid and comfort to the agency's Indians. Leavenworth explained it as dereliction of duty. "He will devote more time and attention in skinning a skunk, or digging round some old rotten stump to discover *some new* species of bug or worm to bottle up and send to the Smithsonian institution," complained the agent, "than he will to a poor sick Indian."[13] The physician's defense was that in the first two months at his post he had made four changes of station and that for private quarters and dispensary he had nothing but a wagon. Of even more concern to Dr. Palmer were the accusations of the "wild Comanches and Kiowas" that he was a "bad medicine man."[14] Some of their people had become ill after his arrival in the area and they held him responsible (some threats to kill him had been made). Interpreter Phillip McCusker did nothing for the physician's nerves by informing him that four years earlier Penetethkas had killed one of their medicine men. Dr. Palmer, formerly hospital steward of the Second Regiment, Colorado Volunteers, retreated eighty miles to Fort Arbuckle and the first Comanche experience with government medical programs ended abruptly.

Back in Washington the Senate was in the process of ratifying the batch of treaties the Peace Commission had arranged with the Indians in the fall of 1867 and the spring of 1868, including those with the Comanches, Kiowas, and Kiowa-Apaches. For months Commissioner of Indian Affairs Taylor had been pleading for funds to be placed at his disposal to meet the commitments of these treaties. He warned that the Indians "will soon lose all confidence in the government" and "an almost endless war will be the result, which will cost millions of dollars to suppress, and to avoid which thousands only are asked."[15] Taylor asked for $1 million to feed the Indians, the Congress appropriated only $500,000 for both subsistence and the civilization programs. Reflecting its ambivalence on the role of the military in the handling of Indian affairs, the Congress that had rejected proposals to return the Office of Indian Affairs to the War Department designated General William T. Sherman to administer the funds.

To discharge his new duties Sherman created northern and southern districts, and to command the southern he selected Major General William B. Hazen. The result was an awkward situation. The Interior Department personnel remained nominally responsible for the tribes, but War Department personnel had charge of dispensing the only substantial fund for the civilization program. For the Comanches and Kiowas the situation was less complicated because A. G. Boone, who returned to replace Leavenworth as their agent, became ill and did not report for duty until December 1868. This left Hazen a clear field with these tribes until then. The general advocated using force, if necessary, to locate Indians on reservations and keep them there. He once justified this by drawing a parallel between the Indian and a leper on a city's streets.[16]

On the southern plains the summer of 1868 had seen more violence. While the Senate was ratifying the treaties that presumably pledged all parties to peace, the Cheyennes were terrorizing settlers in western Kansas and eastern Colorado and the Comanches and Kiowas were continuing their war with Texas. The Comanche raid in the vicinity of Spanish Fork in northern Cooke County on Red River was particularly severe.

The raid was initiated by a son-in-law of the Penetethka Toshaway. He first offered to smoke with the Caddos but they refused him. He then offered the pipe to the son of the Noconie chief Horse Back, who smoked with him, thus pledging himself to the war party. The Penetethka then offered the pipe to others who accepted it, among them a group of Yamparikas who previously had formed their own war party. The final composition of the group reveals one of the difficulties white officials encountered in determining guilt for depredations. As the war party crossed the Red River into Texas it included a total of twenty-eight Comanches (ten Noconies, four Penetethkas, two Cochetethkas, and twelve Yamparikas), two Kiowas, one Wichita, and three Kichais. They returned with many horses and mules, including some stolen in the Chickasaw Nation on their way back, and several scalps. These trophies were celebrated in a dance early in September near the agency in Eureka Valley.

Clerk Walkley passed on to General Hazen the Indian version of one incident during the raid. Coming in sight of a farmhouse, the Indians had put out sentinels and surrounded the dwelling. A scout reported spotting a woman in a rocking chair beyond curtained windows. Checking to be sure no men were around, he signaled his fellows to close in. Whooping and hollering, thirteen of them crashed through the windows and doors. After they had raped the woman, Horse Back's son drove a tomahawk into her head and then Toshaway's son-in-law scalped her. Before leaving the house the Indians reported they killed three or four of her children. They also bragged, according to Walkley, of having "had two white squaws whom they ravished as much as they wanted to and then threw them away."[17]

Such reports of Texas raids were coming in throughout the summer of 1868, but it was the white casualties in eastern Colorado and western Kansas that brought out the troops. Late in August, General Sherman ordered General Philip Sheridan to drive all Indians south of the Kansas line. The problem, as usual, was how to prevent the innocent from suffering with the guilty. Sherman left it to Hazen to provide a refuge for the friendly Comanches and Kiowas and allotted him $50,000 to support them. On the southern plains at least, most of the fund Congress appropriated to launch a civilization program actually would go for rations for those Indians termed friendly while the army strove to locate and punish the hostiles.

Before Sheridan got his campaign under way, he and Hazen met September 20 with Comanches and Kiowas at Fort Larned. The generals told the Indians they must report to their agency in the Leased District, where Hazen would be headquartered at Fort Cobb, or be considered hostile. They promised to provide rations for the Indian trek to Eureka Valley. The generals estimated that it would take ten days to get the rations together and suggested that, in the interim, the Indians should hunt buffalo nearby. At the end of the ten-day period the Comanches and Kiowas did not return and Sheridan was convinced they had joined the hostile Cheyennes and Arapahos. Hazen was more optimistic and lingered at Fort Larned until October, awaiting the return of the Comanches and Kiowas. It was Hazen's guess that the Indians had decided not to risk returning to Fort Larned for the rations and were slowly moving toward Fort Cobb, hunting as they went. This was the case.[18]

Meanwhile the situation at the agencies in the Leased District had deteriorated even further. The ration contractor refused any more credit to Walkley, and in desperation he turned to private traders for cattle to issue to the clamorous Indians. Later investigations indicated that the cattle Walkley obtained from the traders may have been stolen in Texas by Caddo Indians from the Wichita Agency. The clerk's situation had become impossible and he resigned October 10, 1868, when Lieutenant Philip L. Lee arrived on the scene with two companies of cavalry from Fort Arbuckle.

Lieutenant Lee was followed shortly by Captain Henry E. Alvord, who was to be in charge of Indian affairs in the Leased District pending the arrival of General Hazen. The general did not reach Fort Cobb until November 8, having been forced by reports of war parties into a roundabout route by way of Forts Gibson and Arbuckle. Hazen found a very confusing and perplexing situation. Seventeen hundred Indians, 700 of them Comanches, were at Fort Cobb. Delegations from other camps along the nearby Washita and Canadian rivers came in when they heard of the general's arrival. All were hungry and Hazen had the additional task of separating the friendlies from the hostiles. In the latter category Sheridan had lumped the Cheyennes and Arapahos, and when Black Kettle and other Cheyenne chiefs called on Hazen (November 20) he informed them that he had no authority to make peace with Cheyennes, only Sheridan could do that. Black Kettle and his people returned to their camps on the Washita about eighty miles away.

It was in many respects a repetition of what had happened to Black Kettle in 1865. Then he had called at Fort Lyon and asked for peace and was told to go into camp on Sand Creek, where Chivington found him. This time he had not been promised peace but undoubtedly did believe his conference with Hazen assured him some security. Superintendent Murphy was a better judge of coming events. "In all these military movements," wrote Murphy a few days before Black Kettle's interview with Hazen, "I fancy I see another Sand Creek Massacre. If these Indians are to be congregated at Fort Cobb or elsewhere, under promises of protection, and then pounced upon by the military," said the superintendent, "it were far better that they had never been sent for, or any such promises made them."[19] The Cheyenne and Arapaho agent also suspected something of that nature and resigned rather than be involved.

Hazen knew that even as he and Black Kettle conferred, Sherman's columns were engaged in an unusual winter campaign designed to strike the Indians while they were immobilized by the weather. The morning of November 27, 1868, after Black Kettle got back to his camp on the Washita, troops commanded by Lieutenant Colonel George A. Custer struck. The cavalry surprised the Indians and overran the Cheyenne camp, killing Black Kettle and many other men, women, and children and taking some prisoners. There were camps of other southern Plains Indians along the Washita and warriors from them, including some Comanches, came to the aid of the Cheyennes. Custer retreated before he was surrounded, avoiding the fate that befell him under similar circumstances a decade later on the Little Big Horn.

Christmas Day 1868 another of Sheridan's columns found an Indian encampment and the Battle of Soldier Spring ensued. This camp, occupied primarily by Comanches, was at the western end of the Wichita Mountains near the North Fork of Red River. The troops drove the Indians from the camp, killing twenty-five in the fighting, and burned the village. The unrelenting winter campaign was forcing the Indians to report to General Hazen and declare themselves friendly.

The precise situation of the Comanches by the winter of 1868-69 was, as usual, impossible to ascertain. Fewer than 1,000 ever showed up at Eureka Valley. Ten Bear's Yamparikas had been foremost among those who met with Sheridan and Hazen at Fort Larned in September. Presumably those Indians moved south to the vicinity of Fort Cobb and joined other Comanches there, mostly Penetethkas. Sheridan's winter strategy was a shock to the Indians, who were not prepared to wage war at that time of the year, and Comanches from other bands gravitated toward Fort Cobb and the degree of safety Hazen provided. Mowaway (Shaking Hand), the principal Cochetethka chief, reported in to Fort Bascom, New Mexico, and sought to make peace with authorities there. They refused and took into custody the chief and several warriors and women with him.[20]

General Hazen prevented another clash between troops and possibly friendly Indians in mid-December. Hearing that troops were within twenty miles of Fort Cobb, he hurried off messengers to inform them that all the Indians in the vicinity were friendly. In the face of that message Sheridan, who was accompanying the column, refrained from attacking the winter camps. As he made clear when he arrived at Fort Cobb, Sheridan regretted Hazen's intercession. The fiery Sheridan was convinced that the Kiowas and Comanches as a group were hostile and should be punished. In February he was prepared to accept Hazen's suggestion made in December that certain Kiowas and Noconie Comanches be hanged for their activities in Texas. Now Hazen counseled against it on the grounds that the Indians had surrendered after "a kind of tacit pledge to them of security."[21]

Sheridan did have his way about Fort Cobb. A few days there convinced Sheridan that another site would be preferable. Late in December 1868 a party of officers, including Hazen, reconnoitered the area thirty-five miles to the south and decided on a location near where Medicine Bluff Creek joined Cache Creek on its way south to Red River. By the middle of January 1869 the troops had been transferred to Camp Washita, later to be renamed Fort Sill, and Hazen was preparing to move his Indian headquarters there.

By using the army's commissary organization Hazen brought some order into the ration system and at the same time obtained food at a considerable saving over what Leavenworth and Walkley had paid. Also, he was not reluctant to issue rations. "By placing the Indian on prescribed reservations we have assumed the obligation to feed him until we teach him to feed himself in a new way," argued the general.[22] However, even with the improvement he provided (he spent almost $100,000), the ration was inadequate for complete subsistence and the Indians had to supplement it by hunting.

As a step toward making the Indian self-sufficient, Hazen had 1,200 acres plowed and fenced. More than 100 small garden patches and 300 acres of corn were planted. Some fruit trees were set out and a few buildings thrown up. Most of this work was done by white men hired for the purpose. Hazen did see a hopeful sign in the handful of Comanche males, probably Pentethkas, who labored in the fields with the women.

One man who was not pleased with the way things were going was the agent for the Comanches and Kiowas,

A. G. Boone. He had finally arrived at Eureka Valley late in December 1868. He found his position quite frustrating. General Hazen controlled the funds and Boone did not have even a copy of the Treaty of Medicine Lodge. The agent and his family lived in tents throughout the winter and with the coming of spring he described General Hazen as the "Agent in fact" and himself as "a nominal agent." His object in a letter to Superintendent Murphy was to discover "for what purpose I am here."[23] His situation was resolved shortly. Within two weeks another man accepted appointment to replace Boone as agent to the Comanches, Kiowas, and Kiowa-Apaches.

The new appointee was Lawrie Tatum, a Quaker, who was part of an experiment in administration of Indian affairs launched by newly elected President Ulysses S. Grant. As general of the army Grant had favored the replacement of civilian agents by army officers and this continued to be his preference. Large numbers of officers were used in this capacity, in 1869 forty-nine of a possible seventy being military men, but in July 1870 Congress banned the practice. If civilians were to be appointed, Grant seems to have believed that religious bodies should be able to come up with better ones than were available through the patronage process. Between his election and his inauguration he had received two Quaker delegations who urged him to improve the quality of appointments to the Indian Service and stress peaceful and Christian methods in his own Indian policy. To the surprise of the Quakers they were invited to submit nominees for posts in the Indian Service and after his inauguration President Grant turned over two jurisdictions to them, including the Central Superintendency and with it the Comanches. After the congressional prohibition on the use of army officers as agents, Grant expanded the "Quaker policy" to permit other religious groups to nominate agents.

The Quaker policy blended with the peace policy, whose origins lay, together with a little humanity, in the reluctance of Congress to spend the money necessary to impose a military solution on the Indian problem in the West. In the spring of 1869 Congress manifested its concern for a more efficient and realistic Indian policy by other legislation. The Indian appropriation bill passed on April 10 provided $2 million "to enable the President to maintain the peace among and with the various tribes . . . and to promote civilization among said Indians." About $250,000 of this would go for rations for the Indians of the three southwestern agencies, the Kiowa, Comanche, and Kiowa-Apache, the Cheyenne and Arapaho, and the Wichita.

To supervise the distribution of the $2 million Congress also authorized the creation of what would be known as the Board of Indian Commissioners, ten men who for many years would exercise considerable influence through their power to audit the purchase and distribution of Indian supplies and to inspect agency facilities. The presence of only two senators in the chamber while key amendments to this Indian appropriation bill were being voted on suggests that Indian affairs was not one of the principal concerns of Congress.

It remained to be seen whether the Quaker administration of Comanche affairs would serve to implement the policies and promises spelled out in the Treaty of Medicine Lodge. Sheridan's winter campaign had driven many of the Indians to seek the security of the agency, but over half of the Comanches had not yet done so. After witnessing the chaos and confusion of Eureka Valley and the dedication with which the Indians continued to pursue their war with Texas, an observer in Indian Territory in 1869 might have wondered if the mere introduction of Quaker religious and humanitarian zeal would do the job.

4. The Education of a Quaker

The appointment in May 1869 of Lawrie Tatum as their agent associated the Comanches with the Quaker experiment in the administration of Indian reservations. Tatum filled key positions at the agency with fellow religionists and he in turn reported to a Quaker, Enoch Hoag, the central superintendent. Hoag was the link between Washington and a total of ten Quaker agents under his jurisdiction. The purse strings, however, still were held in Washington and it was questionable whether Congress would provide funds on a sufficiently large scale to permit the type of program the Quakers envisioned.

Tatum later stated that the first he knew of his appointment was when he read it in a newspaper.[1] Nevertheless, it could hardly have come as a complete surprise to the forty-seven-year-old farmer, because the Iowa Quaker had evinced much interest in Indian affairs and Hoag also was an Iowan. Tatum signaled to Washington that they had a new type of agent by crossing out "So help me God" and replacing "Sworn" with "Affirmed" on the oath of office form. Correspondence sprinkled with *thee*'s and *thou*'s now began to show up in the Indian Office mail and the Indians observed in their agents a new demeanor.

Tatum, like the good Quaker he was, would not permit swearing and drinking around him, and he discouraged the use of tobacco. The absence of the ubiquitous revolver and knife also served to set the Quakers apart from other white men on the frontier. The new agent was imbued with his sect's belief that kindness begat kindness and that the Indians would respond to just treatment and appeals to their better nature. Never did such lofty principles face a sterner test. The Comanches, Kiowas, and Kiowa-Apaches were warrior peoples leading a life habituated to violence.

59

These Indians practiced among themselves cooperation and sharing to a remarkable degree. However, these qualities dissipated as band lines were crossed, and beyond tribal lines only transitory and uneasy alliances served to soften the harsh face the Comanches turned to the rest of the world. They suffered brutalities at the hands of others and dispensed them with a vengeance when they had the upper hand.

Aside from his Quaker faith it is difficult to discern what qualified Tatum for his new position. Apparently it was the first time he had met Indians such as the Comanches, and he did not have administrative experience or familiarity in dealing with government agencies. Moreover, he was assuming a position of which he was, for all intents and purposes, the first occupant. A. G. Boone had operated under the shadow of General Hazen, who had functioned in the army's chain of command. Leavenworth and his predecessors had done little more than distribute annuities and attempt to maintain a tenuous contact with the far-flung bands. The Treaty of Medicine Lodge specified only that the Indians were to have an agent who would reside among them and process their disputes with the whites. Now Tatum found himself performing all the executive, legislative, and judicial functions for several thousand Indians speaking nine languages and occupying an area the size of Connecticut. The Quaker not only was responsible for the more than 4,000 Comanches, Kiowas, and Kiowa-Apaches but also for the more than 1,000 Indians of the Wichita Agency, which temporarily was assigned to Tatum.

To reach his headquarters adjacent to Fort Sill, Tatum had traveled by wagon over the rolling prairies from Junction City, Kansas, the nearest railhead in 1869. Fort Sill, about twenty-three miles from the eastern edge of his domain, turned out to be little more than a collection of stone and frame structures, built and building, scattered around the perimeter of a parade ground. There were good stands of tall timber near the fort and two streams, Medicine Bluff and Cache creeks. Cache Creek ran between the fort and the site General Hazen had chosen for his agency headquarters, although the general had begun construction of buildings on both sides of the stream.

Within sight of the agency was the eastern end of the Wichita Mountains, a series of rocky elevations that ran through the reservation to within a few miles of its western boundary. Other than an occasional shrub or gnarled tree, little grew on these mountains. The rolling prairies were covered with nutritious grasses and the western half of the reservation was buffalo range. The relatively little good farmland was generally found in the creek and river bottoms. Besides buffalo, the hunter could find deer, antelope, bear, and a variety of small game. The fisherman might try his skill on bass, trout, and drum. The women and children were able to find wild onions and turnips on the prairie, and nuts and berries in the wooded areas.

The reservation had the typical plain's weather extremes. For weeks in the summer the temperature would reach the upper nineties or higher while the hot winds burned the crops and grass brown. During the winter, northers blew in quickly and the thermometer could register a drop of twenty-five degrees in a single hour. Rainfall averaged around twenty inches a year, but too little fell during the summer months for farming as Tatum had known it in Iowa. In many respects it was a harsh country, but a beautiful one for those who admired the awesome sweep of its rolling prairies, broken by tree-lined streams and the bulk of the boulder-cluttered Wichita Mountains.

Tatum had only two weeks to familiarize himself with the reservation and its occupants before General Hazen transferred the responsibilities to him. The Quaker's first concern was for the buildings and other facilities he would need to operate the reservation as he hoped. The two commissary buildings Hazen had erected were already beginning to sag but would be the nucleus of the agency settlement on the west side of Cache Creek, about a mile and a half from Fort Sill headquarters. Tatum decided to abandon the adobe building begun on the east side of

Cache Creek for fear high water would be a problem in the spring of the year.

The general had had some land broken and fencing begun on a modest scale. Tatum's first move was to apply for $14,000 to finish this project.[2] Before he could learn that there were no funds for this purpose, a delegation from the Board of Indian Commissioners, and two Friends inspecting agencies in the Central Superintendency, visited Fort Sill. Perhaps emboldened by discussions with the commissioners and the Friends, the agent submitted an estimate of his needs for the remainder of the current fiscal year and for the next one as well.

The package Tatum asked for must have met with wry amusement from the clerks in the Indian Office. To complete the fiscal year he wanted twenty-seven farmers and fourteen cooks, to be increased to eighty farmers and thirty cooks the following year. In addition he asked for 120 plows, 160 mules, 25 wagons, and a variety of other items. The total bill would run to over $200,000.[3] Superintendent Hoag endorsed the request and sent it on to Washington. The response from the Indian Office was a prompt negative; there were no funds for operations on this scale and the treaty authorized only one farmer, not twenty-seven. Tatum's other proposals were likewise summarily dismissed.[4]

The spring of 1869 had been an unusually favorable one for crops and Tatum had concluded on his arrival: "All the breadstuffs for the Indians, employés, and troops . . . might be raised in abundance."[5] If, however, by some miracle the Indian Office had found the funds and there had been a change in the rainfall pattern, Tatum would have found it very difficult to recruit and keep that many hired hands. Fort Sill was still days away from the nearest settlements and, aside from a few drifters and discharged soldiers, white labor was virtually nonexistent.

To recruit employees for the agency and to purchase a steam sawmill with grist mill and shingle-cutting attachments Congress had appropriated for, Tatum left the reservation in August 1869 for Chicago and did not return until October. He left again in December, this time for Iowa to attend a Friends meeting, and did not return until late January. In his first twelve months as agent he was absent from his post about one-fourth of the time. It is doubtful if Tatum would have been able to accomplish a great deal more had he passed the full twelve months at Fort Sill. The Indians were exhibiting little interest in settling into a farming routine and Tatum discovered very quickly that the Indian's rations would not support them if they did quit hunting.

The United States reservation policy was summarized in 1872 by Commissioner of Indian Affairs Francis A. Walker: "Indians should be made as comfortable on, and as uncomfortable off their reservations" as the government could make them.[6] Three years earlier a circular letter to Indian Service personnel by his predecessor had directed that "Indians who fail or refuse to . . . locate . . . upon reservations, will be subject wholly to the control and supervision of the military authorities, who, as circumstances may justify, will at their discretion treat them as friendly or hostile."[7] In the specific case of the Comanches and Kiowas, Commissioner Walker contended in 1872 that there was no excuse for their hostility: "The United States have given them a noble reservation, and have provided amply for all their wants."[8]

The Comanches would have heatedly denied both assertions. The United States certainly had not "given" them a reservation; at most it had recognized their claim to a fraction of what had been Indian territory before the whites began driving them from it. Tatum would have joined the Comanches in rejecting the government's claim that it had "provided amply for all their wants."

Although their treaty did not call for rations for them, treaties with other tribes negotiated by the Peace Commission in 1868 did carry provisions for rations, and the Comanches, Kiowas, and Kiowa-Apaches were lumped with the "potentially hostile" Indians whom it was cheaper to ration than to fight. Beginning in 1869, Congress appropriated from $200,000 to $250,000 annually to feed the estimated 9,000 Indians of the three southwestern agencies. This was over and above any treaty commitments, and by 1874 the government was rationing in whole or in part an additional 87,000 Indians in other parts of the country. Scandalized congressmen attached a rider to the June 22, 1874 appropriation bill for the Indian Service requiring that male Indians between the ages of eighteen and forty-five be required to work for their rations. This proved impossible to enforce for the Plains tribes and they were promptly exempted from the operation of the law.

Less than a month after he took charge of the agency Tatum was insisting that the ration authorized by the government was inadequate, both in quality and quantity. Corn, which was sometimes issued, was useless to the Indians, who had no method for grinding it into meal. When meal was available it often was so musty the Indians could not eat it. The meat ration was only one pound, which was nowhere near sufficient for a meat-eating people. The Comanches continued to hunt, so the inadequacy of the meat ration did not disturb them nearly so much as the exclusion of sugar and coffee from the ration in the summer of 1869. "It may cost the government one hundred times as much to half feed the Indians," predicted Tatum, "than it would to give them soldiers rations." Nor should the government be sensitive to charges that it would be feeding the Indian too well. "If his stomach is capacious it is no more so than God has made it," said the Quaker, "and it does not become us to virtually say that it has been made too large and must be contracted."[9]

Other agents and superintendents made similar complaints and the government restored sugar and coffee to the ration and increased the beef component from one pound to one and one-half pounds. As defined in August 1869 the daily ration consisted of the beef, three-quarters of a pound of meal or corn, one-quarter pound of flour, with four pounds of sugar and two pounds of coffee per one hundred rations, and salt and soap "when necessary."[10] This became the basic ration for the Comanches although minor changes were made, such as substituting bacon for beef occasionally and adding soda and tobacco. If the full quantity were available and the quality acceptable, it would have been sufficient, but this never was the case.

The beef came from Texas longhorns driven to the agency and kept on pasture until issued. In the summer and early fall they would be in reasonably good shape, but by late winter they were almost starved and when issued to the Indians the cattle were little more than skin and bones. Frequently too weak to walk to the Indian camps, they had to be slaughtered where they collapsed near the issuing corral. To net a pound and a half of beef the United States issued three pounds on the hoof; however, those issued in the late winter produced little more than the hide that the Indians could sell to the local trader. Fortunately the Indians preferred buffalo meat and this was their mainstay for a few more years.

Other items in the ration were frequently substandard. Some of the sugar was of such poor quality as to make the Indians sick. Flour was a particular problem. One wagon train brought in 54,000 pounds that Tatum stigmatized as unfit to eat.[11] As the agent pointed out, the Indians were able to make only poor bread with good flour. Nevertheless, it was himself and his white employees who were Tatum's principal concern. "To require us to use such flour in that remote place, when we have so few of the comforts of life," complained Tatum, "I deem very unreasonable." The agent's solution was to request better flour to be sent "for the use of the school, my employees, and to furnish the Chiefs with about ten rations of bread each."[12] Presumably the rank and file Indians could make do with the inferior flour.

Tatum had a better solution for the corn problem. Whole corn was being issued occasionally to the Indians, who either sold it to whites for a fraction of its value or fed it to their horses. Showing commendable initiative, the agent exchanged some of it with local traders for items such as sugar and coffee, of which the Indians always wanted more.

Rations were not only sometimes of poor quality but short weight as well. Sacks of bacon were found to also contain stones, some barrels of pork were adulterated with lumps of coal. Unless there was collusion between the agency staff and the contractors, these shortages would be reported and restitution ultimately made, but meanwhile the Indians went hungry.

Problems in transporting the huge quantities of provisions complicated the situation. Excluding the beef, which came in under its own power, the three Southwest agencies (Kiowa and Comanche, Cheyenne and Arapaho, and Wichita) required annually in excess of 2.5 million pounds. This did not include the many tons of annuity goods due the Indians and the other freight necessary to maintain the agencies. A contract for the three agencies in 1871 committed the holder to transport nearly 4 million pounds from the railhead between July 1 and December 15.[13] By the middle of August the freighter was complaining that nothing had yet arrived for him to haul and that the best weather for freighting was passing rapidly. Spring, which brought swollen streams and deep mud in a country with no bridges or hard-surfaced roads, practically stopped freight movement. Whenever a train failed to arrive on time, Tatum could try to borrow from another agent, the post quartermaster, or one of the traders. If none of these could or would cooperate, the Indian simply did not receive those components of the ration Tatum was short. If it were coffee or sugar the Indians complained bitterly.

Although the rations were not a part of the commitment the United States had assumed by treaty, the Indians had been led to expect them and once a few issues had been made the Comanches quickly assumed them to be their natural right. Annuity goods were a different matter. The treaty obligated the government to distribute them to the Indians every October 15. Here again there were problems of quality, selection, and prompt delivery.

The Treaty of Medicine Lodge specified that the Indians should receive an annual issue of clothing: coat, pants, shirt, socks, and hat for the man; for the woman a skirt, or cloth to make it, woolen hose, and twenty-four yards of cloth. The children were treated similarly. However, the Indians preferred their native dress and either discarded most of the clothing they received or altered it to meet their needs. Pants had the seats removed, or the legs were cut off for leggings. Woolen hose were worn without moccasins as long as they would last and the coats were usually thrown away. Tatum reported that they would make use of the shirts and recommended that the shirt-tails be made longer because the Indians wore them without pants.[14] Complaints about the quality of the annuity goods were common.

Annuity goods were issued when they became available, despite the October 15 date specified by the treaty. In 1869 the Indians received only about one-fourth of the annuity due them as a result of depredation claims filed against these three tribes. The Treaty of Medicine Lodge provided for reimbursement of losses inflicted by the Indians from "annuities or other moneys due" them from the United States. By 1869 there were more than fifty claims, totaling over $150,000 against the Comanches, Kiowas, and Kiowa-Apaches. That year a single claim for $52,650 by A. M. Adams was approved by the government to compensate Adams for losses suffered from Comanches and Kiowas raiding in Texas in 1867. About $23,000 of this sum was taken from the $30,000 appropriation for annuities for these Indians for 1869, making it a lean year for annuity goods.[15] Shortly afterward Congress stopped this method of reimbursement by providing that depredation claims would require special acts of Congress. This complicated the process, although claims continued to flow in.

Tatum maintained that in four years he had examined 105 depredation claims by Texans, and 123 by Chickasaw Indians, the latter having had the misfortune to live on a direct route between the Comanches and the Kiowas and the closest populous Texas counties.[16] Lieutenant Richard H. Pratt, later to found Carlisle Indian School, was one of the fortunate ones for whose claim Congress appropriated. He received $200 for a horse stolen by Comanches. Most received nothing because the Indians refused to accept the responsibility, or the claimants failed to employ an attorney with the proper contacts in Washington. The favorite tactics of Tatum's Comanches were to blame the absent Quahadas or plead complete ignorance of the incident.

Throughout Tatum's tenure the Comanches and Kiowas continued to raid in Texas and on occasion were guilty of aggressions closer to home. The United States defined as hostile any Indian off the reservation without permission and authorized the withholding of annuities and rations not only from the guilty individuals but also from those tribes and bands that refused to surrender members charged with depredations.

Tatum had been at his post only a few months when he spotted what he considered an inconsistency in the United States policy. He was responsible for administering the affairs of not only the dangerous Comanches and associated tribes but the peaceful Wichitas as well. Only about three hundred in number, they supported themselves by farming and hunting. The Wichitas had never fought the whites and the United States had never troubled to provide them a specific reservation. In 1869 there was no area the tribe could call theirs although Fort Sill and Tatum's agency were located on land the Wichitas had claimed before the arrival of the whites. The Kiowas and Comanches drew the conclusion that their intransigence paid better returns than the meekness of the Wichitas and told their agent so.

Tatum had other evidence that force was more successful with these Indians than generosity. The elusive Quahadas, who were in the vicinity of the agency in the summer of 1869, sent delegations to call on him and General Hazen. What brought them from their usual haunts on the Staked Plains was the capture the previous winter of some of their leaders, together with the Cochetethka chief Mowaway. While these Indians were prisoners the Quahadas and Cochetethkas were on their good behavior. In August the prisoners were released and Mowaway, having seen Kansas City and Fort Leavenworth, seemed impressed with the futility of resisting the whites.[17]

The subcommittee of the Board of Indian Commissioners that visited Fort Sill in the summer of 1869 conferred with representatives of the tribes under Tatum. At the council Mowaway and Esahabbe (Milky Way), the latter a Penetethka chief, spoke for the Comanches in a conciliatory tone. But it was the Kiowa Satanta, speaking in his usual tough tones, who shook up the commissioners. He responded to advice that the Indians "abandon their wandering and savage habits" and become farmers with the comments that corn hurt his teeth and the Indians wanted breech-loading carbines.[18] The commissioners left Fort Sill believing that its garrison should be increased because the Indians were "in a comparatively unsettled state, and are naturally impulsive and easily excited."[19]

When the Comanches were on the reservation they seldom camped close to the agency because of its proximity to Fort Sill. There was insufficient grass for their estimated 16,500 horses, and soldiers annoyed them by slipping into their camps to seek the sexual favors of their women. In the fall of 1869 Comanches were camped as much as thirty-five miles from the agency although still on the reservation. This meant that those farthest removed consumed about four days in simply drawing rations.

The ration issue, made every two weeks, was a colorful scene. Indians by the hundreds, each family with several horses and the usual pack of ill-tempered dogs, descended on the agency. In a bedlam of barking dogs and excited women and children, the "beef chiefs," as they were called, stepped forward to receive the flour and other rations. These men then divided them among the women assigned to their beef bands. White onlookers might be briefly entertained by a squabble among the women that would be quelled by a quirt-swinging warrior, but the beef issue provided the most excitement. The Indians might drive the cattle to their camps to be slaughtered or they might kill them right near the corral. If the latter, each animal was run down by a group of mounted Indians shooting arrows and firing pistol and rifle rounds indiscriminately into the frantic beast until it collapsed. As the clouds of dust and the shouts of the spectators subsided, women would pounce on the fallen animal and quickly skin and butcher it. The reeking hide and meat were then thrown on packhorses and the families would proceed to their various camps.

For those Comanches who remained on the reservation, life settled into a routine. Several days each month was spent drawing rations; the remainder of the warrior's time was devoted to hunting and lounging around the camps. As the Indians made heavy inroads into the reservation's game, there was less incentive for the Comanche males to hunt and they refused to take up the plow and hoe. This meant more time to regale each other with stories of their exploits against the Utes, the Navajos, and the Texans. For a warrior to be unable to boast a herd of fine ponies, or point to a shield festooned with scalps, was to run the risk of being ridiculed as an old woman.

It is little wonder that the Comanche reporting a vision of a successful raid had no difficulty recruiting a war party. With luck the warriors would return with the scalps and plunder that ensured a man's status in Comanche society. This success could spark other dreams and soon another group of warriors would slip away to seek fame and fortune. Nor did fatalities on these expeditions necessarily discourage new ones. The women greeted reports of the loss of their relatives with keening and self-mutilation, gashing themselves and hacking off portions of their fingers. A warrior could respond to the news of the death of a father, a brother, or a friend by swearing vengeance and leading another war party from the camp, thus initiating another round of hostilities.

Eighteen seventy was only a few days old when a party of Comanches and Kiowas led by Satanta intercepted a herd of cattle near the northern boundary of the reservation. The warriors robbed the cowboys and killed nearly 300 head of cattle, stampeding the rest. The cowboys were fortunate to escape with their scalps intact.[20] Other reports from Texas of Indian depredations also were laid at the door of Tatum's Indians. The Quaker admitted that many of his charges had not been to the agency for four months but reminded his superiors that their treaty entitled them to hunt buffalo from south of the Arkansas all the way into Texas. As usual Tatum ascribed to the Quahadas any raids charged against his Indians.[21]

In May 1870 the Comanches and Kiowas met the Cheyennes in a big council on the North Fork of Red River, the western boundary of the reservation. Ten Bears, Horse Back, Toshaway, and Esahabbe spoke for peace, but Black Horse called for war and the young warriors were happy to follow.[22] Not only did raiding parties go into Texas, some struck in the vicinity of the agency itself. Tabananaka (Hears the Sun), a Yamparika chief, headed a party that stole about twenty horses and mules from the vicinity of Fort Sill and chased white farmers from a cornfield. A few nights later some Kiowas invaded the post to drive seventy-three mules from the quartermaster's corral. Emboldened by these successes, other Indians killed two men near the agency and stampeded two herds of cattle. Tatum called his employees together and told them they were free to leave if they so wished and most did, his wife accompanying them.[23]

It was very confusing and perplexing for the earnest Quaker. After a few months at the agency he had concluded he could not take the Indians at their word. If the occasion demanded it their memories went blank and no confidence could be placed in their professed intentions. And too frequently it was only what one warrior referred to as the "coffee chiefs," like Toshaway and Ten Bears, who put in an appearance. At a council Superintendent Hoag had held in March 1870 it was these chiefs and Esahabbe, a Penetethka like Toshaway, who were the bulk of a Comanche audience that heard read a letter from Commissioner of Indian Affairs Ely S. Parker, himself a Seneca, pleading with the Indians to give up raiding and to take up farming.[24]

Clearly this council had accomplished little, but the conferring went on. Tatum talked to delegations who called on him at his office, never knowing whether or not they might have just ridden in with a few Texas horses and scalps. In July, Colonel B. H. Grierson, commanding Fort Sill, joined Tatum in hosting a council at the post. As the colonel reported it, the rhetoric flowed freely. Horse Back spoke piously of his hopes for a "rainbow of peace" to "cover over the blood shed by his red brethern." Ten Bears then described how a Kiowa had swept the road free of all blood stains and Ten Bears hoped the whites would forgive and forget. An army officer added to the unreality of the occasion by insisting that the Indians had no excuse, because the United States had met all its obligations to them to the letter, and that the Indians should bring in the scalps of the whites killed so that they might be buried with their bodies. The session closed with Ten Bears's reference to the bell his Great Father had placed around his neck in Washington and how he had been ringing it for peace ever since.[25]

Meanwhile the raiding continued. Comanches and

Kiowas were supposed to have made up the party that dared in June to launch an attack on Camp Supply, an army base about 150 miles northwest of Fort Sill. Other Indians were busy in Texas, which resounded to demands that the government do something. One letter writer made plain his views on the peace policy: "Give us Phil Sheridan, and send Phil-anthropy to the devil."[26] The Texas legislature did authorize the governor to enlist twenty companies of Rangers.

Tatum's tactic was to reduce the issue of rations or to deny them entirely to those he could identify as belligerent. In a council in August he and Colonel Grierson held with Kiowas, he offered them rations only if they brought in some white captives they held. These included the Koozer family, a mother and five children recently captured in a raid in which the father of the family was killed. The Indians agreed, received their rations, and then refused to deliver the Koozers. Tatum finally had to pay $100 each for them and congratulated himself on having ransomed them so cheaply.[27] When some Kiowas then killed more beef cattle than they were entitled to, the agent cut their coffee and sugar ration in half. The Indian response was to tell Tatum that "they thought it very hard that I should 'get mad, just as they had got entirely over their mad.'"[28]

The Indian view of these differences was much less complicated than that of the whites. Pacer, the principal Kiowa-Apache chief, who owed his rank to Tatum, had a solution for the Comanchero incitement of raids on Texas ranches. Pacer offered to raise a war party and steal horses and mules from the New Mexicans instead![29]

By the fall of 1870 the situation was out of control as far as Tatum was concerned. He reported that all the young men were out raiding or buffalo hunting—he did not know which. The Indians were spoiling for a fight with the cavalry and were confident of their ability to whip the troopers.[30] The only tactics that seemed effective were to hold hostages and to forbid whites to buy stock from the

Indians. Howeah, a prominent Yamparika, had been very cooperative, carrying out several missions for Tatum during the year members of his family, captured in Texas, were held at Fort Richardson. The ban on purchasing horses and mules from the Indians deprived them of one incentive to raid in Texas. It was long overdue because the situation had deteriorated to the point that agency traders and employees were suspected of dealing in the stolen stock.

Tatum's superiors were unable to comprehend the scope of his problem. Superintendent Hoag from his Lawrence, Kansas office hewed to the Quaker line. Even when the irrepressible Satanta told him to his face that the solution for the hostilities was to supply the Indians more ammunition and to move Texas beyond the reach of the warriors,[31] Hoag persisted in his belief that if enough councils were held and enough lectures delivered, the Indians would reform. Officials in Washington were nearly as bad. They thought that councils, plus threats to withdraw rations and annuities, would do the job.

Presumably Tatum felt that his presence at the agency was not critical in the winter. He left again in late December and this time did not return until early March 1871. Acting as agent in his absence was his clerk, George H. Smith, who had had experience in the army's commissary operation. Tatum considered him competent and obviously trusted him implicitly. The Quaker may have misplaced his confidence because Smith was rumored to have made $16,000 in eighteen months while a silent partner in firms supplying the agency.[32]

In Tatum's absence a school was finally opened by Josiah Butler, a fellow Quaker whom he had employed. Butler was aided by his wife as matron and seamstress. Operating as a boarding school, it remained open from February until early July 1871. The average attendance was about seventeen students, none of them Kiowas and only a few Comanches briefly. Four of the seven Comanches to attend were withdrawn when their father, Esahabbe, went into mourning on the death of one of his wives. Two of the other three Comanches were Mrs. Joseph Chandler, the wife of the agency interpreter, and her son, who was too young to be enrolled anyway.[33]

Tatum returned in March to find things had not changed for the better in his absence. Rations remained inadequate, annuities due the Indians the previous October did not arrive until April, and some of his charges were still uncooperative. Commissioner Ely S. Parker's invitation to the Indians of the southwestern agencies to select a small delegation to come to Washington was declined. The Comanche response was that since their only reason to go would be to ask for a larger reservation, it was useless for them to make the trip.

An effort to promote a big council between these Indians and representatives of the Five Civilized Tribes, in the hope that some of their adaptability would rub off on the Comanche and affiliated tribes, was equally unsuccessful. Few of the really influential Comanches and Kiowas could be prevailed upon to attend. Then Mowaway brought his 300 Cochetethkas into the agency for their share of the annuity goods and rations and left in a surly mood without them, having refused to surrender a young white boy one of his warriors had bought from an Apache. Tatum knew that his Indians were still organizing expeditions into Texas and he was afraid the summer of 1871 would be worse than the previous one.

The raiders were quite active. Late in April the stagecoach line running southwest from Sherman, Texas suspended operation because of Indian activity. At Jacksboro, about 120 miles farther west on the line, a public meeting of citizens of Jack County drafted resolutions and a statement of Indian depredations. Blaming the Fort Sill Indians —the term increasingly employed by Texans who could not identify their attackers but were convinced they were Comanches or Kiowas from Tatum's agency—the citizens claimed they had lost $50,000 worth of horses in the month of April alone and a total of more than 2,000 head in the past two and one-half years. They set their losses in lives in the same period as 42 not to mention wounded and missing, and this in a county whose population had never exceeded 600. Their plea was that the United States authorize troops to pursue suspected hostiles onto the reservation, thereby eliminating their sanctuary.[34] Such an order would violate a cardinal principle of the peace policy: that those Indians on a reservation were immune from attack. It was apparent, however, that Colonel Grierson's stationing of a few score troops along Red River had not served to discourage the Fort Sill Indians from going back and forth at their pleasure.

The issue was resolved May 18, 1871, by the action of a Kiowa war party that included some Comanches. Led by Satanta, Big Tree, and Satank, 100 warriors ambushed a train of twelve wagons loaded with corn about twenty miles west of Fort Richardson. Seven of the twelve white men were killed, one of them being found with his tongue cut out, chained to a pole, and horribly burned. General Sherman heard the news at Fort Richardson, where he had stopped en route to Fort Sill on a tour of inspection. He issued orders for a pursuit of the party even if the trail led into the Comanche and Kiowa reservation. Heavy rains washed out the trail the cavalry followed, but Sherman went on to Fort Sill determined to make an example of this war party.

Meanwhile Tatum had learned of the fate of the wagon train and had suspected that, because they were off the reservation, Satanta and other Kiowas might be guilty. He wrote Hoag asking permission to have Indians guilty of depredations in Texas transferred to that state for trial. Before he could get a response the Kiowas, Satanta among them, showed up for rations. When the agent questioned them about the wagon train Satanta freely admitted his role, even boasted of it, and implicated others.

After requesting that General Sherman arrest Satanta, Big Tree, Satank, and Eagle Heart, Tatum succeeded in getting the principal Kiowas involved to meet with the general. In a dramatic confrontation that almost turned into a bloodbath, Sherman took the first three chiefs into custody and dispatched them to Texas for trial. Barely out of Fort Sill, Satank chose to die attempting to escape. The other two were tried at Jacksboro, found guilty, and sentenced to death. However, Governor E. J. Davis of Texas commuted their sentences to life imprisonment. Tatum had urged this course of action on the grounds that if the chiefs were executed, the Kiowas would seek vengeance, whereas if the chiefs were held prisoner the Kiowas would behave in an effort to get them freed. Satanta could not understand why the whites continued to agitate about the destruction of the wagon train. Sherman reported that the Kiowa told him that because the Indians had had three warriors killed and three wounded in the assault, as well as another killed at the time the three chiefs were arrested, "the account is even and therefore I ought to be satisfied."[35]

Seizing the chiefs represented quite a change in policy. Heretofore, Comanches and Kiowas had returned openly to the reservation with scalps and prisoners and at most had been denied rations and annuities. They had been able, if they wished, to trade any prisoners they held for hundreds of dollars worth of goods. A new hard line had emerged and all the Fort Sill Indians were to suffer to some degree, if only by having their movements more closely circumscribed. The secretary of the interior, at General Sherman's suggestion, gave blanket authorization to military authorities to enter the Comanche and Kiowa reservation "in the pursuit and arrest of predatory and criminal Indians."[36]

Superintendent Hoag had not lost any of his enthusiasm for the peace policy. He was willing that if raiding continued the culprits should be arrested and tried, but he rejected Tatum's suggestion that the raiders be turned over to the jurisdiction of Texas, arguing that in the Border States "prejudice strongly exists against all Indians."[37] The superintendent and Agent Tatum were drifting further apart in their ideas on how the Comanches and

Kiowas should be handled. Tatum had reached the point where he thought the Indians themselves had nullified the Treaty of Medicine Lodge and should be treated by the United States not as nations but as "wards and paupers."[38]

Tatum's increasingly tough line was causing concern in Quaker circles. The Friends Indian Committee wrote the agent "to urge the necessity of fully upholding our peace principles in the administration of thy agency."[39] Tatum was sufficiently disturbed to seek the opinion of another Iowa Quaker. The Iowan's response was that their principles ruled out asking the military to arrest raiders because the soldiers would go "armed with deadly weapons, *Guns, Swords,* and *Bayonets,* and if Resistance is offered . . . these weapons will be used to the taking of life."[40] Tatum soon would have to choose between open rupture with the philosophy of the Society of Friends and giving up any hope of restraining the militants among the Comanches and Kiowas. The Kiowa murder of two of his employees, one of whom was not only scalped but had his ears cut off, put additional strain on the agent's pacifism.

Comanches were reacting to the turmoil in diametrically opposed fashions. Some resumed their old roaming ways. After the release of their people captured in New Mexico with Mowaway, the Quahadas had not ventured near the agency again. Mowaway and his Cochetethkas had not been back since May, when they had been refused rations and annuities for not surrendering the white boy. Paracoom (He Bear), another prominent Cochetethka chief, and Tabananaka and his Yamparikas were last seen by Tatum in the fall of 1870. The reaction of some of the Penetethkas was not to flee to the plains but rather to seek assignment to the Wichita Agency to get out of the line of fire. The Indian commissioner approved and Toshaway with 75 and Esahabbe with 121 began to draw rations at the new Wichita Agency on the north side of the Washita, about thirty-five miles from Fort Sill. Three other Penetethka bands totaling 135 people were still assigned to

Tatum. In the following months other Indians complicated the situation by seeking to avoid punishment by taking shelter at the Wichita Agency with Toshaway and Esahabbe.

As cold weather came to the southern plains Tatum as usual headed for Iowa. He left in late October and did not return until January 1872. No one acquainted with affairs at Tatum's agency in 1871 had found much comfort in the workings of the peace policy, but President Grant in his annual message to Congress in December maintained that it had generally enjoyed success and should be supported "not only because it is humane, Christianlike, and economical, but because it is right."[41] The president could hardly have been thinking of the Comanches and associated tribes when he wrote those words.

The Fort Sill Indians did not entirely give up their depredations in Texas during the winter of 1871–72, and as the new spring grass restored the energy of their ponies they redoubled their activities. In seven months Kiowa-led parties stole 125 mules from an army detachment on the open prairie near Camp Supply, captured nine wagons of small arms and ammunition and killed the 17 teamsters on the road between San Antonio and El Paso, relieved a trader at the Wichita Agency of 37 head of horses and mules, and killed and scalped a white man only a mile and a half from Fort Sill. They also attacked the Abel Lees, a farm family living sixteen miles from Fort Griffin, killing the parents and one of the children and abducting three others. Only two depredations clearly could be pinned on the Comanches. Late one night in June a few Cochetethkas embarrassed the garrison of Fort Sill by taking over 50 horses and mules from the quartermaster's corral. The Comanches were also charged with the theft of 47 head of horses from the Chickasaws.

These, however, were only the depredations for which responsibility could be ascribed. There were many others, such as the murder of the justice of the peace of Texas's Palo Pinto County by Indians who took his scalp and cut off his nose and ears. Tatum estimated that Indians of his agency had killed twenty-one Texans between September 1871 and September 1872.[42]

The Texans were desperate. What drove them to fits of fury was the knowledge that at least some of the raiders came from the Fort Sill Reservation and returned to its relative security to draw rations. A Texan writing President Grant gave the gory details on the Lee family and the Palo Pinto County justice of the peace, denouncing the "bloody Quaker pets" and the "dread *Insane* Pseudo humanitarian Policy."[43] Texas cattlemen took matters into their own hands after the Comanchero trade took an upturn at the expense of their stock. A party of about ninety heavily armed Texans crossed into eastern New Mexico, scoured the area, and recovered 6,000 of their cattle the Indians had driven off and then traded to New Mexicans.[44]

Tatum and army personnel wanted force employed. Tatum had come a long way since the day when he thought he could handle these warriors if he just received larger quantities of coffee and sugar. "We had as well attempt to hire the murderers and desperadoes in our large cities to cease their depredations" was now the agent's opinion. The Indians, as the Quaker phrased it, regarded the leniency of the government as "cowardice or imbecility."[45] General Phillip H. Sheridan, whose Division of the Missouri now included Texas, was sure he had the solution. "If the Government will give me the promise of non-interference and non-protection to those Indians next winter," wrote Sheridan, "I will settle their hash for them when their ponies are poor."[46] The general obviously was thinking in terms of another Battle of the Washita, or Sand Creek Massacre. Meanwhile, Colonel Ranald S. Mackenzie and his Fourth Cavalry Regiment headed for the Staked Plains in the hope of convincing the bands there that no place was safe from pursuit.

At Lawrence, Kansas, Superintendent Hoag and his chief clerk Cyrus Beede continued loyal to the peace policy. In the face of incontrovertible evidence of Indian

Esahabbe, 1872. (Smithsonian Institution, National Anthropological Archives)

Horseback, circa 1872. (Fort Sill Museum)

Toshaway, circa 1872. (Fort Sill Museum)

Ten Bears, circa 1872. (Fort Sill Museum)

depredations they claimed the reports were exaggerated, or they ridiculed the army for loss of its own stock, as at the Fort Sill quartermaster's corral. Beede accused the military of "gross neglect or carelessness"[47] and Hoag spoke of their "inefficiency to protect themselves to say nothing about protection to citizens and management of Indians."[48] The answer, in the superintendent's opinion, was to remove the agency from the corrupting influence of Fort Sill and to repose in the Indians "full confidence and trust in their integrity." Then, according to Hoag, "the same virtues are most invariably reciprocated."[49] He insisted that the use of troops to arrest Indians guilty of murder, as Tatum was proposing, "would, undoubtedly instigate fresh hostilities."[50] To recover property, Beede proposed to use friendly Indians who would be paid to perform this function. On one occasion he bought $75 worth of clothing for Esahabbe and several of his young men to ensure their cooperation, and on another he suggested $10 an animal as a fair reward for the return of livestock. Had this policy been adopted the Indians would have had yet another inducement to raid.

Officials in the Indian Office refused to openly countenance any payment for prisoners or livestock, but accounts run up in the process of securing the release of captives were paid. None of the Quaker aversion to the use of force was apparent in the Indian Office, although there obviously was a reluctance to call on a rival department for help. Threats to visiting delegations, or sent out by emissaries from Washington, were resorted to although they had become rather hollow after several years' repetition. Nevertheless, in June 1872 Interior secretary Columbus Delano's decision was to "send a Commissioner with an 'Olive Branch,' as we have done in Arizona."[51] An effort also would be made to recruit a delegation to visit Washington, where, hopefully, the Indians would be overwhelmed by the power and majesty of the United States.

To represent the government, Commissioner of Indian Affairs Francis A. Walker chose a Quaker, Professor Edward Parish of Philadelphia, and Henry E. Alvord, now retired from the army, who had represented General Hazen at Fort Cobb in the fall of 1868. Before they could reach Indian Territory the Quakers in the Lawrence office had engineered a council at old Fort Cobb designed to bring the Comanches and Kiowas into contact again with representatives of the Five Civilized Tribes, and particularly to try to effect a reconciliation with the Kiowas.

There was a good representation at Fort Cobb of the less belligerent Comanche chiefs to hear the delegation from the Five Civilized Tribes. Toshaway, Horse Back, Esahabbe, and Ten Bears were there, the last complaining he was getting old, "when my horse trots I grunt."[52] Conspicuous by their absence were Mowaway, Paracoom, and Tabananaka.

Beede and Hoag claimed a huge success. Comanches did turn in most of the horses they recently had stolen from the Chickasaws. The Kiowas produced the Lee orphans and agreed to join the delegation to Washington to bring in some of the stolen government stock. However, Beede and Hoag did not pass on some of the disquieting remarks of the Indians in and out of council. Neither the Comanches nor the Kiowas appeared to fear acknowledging their participation in raids. Nor did they make sweeping promises of good behavior in the future. Some Yamparika warriors with a sense of humor pledged to give up raiding when the white men gave up paper and books. They spoke disparagingly of the Creeks, Cherokees, and Seminoles brought to Fort Cobb to impress them. "They are an old dirty inefficient looking set," the interpreter had the Yamparika spokesman saying, "hardly capable of managing their own affairs, we don't take much stock in them."[53] It was clear that what cooperation the Kiowas provided during and after Beede's council derived from the impression they gained from him that if they behaved, Satanta and Big Tree soon would be released by the Texas authorities.

Three weeks after Beede concluded his council, Edward Parrish and Henry Alvord arrived for theirs with the tribes of the three southwestern agencies. Professor Parrish went to bed on his arrival at the agency and died there of typhoid fever two weeks later. The expense of returning his body to Philadelphia was charged to funds appropriated for the benefit of the Comanches and Kiowas, needless to say without seeking the concurrence of the Indians. Alvord, who had predicted that he and Parrish would have trouble because the professor was "a very consistent *Friend*,"[54] now had the mission to himself.

Although the Kiowas had loomed particularly large in the drafting of his instructions, Alvord had trouble assembling a good representation of that tribe, and no Cheyennes put in an appearance. The Comanches, on the other hand, turned out in substantial numbers, among them such wary chiefs as Mowaway and Tabananaka. After a series of conferences in which Alvord warned them of incurring the wrath of the United States if they continued their raiding, he issued the invitation to the tribes of the three southwestern agencies to send representatives to Washington. A delegation of forty was assembled, including the Comanches Ten Bears, Mowaway, Esahabbe, Asatoyet (Gray Leggings), Quirtsquip (Elk's Cud), and Cheevers (Goat). Ten Bears, Mowaway, and Esahabbe we have met before. Asatoyet was a Penetethka whose chief claim to fame was that he had guided the party of officers who selected the site of Fort Sill in 1868. Quirtsquip and Cheevers were younger Yamparika chiefs of whom more would be heard.

The delegation traveled by army wagons to Atoka, the railhead of the Missouri, Kansas, and Texas. There they were met by Satanta and Big Tree. The Kiowas had been working on a chain gang building a railroad near Dallas until Alvord asked to have them brought up to satisfy their fellow tribesmen on the delegation. At St. Louis, Satanta and Big Tree were left to be returned to Texas; Alvord and his party went on to Washington.

President Grant received them at the White House in the presence of a number of spectators, including the secretaries of the interior, treasury, war, and state. After a brief lecture on the advisability of their giving up the roving life, the president dismissed them. The delegation wound up their stay in the East with a call on Commissioner of Indian Affairs Francis A. Walker. The commissioner was stern, informing the Comanches and Kiowas that by December's full moon they must take up residence within ten miles of the agency and surrender all stolen government stock or replace it with animals of equal value. The alternative was to be labeled enemies of the United States. Walker said there would be no more messages sent to the Quahadas, who were unrepresented in the delegation; the next time troops would be sent. "The Great Father's heart is kind," said the commissioner, "but his hand is very heavy."[55]

Although he did not choose to share the news with the Indians, Commissioner Walker knew that Colonel Mackenzie's command had struck a Comanche village of 262 lodges in the Texas Panhandle on September 29. The troops, at a cost of only 4 casualties, had killed 24 Indians and taken 124 prisoners, almost all women and children.[56] They also burned the lodges, destroyed Indian property in the village, and captured the Comanche horse herd. In the first two nights after the fight the Indians managed to recapture most of their horses, but they had suffered a serious blow. The decision was made almost immediately, on Mackenzie's recommendation, to hold the prisoners as hostages for the good behavior of the Comanches.

Tatum knew of the battle on McClellan Creek before Mackenzie's superiors had learned of it. Refugees from the burned village came straight to the agency. Some of them vented their wrath by putting to the torch the houses of two chiefs on the Washington delegation, Toshaway and Esahabbe. It must have been quite a disappointment to old Toshaway to return from Washington and find in ashes the home for which he had pled for years.

Despite this flareup, the conduct of the Comanches in the next few months reflected their concern for the hostages. Several bands were affected although Mackenzie assumed he had attacked a Quahada village. The identity of the prisoners revealed that the term *Quahada* had come to be applied loosely to all Comanches who insisted on remaining on the Staked Plains. Of 105 from this one village still held at Fort Concho in April 1873, 30 were Quahadas, 37 Cochetethkas, 18 Yamparikas, 11 Noconies, and 9 Penetethkas.[57]

Horse Back, the Noconie chief who had helped ensure attendance at the councils of both Beede and Alvord in the fall of 1872, secured the release of four white prisoners held by the Indians in hopes of freeing some of his relatives held at Fort Concho. Commissioner Walker rejected Tatum's proposal to thus reward Horse Back, preferring to wait until more Comanches and Kiowas had manifested a change of heart. The agent, however, had contacted the military directly, and the commanding officer of the Department of Texas ordered five of Horse Back's family freed.

As winter closed in it appeared that almost all Comanches had reported to the reservation. Their camps spread over a large area and some were thirty-five or forty miles from the agency headquarters. This led Tatum to refuse to comply to a directive from the commissioner of Indian Affairs that rations be issued once a week at the three southwestern agencies rather than semimonthly. Moreover, they were to be issued on the same day as it was suspected that some of Tatum's charges had been drawing rations at both his and the Wichita Agency. If he had complied with the commissioner's order, some of Tatum's bands would have had to be on the road three or four days a week because camp sites with grass enough for their huge horse herds were not that plentiful near the agency. Moreover, the Indians did not like to come so close to Fort Sill. Tatum was aware of this and had proposed the agency be relocated ten or twelve miles from the post.

With the surrender by the Comanches of five Mexican children, Tatum believed he had obtained all the captives they had held. The origin of the Mexican children gave some idea of the scope of Comanche operations. One of them had been seized near San Antonio, two about 250 miles west of there, and the remaining two were believed to be from south of the Rio Grande in Mexico.

The Quaker agent had learned of some of these children being in the possession of the Comanches from a Mexican girl of about eighteen who escaped her owner, a Quahada warrior named Black Beard. The girl (Tatum called her Martha Day) had been captured near San Antonio two years earlier. She fled to the agency one night despite Black Beard's threat to kill her if she attempted to escape. He told her that as a Mexican she would just be returned to the Indians by Tatum. While armed warriors lurked near the agency on the lookout for the girl, wives of the white employees transformed her from the dirty, slovenly creature who had fled the Indian camp into a well-dressed, attractive young woman. Heavily veiled, Miss Day was smuggled into a stagecoach and started for San Antonio in the charge of a Texan who had come to the agency to pick up his own child, a captive of the Indians for a year and a half.

The folowing day some Comanches called on Tatum and told him one of their women was missing. He surprised them by the news that Martha Day had left the agency by stage the previous evening. They then asked payment for her and he refused, reminding them that they earlier had assured him they held no more captives.[58]

The day following this minor triumph, which the Quaker attributed to divine intervention, Tatum penned his resignation to take effect March 31, 1873.[59] The agent believed things were going better than at any time since he came to Indian Territory in June 1869. All the major bands were on the reservation and the Indians were generally more cooperative. Tatum attributed the improvement to Mackenzie's capture of the Comanches on McClellan Creek and his own refusal to continue to recognize as chiefs a few of the most recalcitrant Kiowas and Comanches. Contributing to the agent's decision to resign was the degree to which he found himself at odds with Hoag and Beede and the Friends Indian Committee. Sent to the Comanches to win them by kindness and a Christian example from a life of raiding and roving, Tatum had gravitated to the position of Phil Sheridan that the Indians would have to be forced into the new life. Unfortunately, Lawrie Tatum and Phil Sheridan were more realistic in their appraisal of the situation than were Enoch Hoag and Cyrus Beede—or Tatum's successor James M. Haworth.

5. Comanche Freedom Ends

Late in March 1873 Cyrus Beede, representing Central Superintendent Hoag, summoned the leading Comanches and Kiowas to a council at their agency. After hearing the chiefs and headmen blame a recent killing of a Texan on a few Comanches over whom they had no control, Beede proposed that the Indians sign a pledge to make no further raids and to stay out of Texas. The X's of nearly fifty Indians were obtained and Beede then promised that within two months the United States would liberate Satanta and Big Tree from the Texas state penitentiary.[1] Actually it would be six months and only after considerable haggling between federal officials and the governor of Texas before the two Kiowas would be free.

Beede also introduced their new agent, James M. Haworth, to the assembled Indians, who would soon be referring to him as Red Beard. The forty-one-year-old Quaker had once strayed from the Society of Friends. But after entering the Methodist church and serving as an officer in an Ohio regiment (1861–63), he resigned his commission, left the Methodists, and rejoined the Society. He came to Fort Sill firmly committed to the peace policy, a Quaker who had strayed once but did not intend to do so again.[2]

Arriving at a time when the Comanches and associated tribes were on their relatively good behavior—the Comanches seeking the release of their people captured by Colonel Mackenzie and held at Fort Concho, and the Kiowas hoping for the return of Satanta and Big Tree—Haworth had confidence that the peace policy would work. "I verily believe," said their new agent, "it is the only way by which these ignorant, suspicious and supersticious [sic] people can be brought to change the spear into the pruning hook."[3] As an expression of his faith in the efficacy of kindness and trust, Haworth dispensed with the agency's day guard from Fort Sill. Then new post commander Lieutenant Colonel J. W. Davidson, in a fit of pique, withdrew the night guard and declined to replace it without a written request from the agent. Haworth found himself embarrassed into a more complete adherence to Quaker policy than he had originally intended. Throughout his tenure as agent, Haworth was at odds with the military whereas Tatum had gotten along well with them. The bickering further complicated the administration of Comanche affairs and confused the Indians as to who actually represented their Great Father.

Haworth early protested the practice of Colonel Davidson sending out small scouting parties without consulting him. He also was disturbed by Davidson's claim that he had the authority to pursue raiders right back to their lodges on the reservation. The Indian Office straightened the agent out on that, citing the policy established in 1869 authorizing hot pursuit onto a reservation. Haworth likewise was informed that the colonel did not need to clear with him the dispatch of scouts and patrols.[4]

The level of raiding in Texas was lower in the spring of 1873 than in previous years. But the level of expectation of Texans was higher and the fact that things were relatively better was little consolation to them. Texans did not receive kindly the proposals that the Comanches at Fort Concho and the Kiowas Satanta and Big Tree be liberated. Nevertheless, in view of the Indians' cooperation in returning stock and women and children seized in Texas, in April General C. C. Augur, commanding the Department of Texas, ordered the release of the Fort Concho prisoners. The commissioner of Indian Affairs had been agreeable, in part because the forage the stock of the Fort Concho prisoners were consuming at an alarming rate was being charged by the army quartermaster to the Indian Service.[5]

Haworth notified the Comanches that the prisoners would be delivered to them at Fort Sill. Over a month passed without their appearance and the Comanches grew restless. The agent described the friendly Noconie chief Horse Back as saying, "If they don't come by the time this moon dies he will close his ears against white men's promises and his heart will not feel like laughing *any more*."[6]

There was great rejoicing among the Comanches when a small detachment of cavalry escorted their hundred fellow tribesmen into Fort Sill June 10, 1873. The wagon train had had to detour around Jacksboro, where a mob of white settlers had been a threat to the Indians.[7] However, the prisoners reported having been well treated at Fort Concho and on the tedious seventeen-day trip to Fort Sill. In their delight at being reunited with their wives and children the Indians were prepared to promise anything and Haworth warned the Comanches of the necessity of their continued good behavior.

The Comanches were involved also in the release of Satanta and Big Tree. Texas authorities regarded the two Kiowa chiefs as hostages not only for their own tribe but for the Comanches as well. Haworth and Hoag did not seem to comprehend this and in their eagerness to get Satanta and Big Tree freed were prone to attribute any Indian hostilities in Texas to the Comanches. What the Texans were looking for was a complete cessation of depredations by all Fort Sill Indians.

Apparently, officials in Washington did not entirely grasp the situation either. They always seemed to have difficulty appreciating what Texans were suffering at the hands of the Indians and the depth of Texas feeling on the subject. Governor E. J. Davis had made clear to Washington that he would demand the disarming and dismounting of the Kiowas and Comanches before releasing Satanta and Big Tree. Agent Haworth and Superintendent Hoag were not informed of this and their ignorance helped set the stage for an embarrassment to the federal government.

In March 1873 Secretary of the Interior Columbus Delano requested that Governor Davis pardon Satanta and Big Tree. The secretary set "on or about" April 15 as the date for freeing the Kiowas.[8] Before Davis had agreed to this, Beede in his council with the Indians at Fort Sill informed them Satanta and Big Tree would be released in two moons. Events 1,500 miles west then intervened. The Modoc War was getting underway and Secretary Delano asked the governor to delay, presumably believing that it would be poor public relations to free Satanta and Big Tree while an Indian war was in progress. Davis himself preferred postponing the release until May 20, when the Texas legislature would have adjourned and he would be free to visit Fort Sill.

In the next few weeks the governor spelled out the terms under which he would agree to grant the pardons. "There will be no peace on the frontier until the Indians are put on foot, disarmed, and kept under close surveillance," wrote Davis.[9] The Republican governor was facing a strenuous campaign for reelection. David knew that his political opponents would exploit any weakness he exhibited in maintaining the authority and interests of Texas in its dealings with the federal government and its Indian charges.

The view from Fort Sill was different. The Indians had been made a promise, and if it were not fulfilled it was easy to conjure up unpleasant repercussions. Cyrus Beede, ignoring the fact that the secretary had erred in making a commitment he had no authority to implement, asked, "Can the Govt. afford to risk the chances of an *Indian War,* as a legitimate result of a refusal to deliver these chiefs, in accordance with its promises?"[10]

One vehement objector to releasing the Kiowas was General Sherman. He had protested when the proposal first had been made and expressed his opposition again on hearing that a Comanche war party had returned to the reservation with a herd of mules stolen in Texas. Referring to them as "the Indians to conciliate whom Satanta and Big Tree are to be turned loose," Sherman harked back to two years earlier when he had seized the Kiowas at Fort Sill. "I have no more faith in their sincerity than I have in the prairie wolves," snarled the general, "and as I once risked my life to prove their sincerity, I do not propose to again expose others to a like danger."[11]

Governor Davis strengthened his political position by obtaining a resolution from the Texas legislature endorsing his policy. He then agreed to turn over the prisoners to be held at Fort Sill pending arrangement of satisfactory conditions for their release. The governor left no doubt that he would go to Fort Sill for the final negotiations and would like Secretary Delano to meet him there.

For Agent Haworth the summer of 1873 was a long one. He knew that some of his Indians, although fewer than usual, were raiding in Texas. While reporting it, he played it down and emphasized the success he had enjoyed in getting some of the stolen stock returned. Haworth would have found few supporters south of Red River, where Texas settlers still dreaded seeing a moon grow full. There were incidents, such as the one on a fork of the Brazos in June, that explained their apprehension. Indians had attacked a farm family, killing a baby and riding off with a seven-year-old girl who was later found scalped and hanging from a tree. Texans could only regard with shock and disgust the Quaker agent's conviction of the "wisdom and righteousness of the present peace policy."[12]

For the great majority of Comanches who did abstain from raiding, Haworth had little to offer. A bad drought and blazing heat eliminated any hope of crops for the handful of Indians who had worked in the fields. The flour the agent had for issue was of a very poor quality and he had to borrow in July to provide even part rations of sugar and coffee. Because he was permitting them to hunt and buffalo were plentiful that season, the Indians had plenty of meat. Indeed their only interest in the beef cattle issued was in the hides that they could sell to traders.

More disturbing to the Indians than the poor quality of flour, or even the reduction in the sugar and coffee ration, was the rumor that they would be dismounted and disarmed. Old Horse Back said that dismounted and disarmed Comanches would be left *"sitting like poor dogs on the prairie.*"[13] No self-respecting Comanche would permit that in 1873 and Haworth knew it.

With incredibly poor timing, someone chose July to send a party of surveyors to the reservation to subdivide it. The explanation offered was that the Indians thus would be enabled to select their allotments if they wished to begin farming. Although their overly optimistic reports had helped bring it about, the Quakers realized how disturbing to the Indians the surveying could be and both Beede and Hoag wired Washington to suspend the project. At Haworth's request Colonel Davidson already had withdrawn the military escort from the surveyors, effectively stopping them. After an initial refusal, an acting secretary of the interior agreed to a delay until Satanta and Big Tree were delivered to Fort Sill.

Early in September the two Kiowas were delivered to the post and placed in its guardhouse. A month passed before Governor Davis and a delegation of Texans from the border counties arrived at Fort Sill to discuss with Commissioner of Indian Affairs Edward P. Smith and Superintendent Hoag terms for the release of Satanta and Big Tree.

In the presence of the settlers from northern Texas, Governor Davis had no choice but to adhere to the tough conditions he had spelled out earlier. Shortly before he left for Fort Sill, Indians had killed and mutilated a father and son a few miles from Jacksboro. As one of the village's residents wrote the governor, "If Satanta and Big Tree are given up *without adequate Security* for the protection of the frontier, the Republic Party is *defeated*—and *you* will be *unjustly censured.*"[14]

At Governor Davis's insistence the council convened October 6 in front of Colonel Davidson's headquarters, although the Indians had protested the location. The governor specified the terms under which he would release the two Kiowas—subject to rearrest if their tribe misbehaved. All Indians must settle on farms, give up their horses and weapons, draw their rations in person at three-day intervals, turn in any stolen stock, and surrender to Texas authorities those Comanches recently raiding in Texas. These terms, with the possible exception of the last, were already familiar to Commissioner Smith, Superintendent Hoag, and Agent Haworth. Nevertheless, Commissioner Smith hastened to interject that neither he nor Hoag and Haworth had been aware of these conditions.

Kiowa spokesmen, prepared to promise anything to free their leaders, indicated a willingness to comply. The Comanches were indefinite. Horse Back expressed the hope that the Kiowas would be released and admitted that "some of our foolish young men go off on the warpath."[15] Asatoyet and Quirtsquip expressed their resentment at being denied free access to Fort Sill, contrasting their treatment at the post with that accorded them in Washington. There, said Quirtsquip, "I saw pretty things . . . and better houses than here and was allowed to go in."[16] Both maintained the United States had failed to meet its obligations to them. "I saw my Father in Washington and have been true to my promises and wait my Father to Keep his to us," said Asatoyet,[17] and Quirtsquip told the assembled whites that if they wanted him "in the white man's road, let me see the things promised."[18] When Commissioner Smith asked Quirtsquip if he had not had land plowed for him in the spring, the Comanche attributed his failure to farm to "bad medicine." When he had gone to his farm thunder and lightning greeted him and clouds appeared only over his land.[19]

Despite the pleas of the Indians that they could not control their young men and that the government was reneging on its promises, Governor Davis held firm. Not even a public appeal from Hoag could shake him. Commissioner Smith saw the futility of attempting to change Davis's mind and concluded the council by giving the Indians an ultimatum. Indicating a point in the heavens roughly equivalent to the sun's location at 3:00 P.M., the commissioner told the Indians he would give them until that time the next afternoon to surrender the Comanches involved in the recent raids.

The Indians ignored the ultimatum, but it did produce
negotiations between Commissioner Smith and the governor and a clarification of the latter's terms for the benefit
of Colonel Davidson. Smith promised that all Comanche,
Kiowa, and Kiowa-Apache males would be placed on a
roll and checked frequently. The commissioner even
pledged "to compel the Comanches to surrender not less
than five of the recent raiders." In conclusion he appealed
"to the courtesy of the Chief Executive of Texas, to re-
lieve the embarrassment of the Government." If the two
Kiowas were not released, the commissioner predicted,
"We shall have to fight all the Kiowas . . . together with
the Comanches."[20]

When the council reconvened on the morning of October
8, 1873, the Kiowas came prepared, bows strung and firearms loaded. Fort Sill was alerted and some of the cavalry
were standing by ready to go into action. The Indians
were deadly serious. Kicking Bird, a normally complaisant
Kiowa, said that his "heart was a stone; there was no soft
spot in it," and that the United States had deceived them,
"Washington is rotten." Lone Wolf, a fierce Kiowa raider,
observed ominously: "I know that war with Washington
means the extinction of my people, but we are driven to
it."[21] If the Kiowas had attempted to liberate Satanta and
Big Tree, the Comanches would have been drawn into the
fighting and Commissioner Smith's worst fears would have
been realized.

Governor Davis relieved the tension by announcing that
he was freeing the Kiowas on the guarantee of Commissioner Smith to enforce the Texan's conditions. The following day Smith met the Comanches in council at the
agency and demanded within thirty days the surrender of
at least five Comanches guilty of raiding, or the tribe's
rations and annuities would be stopped. When the chiefs
said they were unable to produce the warriors the commissioner denounced them as cowards. The chiefs responded with some heat that if Smith wanted warriors
captured he could take troops from Fort Sill and do it

himself. Calmer heads prevailed and a compromise was reached. Cheevers, the Yamparika, agreed to recruit Comanches to act as guides for a detachment from Fort Sill that would scour the plains for the raiders.[22]

Thus the Fort Sill conference ended. Governor Davis could claim he had forced the federal government to accept his terms. Commissioner Smith could claim he had a promise from the Comanches to cooperate in securing their warriors guilty of the recent raids. The Kiowas were satisfied because Satanta and Big Tree were back with them at last. The Comanches must have been quietly amused at the gullibility of the white chiefs.

Captain Phillip L. Lee rode from Fort Sill on October 12 at the head of fifty cavalrymen and twenty Indian scouts from the bands of Cheevers, Quirtsquip, and Esahabbe. His orders were to run down the Comanche raiders, reportedly in the vicinity of Double Mountain in Texas. General Sherman, with his usual bluntness, accurately characterized the mission:

> I think the Commissioner of Indian Affairs has imposed on the military a costly and impossible task. To chase a small band of raiding Comanches in all western Texas, a country three or four times as large as the State of Pennsylvania, utterly devoid of supplies, and even grass, will wear down the horses and the men, and result, as hundreds of similar attempts, in failure.[23]

Captain Lee and his men returned in twelve days, having traveled about 150 miles and scouted thoroughly the area that Cheevers had suggested as the most likely location of the marauding Comanches. To the surprise of few, Lee reported having seen no hostile Indians.

Nevertheless, throughout the fall and winter Texans continued to report stock stolen and occasionally scalps lifted. Apparently several small parties of Indians were involved. They drove off more than a hundred horses and killed at least twenty-five people. Troops from Fort Clark caught one raiding party and recaptured some of the stock, but usually the warriors got away with their plunder. One Texan writing to the editor of the *San Antonio Express* asked, with the heavy sarcasm and classical allusion popular among letter writers of his day, "Will these reservation equipped gentry be graciously received or summarily punished on their return from this pleasure excursion, will Regulus return to Carthage, or Satanta to Huntsville [site of the Texas penitentiary] ?"[24]

Governor Davis responded to the reports of depredations by telegraphing the information to Commissioner Smith and putting six companies of state militia in the field. The Texas troops made no appreciable impact. Early in December the governor complained bitterly to the commissioner that Indian raids were more frequent than before the Fort Sill conference and that none of the promised restrictions on the Comanches and Kiowas had been imposed.

Commissioner Smith in turn complained that Texans were stealing horses from the Fort Sill Indians! Within a month of the end of the Fort Sill conference over 250 Indian ponies had been stolen. The first theft had been of 120 taken from the bands of Cheevers and Quirtsquip while warriors from those bands were accompanying Captain Lee's column searching for Comanche hostiles. The horse thieves apparently had been part of the delegation of Texans accompanying Governor Davis and had lingered a few days after he had departed.[25] And this was just the beginning. Other white men and Indians from neighboring tribes became involved, inspired either by a spirit of revenge (a Texan had identified one of his horses in the possession of a Comanche at the time of the conference and had been unable to reclaim it) or unable to resist the temptation of so many horses so readily accessible.

His experience at the Fort Sill conference had brought Commissioner Smith to a sterner line on the Indians. "The reservation cannot be made a refuge for thieves and murderers," he proclaimed in his 1873 annual report. Recognizing the risk of making the innocent suffer with the guilty, the constant concern of the Quakers, Smith declared, "Yet I am persuaded that vigorous treatment will be kindness in the end."[26] Late in November he telegraphed Haworth to issue no more annuities to the Comanches and to give them ten days to fulfill their pledge to surrender the five raiders. If they did not comply, the Comanches were to be "handed over to the Military."[27] Anticipating Haworth's reaction to his orders, the commissioner told the Quaker that he could be relieved temporarily if he did not care to act as agent during military operations.

Haworth summoned the Comanche leaders to a council and gave them the commissioner's ultimatum. As usual, the chiefs present were, like Cheevers and Asatoyet, those who were least guilty. The latter said he would move his band over to the Washita to be near the Wichita Agency and away from any possible fighting. The night after the council Haworth was wakened by one of his employees with a warning that some of the Indians had decided to attack the agency. Most of the Comanches had taken the ultimatum as a declaration of war against them, and more of them were seen now with bows strung and carbines in hand. The agent concluded it would be wise to dismiss the school for a few weeks.

Haworth was not at all in sympathy with the approach Commissioner Smith was taking. The agent continued to explain away raids in Texas as highly exaggerated or the work of Cheyennes or Indians from New Mexico. Superintendent Hoag took the same line, asking that the demand for the five Comanche raiders be remitted and that the issue of annuities to the Comanches resumed, if they just returned some of the stolen stock. The superintendent blamed the thieving Texans for keeping the Indians on edge and inspiring them to retaliate. "A large number of the citizens on the frontier of Texas," declared Hoag, "are really worse, and meaner than the worst Comanches."[28] To cure the "few raiders from their bad habits," the

Quaker continued to place his confidence in "appeals to their better nature."[29]

The Quaker viewpoint might make little sense on the frontier, but there were eastern groups supporting it. Hoag had alerted the Executive Committee of Friends because "they stand responsible to the Govt. for their administration of the cause entrusted to their care."[30] Felix R. Brunot, chairman of the Board of Indian Commissioners, protested the ultimatum before Haworth had even received it. Brunot called it a "return in its very worst form to the old plan of managing the Indians which kept up perpetual wars."[31] Commissioner Smith might have stuck to his guns had he not received additional opposition from an unexpected quarter, the army. General Sheridan passed on with his approval General Augur's opinion that a recall of the ultimatum would be best in view of the trouble it might produce. Smith executed a strategic withdrawal, notifying Haworth he could resume distribution of annuity goods to the Comanches if they just returned stolen stock. The demand for the five Comanche raiders that had been made as part of the deal to free Satanta and Big Tree back in October was quietly forgotten.

The Comanches who were innocent of any direct participation in the Texas raids (and this was most of those on the reservation) had been placed in a distressing situation. Until the lifting of the commissioner's ultimatum only those Comanches assigned to the Wichita Agency had received their annuity goods. They might have little use for the coats, pants, and wool socks that continued to be issued in the face of earlier protests about their uselessness to the Indians, but the axes, frying pans, iron kettles, needles, butcher knives, and blankets were needed. These were finally distributed three months late. The rations promised the Indians (without which it was impossible for them to remain near the agency as ordered) were in short supply all winter. Haworth had received considerably less than he had estimated he needed for the year. For the

fiscal year ending June 30, 1875, 2.5 million pounds of
beef and 500,000 pounds of flour had been contracted for
as opposed to his estimate of 4 million pounds of beef
and 730,000 pounds of flour required.[32] The agent got
through the winter by dispensing partial rations to his
hungry Indians. With the coming of spring and the real
raiding season it was particularly necessary that, in Cyrus
Beede's words, "Congress in its economy will not force
these Indians into Texas or elsewhere to commit depredations,"[33] a policy he dubbed "most suicidal."[34] After
assessing the situation at the three southwestern agencies
Beede was sent by Hoag to Washington to convince the
commissioner of the gravity of the situation.

Despite the very real problems that faced them, Colonel
Davidson and Agent Haworth found time to squander
energy and vitiate any hope of their cooperating by quar-
relling over the practices of the Fort Sill sutler, J. S. Evans.
Haworth had complained to Secretary Delano that Evans
was maintaining open bar at the post and some of the
whites got drunk there and then robbed his Indians. Davidson heatedly denied this when it was called to his attention
by the secretary of war. The colonel proceeded to accuse
the agent of violating the law requiring the presence of an
army officer at every annuity issue. Haworth tried to conciliate Davidson, whom at least one subordinate believed
to be subject to periodic insanity,[35] but to no avail. Both
ended up calling on colleagues for supporting letters and
still more energy was wasted. Beede, always happy to
damn the military, supported Haworth and charged the
colonel with opposing the president's entire peace policy.

The winter of 1873-74 was a bad one. On the reservation the Indians had gone hungry and only received their
annuities after the scare produced by the ultimatum. Off
the reservation some Indians died in two clashes with
United States troops in Texas. Cavalry from Fort Clark
guided by Seminoles had caught a party of thirty to forty
Comanches and Kiowas in December and killed several, including a son and a nephew of the Kiowa chief Lone Wolf.

Early in February 1874 troops, this time from Fort Griffin and guided by Tonkawas, killed eleven Comanches near Double Mountain.

According to the Indian code these deaths must be revenged and everyone at the agency expected a new round of raids when the grass could better support the Indian ponies. Especially disturbing to the whites was the knowledge that the Indians had been trading their buffalo robes for arms and ammunition. When Otter Belt, a young Quahada warrior, was denied them by a clerk of J. S. Evans, he showed up a few days later with a new revolver and a mule load of ammunition obtained from Evans's Cheyenne Agency competitor. And there were other signs of tribal tension.

In the spring of 1874 the Comanches decided to hold a Sun Dance, although unlike the Kiowas they had no tradition of an annual dance for the entire tribe. This coincided with the emergence of a young Comanche medicine man, Eschiti, and betrayed the sense of anxiety that had gripped the Comanches. Eschiti (Coyote Droppings) was only about twenty-seven years old.[36] A Quahada, he had engaged in the vision quest common among the Plains Indians and had been granted unusual powers. Early in May an agitated Horse Back came to the agency to report the new developments to the agent. From the old Noconie Haworth learned that the Comanches planned to hold their dance soon at the western end of the reservation and that Eschiti was capable of vomiting up all the cartridges the Indians might need for any make of gun. The medicine man also had demonstrated his capacity to raise the dead and he could make himself and others bulletproof.[37]

During the next two months the whites kept abreast of developments at the western end of the reservation through friendly Comanches such as Horse Back, Quirtsquip, and Esahabbe and the Kiowa, Kicking Bird. Eschiti was more than the usual medicine man. His message to the Indians had taken on a messianic note. He reminded them that the Indians' fortunes were declining rapidly (witness what had happened to the Caddos and Wichitas, who had taken the white man's road). He, Eschiti, had been sent by the Great Spirit to deliver them from white oppression.[38] His pronouncements were for all the Indians of the southern plains, although outside the Comanches he attracted support only from a number of the Cheyennes and a few Kiowas and Arapahos. Even among the Comanches the Penetethkas generally held aloof, despite threats to their life and property from Eschiti's followers.

The Comanche Sun Dance, their only recorded one and dramatic evidence of tribal trauma, took place late in May 1874. It was preceded and followed by much conferring among the several camps of Comanches, Kiowas, and Cheyennes along the North Fork of Red River. Comancheros brought in whiskey and the deliberation grew heated. Several plans of action were proposed. As an interpreter heard it from Quirtsquip, "They have a great many hearts, could make up their minds at night for one thing, and get up in the morning entirely changed."[39] Some Indians demanded a general attack on the whites, others advocated hitting the Texans only. The Tonkawas, having provided the scouts for the detachment that had killed the Comanches near Double Mountain, were the preferred targets for many. White buffalo hunters, drawn to the plains in increasing numbers since the development of a new tanning process had made buffalo hides as valuable as cow hides, were the choice of others.

The white hunters were killing the buffalo at a shocking rate. Kicking Bird, on whom Haworth depended so heavily, shared the feelings of all Plains Indians on this issue. The Kiowa urged his agent to take action, pointing out that the buffalo were the only resource of the Indians, their hides the "money" with which they purchased from the trader the things they had come to depend upon.[40] Haworth sympathized with the Indians' position, as did Cyrus Beede; however they were powerless to halt the slaughter.

At the agency headquarters hopes rose and fell during May and June. Rumors of impending attack alternated

with assurances that at most the Comanches would engage
in a little horse stealing and then come in. There was positive evidence that the Indians were becoming more reck-
less. Late in April Comanches began taking horses and
mules from the agency and its neighbors, including twenty-
eight head of stock seized earlier in Texas and then surrendered to Haworth. They even stole from the Kiowas,
Kicking Bird losing several horses to them.[41] A Caddo
Indian and an interpreter recovered some of the stock and
brought it to the agency, only to have it taken from them
again by Comanches who had followed them in. One report was that the Comanches had decided to retain the
best horses and mules to bargain for peace in the fall at the
conclusion of the raiding period.

Haworth, as usual, refused to recognize the basic drives
of these warriors for whom he was responsible and attributed their restlessness to the ration situation. It was bad.
In the critical period from late April into June he sometimes had no coffee or sugar to issue and only partial
rations of beef and flour. Nevertheless, it was unrealistic
for him to contend that given "plenty of supplies . . . I will
exert a controlling influence over them."[42] More practical,
if humiliating for him, was Haworth's request of Colonel
Davidson that he again provide a night guard for the
agency.

Late in June Haworth permitted himself to be mildly
optimistic about his "recreant children."[43] The Kiowa Sun
Dance was under way and they had assured him that they
would make "good medicine."[44] The agent hoped the
Kiowa example would keep the Comanches off the warpath. Also, Hoag and Beede were making strenuous efforts
to improve the ration situation, and supplies of sugar and
coffee were on their way. What Haworth did not know was
that a war party of 300, mostly Comanches and Cheyennes
with a few Kiowas and Arapahos, had left the camps in the
western part of the reservation and headed for Adobe
Walls in the Texas Panhandle. Among the Comanche
leaders involved were the chiefs Tabananaka, Wild Horse,

Mowaway, and Black Beard, and a rising young warrior, Quanah.

At dawn on June 27 they launched an attack against a party of buffalo hunters and merchants, twenty-eight men and one woman, who had recently installed themselves in some log and sod buildings near the site of Kit Carson's battle with the Comanches in 1864. Confident in their numbers and Eschiti's power to render the guns of the whites harmless, the Indians charged in for the kill. Only the chance breaking of a building's beam, which had roused some of the hunters shortly before daybreak, saved the whites. As it was, two of them were still asleep in a wagon and were killed when the charge broke over the little community. But some of the Indians became casualties in the first few minutes and having survived the initial rush the whites settled down to withstand a siege. Most of them were fine marksmen, and with plenty of ammunition at hand and firing from the cover of the buildings, they survived repeated charges. In the middle of the afternoon the Indians drew off to confer. During the council Eschiti's horse was killed by a lucky shot from the beleaguered whites, completing the deflation of the warriors. The whites had won, although there would be Indians lurking in the area for the next twenty-four hours. A third white man had been killed, and an estimated six or seven Comanches and several Cheyennes lost their lives. Eschiti attributed the failure of his medicine to a member of the war party violating a taboo by killing a skunk.

Even as the warriors had made their way toward Adobe Walls, Colonel Davidson had been assured by Commissioner Smith that he had authorization to follow any raiding parties back to the reservation and punish them. It would take more than the few hundred troops at Fort Sill to cope with the large number of Indians hostile by the summer of 1874. Additional troops would be ordered into the field in July.

The orders were issued after Cheyenne warriors returning from the Adobe Walls battle frightened their agent,

John D. Miles, into asking for a guard of troops from Fort Sill. Abandoning his post, Miles hastened east to impress authorities with the magnitude of the uprising. En route he found the still-burning remains of a small wagon train and the bodies of its four teamsters. One of them had been tied to a wagon wheel and had been virtually consumed by the fire. Ironically, the three wagons had carried the coffee and sugar Hoag and Beede were rushing to Haworth. These developments gave credence to Agent Miles's reports, and major troop movements were set in motion by Generals Sheridan and Sherman.

The assumption of the officers was that the hostile Indians would retreat to the headwaters of the Red River. To invade this area from the north and west with three columns was the responsibility they assigned General John Pope's Department of the Missouri. From General Augur's Department of Texas three columns would operate north and west, one of them from Fort Sill under Colonel Davidson. If all went according to plan, the six columns would converge and trap the hostiles. To differentiate the guilty from the innocent, by August 3 all friendly warriors were to be enrolled at their agencies and daily musters would be held from that time. Indians out were subject to attack anywhere they were found. If they came in to the agency after the deadline they were to be dismounted and disarmed.

The only violence near Fort Sill had been the murder of a woodcutter, but Colonel Davidson did not intend that his small garrison should be overrun by any surprise attacks. He delegated Captain G. K. Sanderson to assist Haworth in enrolling the Comanches from whom the most trouble was expected. By August 8 only thirty-eight Yamparikas, six Noconies, and sixteen Penetethkas were listed for daily muster, and no Cochetethkas or Quahadas.[45] The muster did not include the bands of Penetethkas at the Wichita Agency. Their numbers swelled that summer as friends and relatives sought safety with them.

Captain Sanderson and Agent Haworth represented different approaches to the problem. The Quaker was concerned that innocent blood not be shed and strove to liberalize admission to the sanctuary of the agency. The captain feared that guilty Indians would escape punishment by slipping into the camps of the enrolled warriors and their dependents. When Cyrus Beede arrived at the agency in August, Captain Sanderson happily conveyed to Haworth Colonel Davidson's edict that Hoag's subordinate could have no intercourse with the Indians without prior approval of the colonel. Sanderson believed that the tribesmen "at present . . . pretty thoroughly understand all that has been said as serious war talk. And it will not do," the captain went on, "to upset their minds with any peace promises. There is plenty of time for that in the future."[46]

Colonel Davidson also was disturbed at Haworth's performance during the enrollment. The colonel described him as "anxious to carry out the peculiar views of the Lawrence superintendency and to shift all responsibility of fixing the selection of the guilty parties upon the military."[47]

Among the Comanches there were equally divergent opinions. Some, notwithstanding the fiasco at Adobe Walls, still were confident of their power to either defeat or elude any troops sent against them. Others lacked this assurance and daily in the first three weeks of August they slipped into the reservation.

The weather in the summer of 1874 was a major factor in the operations of both Indians and troops. Between late June and early September there was no rain worthy of note on the southern plains, Eschiti taking credit for arranging the drought. As the temperature soared over 100 degrees, finally reaching 112 in the shade, the streams dried up and the grass died. The mobility of the troop columns was handicapped and two of the six did not even begin their portion of the pincer movement until a few days after it finally rained (September 6). The Indians, however, also had great difficulty in maintaining them-

selves and their large pony herds. About fifty lodges of
Noconies, not wishing to remain out, but not wanting to
surrender their arms and ponies either, sought a way out
of their dilemma by going to the Wichita Agency. Here
they permitted their stock to invade the fields of the
Wichita and affiliated tribes. These Indians protested to
their agent, who requested help from Colonel Davidson.
The colonel was concerned about two cowboys killed the
day before about twelve miles from the fort, but the call
for help from the Wichita Agency took priority.

Davidson arrived at the Wichita Agency August 22 with
four companies of black cavalrymen. It was ration day at
the agency and hundreds of Indians were around, including
a number of Kiowas who had come over without permission. The colonel talked with Red Food, the principal
Noconie chief present, who agreed to be escorted with his
warriors to his camp, where they would surrender their
weapons preparatory to being taken to Fort Sill. What almost resulted was the Wounded Knee Massacre of 1890
in reverse.

At the Noconie camp the warriors produced only one
rifle and two pistols. When the officer present demanded
the Indians' bows and arrows as well, Red Food gave a
whoop and led his warriors away at a trot. The officer
ordered his detachment to open fire but they hit no Indians. The troops then found themselves under fire from
the Kiowas as well as the Comanches. In two days of
skirmishing the Indians under Lone Wolf and Red Food
wounded only four soldiers. But they killed six civilians at
the agency, burned a number of public buildings and
houses belonging to the local Indians, and looted the
trader's store. The troops killed several Kiowas and Comanches, possibly as many as ten, although only two
bodies were found and one of them was of an old woman.
Colonel Davidson ordered the Noconie camp put to the
torch and all the band's belongings went up in smoke.

Panic gripped Haworth's Indians. Many of the Indians
hurriedly struck their lodges, rounded up their pony

herds, and headed west. As their initial fright faded most of them trailed back, followed by Esananaka (Howling Wolf), a Yamparika chief with a band of about seventy-five people. These Indians had to surrender their arms before they would be accepted into the agency by Davidson.

During the fall and winter other bands trickled in as the troops stayed in the field and gave the Indians no rest. A number of bands were driven from their camps and lost their lodges and winter meat supply. In September Colonel Ranald S. Mackenzie did great damage to a large group of Comanches and Cheyennes encamped in deep Palo Duro Canyon in west Texas. Although he inflicted only a few casualties on the Indians, Mackenzie destroyed their lodges, food, and equipment and captured over a thousand of their ponies, which he shot except for a few given to his Tonkawa Indian guides. The next month Tabananaka came to the agency and surrendered a small party. Red Food, Little Crow, and White Wolf—all Comanches—sent in word that they were ready to give up. When the 300 Indians came in to Fort Sill, they surrendered their arms and about 2,000 horses. As sleet and snow came to the southern plains and 100 of his horses froze to death, Colonel Davidson withdrew his column to Fort Sill. Other columns continued to crisscross the area, keeping the Indians on the run. The troops, in all their operations, killed only ten Indians and captured twenty. Texas Rangers trapped one small party of six Comanches, killing five whose heads were put on display by a Jacksboro, Texas physician.[48]

As the former hostiles gathered at the three southwestern agencies, authorities debated the proper policy to pursue toward them. For Satanta, who had been drunk at the Wichita Agency when the fight there took place and had then fled to the plains only to surrender in October at the Cheyenne Agency, the decision was easy. Unlike Big Tree, who was confined only briefly and then released as harmless, Satanta was returned to the Texas penitentiary on the grounds that he had violated his parole. Four years later he committed suicide by jumping from an upper story of the penitentiary.

General Sherman originally wanted a military court created to try warriors accused of particular crimes. It also was proposed that, without trial, the ringleaders be identified and then imprisoned at Fort Leavenworth in Kansas, Fort Snelling in Minnesota, or Florida's Fort Marion. General Sherman favored placing them among one of the northern tribes, such as the Chippewas, where they could help support themselves by "fishing or engaging with the Fur Companies who will tame them."[49] By spring the military had reached a decision on Fort Marion. Lieutenand R. H. Pratt was selected by Colonel Mackenzie to escort the "criminal Indians" to Fort Marion. As late as April, Pratt had been of the opinion that "some of them should be tried and executed here in the presence of their people," and others sent to Texas to be tried for murder.[50]

As was to be expected, Enoch Hoag and Cyrus Beede opposed any trials that might result in executions and belittled the charges of Indian violence. Hoag had coined the euphemism "retaliatory depredations" to describe Indian violence.[51] Agent Haworth found himself at odds with both his fellow Quakers and the military. He would imprison fewer than the military, but on the other hand he did not like a proposal originated by William Nicholson of the Executive Committee of Friends.

Nicholson had proposed that the southern Plains Indians be moved east of the ninety-sixth meridian. This Quaker had lost faith in the efficacy of any program for these Indians until they had been broken of their roving habits, dismounted, and disarmed. Hoag endorsed the proposal if it were limited to the Indians the army captured or forced into the reservation. Haworth opposed even this because it would divide families and be impossible to enforce.

As a stopgap, warriors of Haworth's agency surrendering or captured were encarcerated in the Fort Sill icehouse. A few of the more notorious, such as the Comanches Tabananaka, Red Food, White Wolf, and Little Crow and the Kiowa Lone Wolf, were put in irons and lodged in the post's guardhouse. The women and children of all the prisoners were placed in camps nominally run by the military but actually under the charge of friendly chiefs such as Cheevers, Horse Back, and Kicking Bird.

The icehouse, a structure 150 feet by 40 feet, of which only the stone floor and walls had been completed, held up to 130 prisoners. A visitor to the post in January toured it and found Indians living in pup tents placed against the walls with their campfires down the middle. The warriors were passing the time by gambling and appeared happy to see the visitor, from whom they begged some tobacco.[52] Owing to the arrival of new prisoners and the discharge of old ones the population of the icehouse was constantly changing. Those released were turned over to the custody of the friendly chiefs.

The saddles and bridles, bows and arrows and firearms were taken from the warriors as they came into Fort Sill and burned or stored in warehouses. Of the 2,000 ponies and mules the Indians surrendered in October, some were stolen by white and Indian thieves and 650 were awarded to Tonkawa and white scouts. Many of the ponies were in such bad condition when they came in, and the pasturage around Fort Sill was so poor, that they died. Others were shot on Colonel Davidson's orders and soon the stench from 760 dead animals suggested that this was not the best solution. The colonel then auctioned off 590, the paucity of buyers and the poor condition of the stock keeping the average price down to $6 an animal.[53] The money was held in escrow, Colonel Davidson hoping to use it to buy cattle and sheep for the Indians.

In February 1875 a hunting party of Comanches from the agency, headed by Esahabbe and accompanied by interpreter Philip McCusker, encountered about 250 Kiowas and arranged their surrender. This virtually ended that tribe's resistance. In March it was the turn of the Cheyennes, 1,600 of whom surrendered at their agency. By the first of April the only significant groups of Indians absent from the three southwestern reservations were nearly 600 Comanches, mostly Quahadas and Cochetethkas, and a few Kiowa-Apaches, the latter having fled in panic at the time of the Wichita Agency fight.

Colonel Mackenzie had assumed command of Fort Sill April 1, 1875, replacing Colonel Davidson, and he made plans to catch the Comanches still roaming the Staked Plains. To trap the wary Indians Mackenzie was prepared to exploit their confidence in Comanchero José Piedad or the Kiowa chief Kicking Bird. The colonel first had arranged with Piedad to lead a trading party to the plains in the spring and, after having established contact with the Quahadas, to report their location to Mackenzie.[54]

After coming to Fort Sill the colonel turned to Kicking Bird for help. In return for a promise of a generous number of ponies from the Quahada herd—the same offer made to Piedad—the Kiowa agreed to cooperate. With only Mackenzie aware of his real purpose, Kicking Bird was to secure permission to take his band buffalo hunting. They would then "accidentally" contact the Quahadas, and Kicking Bird would get the information to Mackenzie, who would be trailing him by a day or two.[55]

As things developed, Mackenzie did not have to resort to either of these schemes and Kicking Bird did not live to see the Quahadas surrender. As he was bidding good-bye to his fellow Kiowas who were en route to prison in Florida, one of them placed a curse on him. Shortly afterward Kicking Bird was dead; the post surgeon said from strychnine poisoning, Kiowa tradition says from the curse. There certainly were Kiowas—and Comanches—on whose relatives and friends Kicking Bird had informed, who were happy to see him dead.

Colonel Davidson also had turned to Indians for aid. Before he left Fort Sill he dispatched three Comanches, one of them White Wolf, the Noconie chief who had come in the previous October, and army scouts Jack Kilmartin and Jack Stilwell, to see if they could contact any of the

out bands. In the middle of April they returned with Ka-
wertzen (Long Hungry) and Mowaway, both Cochetethkas,
and Wild Horse, a Quahada, a total of about 175 men,
women, and children, together with their 700 ponies and
mules.

It was Colonel Mackenzie who received their surrender.
He promptly recruited Wild Horse and two other Comanches to return to the plains to aid in trying to locate the
remaining Quahadas. J. J. Sturm, who had been serving
Mackenzie as an interpreter, volunteered to accompany
the Comanches and bear a message to the Quahadas from
Mackenzie.

Sturm, who usually affected the title Doctor, was a rather
flamboyant character who had been acquainted with the
Comanches since employed on the Texas reservation of the
Caddo and affiliated tribes in 1857. Moving with them and
the Comanches to the Washita in 1859, he had married a
Caddo and over the years held a variety of jobs at both the
Wichita and the Comanche agencies, as well as with local
traders. It is fortunate that Sturm was the atypical fron-
tiersman who could savor the romance of his mission, for
the journal he kept and the letters he wrote are our only
record of the circumstances surrounding the Comanche's
last days of nomadic life.[56]

Dr. Sturm, Wild Horse, and the two warriors left Fort
Sill on April 23. Traveling southwest they were two days
out when ravens flying around their camp signaled to the
Indians the proximity of buffalo. Shortly afterward the
party did see large herds and took time to kill two cows.
The Comanches knew the country well and the Doctor
recorded in his journal their names for the terrain features.
Buffalo continued to be plentiful and the Indians varied
their diet with milk from the stomach of a calf they killed.
Sturm observed that Indians frequently did this although
he was not tempted to indulge.

Six days from Fort Sill the party followed a trail to the
camp of Black Beard, a Quahada chief. Black Beard welcomed them with a hearty meal of buffalo meat and a

ceremonial pipe. When Sturm conveyed Mackenzie's surrender demand, the Quahada indicated his readiness to comply and directed the Doctor to the main body of Quahadas "two sleeps distant."

Resuming their mission the next day, Mackenzie's emissaries crossed a fork of the Brazos and ascended a steep bluff to the *Llano Estacado,* the Staked Plains. Twenty-four hours later, nine days out of Fort Sill, they came in sight of the main Quahada camp. Surrounded by curious Indians, Sturm and his companions were ushered into an immediate council. When the Comanches learned Mackenzie's message, they asked that the meeting be postponed until the following day to give some of their principal men who were out hunting a chance to participate in the deliberations.

On May 2 they reconvened. Several Indians spoke, among them Quanah, the son of Cynthia Anne Parker and the Quahada chief Peta Nocona. Described by Dr. Sturm as "a young man of much influence," Quanah advocated surrender.[57] Wild Horse, for whom he had a great deal of respect and to whose band he normally belonged, may have helped Quanah reach his decision. However, it was the medicine man Eschiti, whose authority seemed unimpaired a year after the Adobe Walls debacle, whom Sturm credited with the Indians' deciding to head for Fort Sill and captivity.

Eschiti impressed Dr. Sturm. The first night the emissaries were in the Quahada camp he had invited Sturm to his tepee and had assured him that he would take his people to Fort Sill. True to his word Eschiti led them northeast the morning of May 3. The Doctor noted, "When he says move, we move and when he says stop, we stop."[58]

The Comanches were almost a month getting back to Fort Sill. Their ponies were in poor shape and the Indians stopped along the way to allow them to graze and to give the hunters a last chance at the buffalo and antelope.

Under way, the column of over 400 Indians and 2,000

ponies stretched for miles over the prairie. Dr. Sturm rode
with the warriors, joining in the buffalo hunts and sharing
in the excitement of chasing wild horses, of which they
killed three and captured one. The Doctor's journal suggests that he had adapted well to the nomadic life, thriving
on a diet of meat and coffee: "My health is good and I
never feel so delighted as when mounted on a fleet horse
bounding over the prairie."[59]

When they stayed in camp for a day or two to permit
the women time to dry meat and prepare new tepee
covers, the men raced horses and conversed around the
campfires. It was an idyllic life as Sturm described it. The
children chased chaparral hens, and an occasional buffalo
ran among the tepees, providing a flurry of excitement.
Once the Indians found an abandoned wagon. Improvising
harness for a team of ponies, they drove it careening across
the prairie loaded with every Indian who could find a spot
to hang on.

The only unpleasantness occurred when a young Comanche warrior and an intermarried Mexican disputed the
ownership of a horse, a handsome pinto. The Comanche
came upon the Mexican on the open prairie, killed the
horse his opponent was then riding, and forced the Mexican to walk into camp carrying his saddle. When the
Mexican got in he rallied his supporters and went looking
for the Comanche, who also had friends. Arrows and lead
flew briefly before the chiefs managed to stop the skirmish.
The chiefs then killed the pinto, effectively eliminating
that source of contention. The only other casualty of the
dispute was the Mexican, who suffered two slight arrow
wounds.

As the migration to Fort Sill entered its second week,
Dr. Sturm decided to reassure Colonel Mackenzie that all
was going well. On May 11 a party of several Comanches,
including Black Beard and Quanah, rode for Fort Sill with
messages to the colonel. They brought Mackenzie the first
word he had had from Sturm since the Doctor left the post
three weeks earlier. Other reports arrived in succeeding

days, confirming that all was going well and that the Indians realized they must surrender their arms and the warriors accept imprisonment in the icehouse. One of these messages was carried by Wild Horse and Eschiti. Sturm spoke again of how dependent he had been upon Eschiti and expressed the hope that Colonel Mackenzie would permit the medicine man to retain a favorite gray horse: "He says he loves him as he does his people."[60]

Not until June 2, 1875 near Signal Mountain, about twelve miles from the post, did Mackenzie finally take the Quahadas into custody. The surrender, nearly eight years after the Treaty of Medicine Lodge, marked the cessation of Comanche hostilities and the end of their free existence as nomadic warriors dominating the south plains.

6. The Civilization Program
Is off to a Slow Start

James M. Haworth presided over United States efforts to launch the Comanches on careers as farmers and cattlemen during the first three years that all of them were on their reservation. He also was a participant in the acrimonious debate on the proposal to move the agency from the vicinity of Fort Sill to the Washita River. The Indians' paramount interest in this period was trying to get enough to eat.

Compared with the Kiowas or the Cheyennes, the Comanches were not treated harshly by the United States when they surrendered. Colonel Mackenzie was particularly lenient with the Quahadas, who came in with Eschiti. Unlike other bands that in the years 1870–74 had alternated between drawing rations on the reservation and eluding troops to escape to the plains, the Quahadas had steadfastly refused to give up their nomadic life. The colonel admired them and had decided "to let them down as easy as I can"[1] Although they were disarmed and dismounted when they arrived at Fort Sill, the Quahadas were returned 500 of their 2,000 ponies and few of their warriors spent any time in the icehouse. The Comanche bands provided only ten of the prisoners who had been shipped off to Florida before the Quahadas had even come in. In contrast, thirty-two Cheyennes and twenty-six Kiowas were incarcerated at Fort Marion.

Army personnel also used their influence to block the movement of 3,000 of the recently hostile Comanches, Kiowas, Cheyennes, and Arapahos to the Quapaw Reservation in the northeastern corner of Indian Territory. This scheme had originated with William Nicholson and the Executive Committee of Friends and had been backed by Congress with an appropriation of $300,000. The Quapaws had been persuaded to sell 40,000 acres for the purpose.

It sounded good in theory. As Commissioner of Indian Affairs Affairs Edward P. Smith pointed out, "Experience has shown that you can not . . . induce [Indians] to make any effort worthy of the name toward civilization so long as they are mounted armed and within two days march of the buffalo grounds."[2] The commissioner intended to conduct the "experiment of enforced civilization" by seeing to it that the Indians "come to daily toil or suffer hunger."[3] To execute the plan the Special Agency for the Captive Indians was created, some buildings were erected, and a few hundred of the 40,000 acres plowed.

The army, however, had released to their agents nearly all of the Indians shortly after they surrendered. Also, the warriors had not been completely disarmed and dismounted. Nor could they have been so long as they continued to have to hunt to supplement government rations. And once out of army custody, the recently hostile elements mingled with those who had remained on the reservation. If 3,000 somehow could be identified and removed to the new agency it would be impossible to prevent them from slipping away to rejoin their friends and relatives at the southwestern agencies. Kansans appalled at the prospect of having these raiders as neighbors added their voices to the chorus of opposition, and the scheme was finally shelved after costing the United States $200,000. Some inkling of the problems it would have presented was provided subsequently by the flight of Standing Bear from Indian Territory when the relatively amenable Poncas were moved from Dakota Territory to the tract obtained from the Quapaws.

The decision to leave the southern Plains Indians at their original agencies spared Kansans any possible problems with Comanches. Texans and Comanches, however, continued to clash and the whites now were more frequently the aggressors. Their targets were the loosely herded Indian ponies. A rustler operating from Texas or the Chickasaw Nation could cut out a herd of fifty or sixty early in the evening and by dawn be across Red River into Texas or back to the thinly populated nation. The Fort Sill garrison was kept busy trying to run down the thieves, some of whom were former post employees. These were men who had taken temporary jobs with hay and wood contractors at Fort Sill and then quit abruptly to ride home in style. In 1874 the Fort Sill Indians had lost almost 2,000 ponies and mules in this fashion.[4]

The height of the rustlers' activity came in the summer of 1875, when more than twenty were arrested and dispatched to Fort Smith for trial before Judge Isaac Parker. An appearance before the "Hanging Judge" held little fear for these criminals because the federal law restricted punishment of theft of a horse from an Indian, in Indian Territory, to one year's imprisonment. The Fourth Cavalry's Captain Wirt Davis may have resorted to more direct methods. In September 1877 while on a scout from Fort Elliott he captured five horse thieves and recovered 133 horses they had stolen from the Kiowas. Fort Sill authorities declined to take two of the thieves into custody and Davis headed back to Fort Elliott with them. En route the horse thieves reportedly escaped, but a few days later soldiers from Fort Sill found them hanging from a tree.[5]

The Indians also ran down thieves—or tried to. In early August 1879 Quanah pursued white thieves who had made off with forty-seven ponies from the band's herd. Near the Texas panhandle line the Comanches not only recovered their stock but also captured four of the rustlers' horses. A few weeks later the same rustlers struck again and this time pursuers led by Black Horse overtook them 150 miles from Fort Sill. The Indians captured the thieves and brought them and the stolen ponies back to Fort Sill.

Texas judges were even less of a menace to white thieves than was Judge Parker, as Otter Belt, a young Comanche chief, found out in 1877. He lost nineteen ponies to two

Texas brothers who drove the herd to Denison, just south of Red River. They were trailed there by a Fort Sill detachment headed by a sergeant, who discovered that the Texans had auctioned off four ponies to local citizens and had taken the remainder of the herd deeper into Texas. The sergeant managed to identify two of the stolen horses. Nevertheless the Texans who had bought them refused to surrender them. A lieutenant was sent to take charge of a court action, but to no avail.[6] The citizens of Denison declined to cooperate, clearly not regarding stealing horses from Comanches to be theft in the usual sense. They rationalized that they were only taking horses previously stolen from other Texans. In view of these obstructive tactics and faced by a long court proceeding in a hostile environment, the army gave up its effort to recover the stolen stock.

Such incidents did nothing to build Comanche confidence in the United States. The 1867 treaty specifically provided for reimbursement of Indians for property lost to whites, just as it provided for compensation to whites who lost property at the hands of Indians. If the whites stole only from Indian raiders it might have boasted an element of justice. However, the innocent on both sides usually were the victims. Congress proved sensitive only to the fears of the whites.

Texas congressman Roger Q. Mills took the initiative in 1876 with a strange piece of legislation. A rider to the Indian Service appropriation bill specifically forbade the Comanches and other southern Plains Indians to cross into Texas. The agents must have made an effort to impress the Comanches with the law barring them from the state because several years later Quanah sought permission from the governor of Texas to cross the Red River to visit white relatives.

Quanah and his fellow Comanches, in their first three years on the reservation, made very little progress toward the government's goal of making them self-sufficient through agriculture and stock raising. But meanwhile the buffalo herds that had been the mainstay of Comanche existence disappeared from the southern plains.

The Indian trade reflected what was happening. Traders for the tribes belonging to the Kiowa, Comanche, and Wichita Agency purchased $70,400 worth of robes and furs from the Indians in 1876. In 1877 the figure dropped to $64,500, and then plummeted to $26,375 in 1878 and $5,068 in 1879.[7]

Until the buffalo disappeared from the southern plains, small parties of Indians had slipped away from the reservation in the hope of a return to the old life. On some of these occasions the Comanches stole Kiowa ponies to make their getaway. In every instance they were pursued by troops, although these detachments were no more able than their predecessors to run down Indians on the open plains. Prominent Comanches such as Quanah, Black Beard and Eschiti (now identified as White Eagle) performed valuable service to the United States in seeking out the runaways and persuading most of them to return. In the summer of 1877 Quanah brought in twenty-one and helped persuade Colonel Mackenzie to hold them in custody at Fort Sill rather than ship them off to Florida. Among the runaways was Rudolph Fisher, a white man in his late twenties whom the Comanches had captured near Fredricksburg, Texas, thirteen years earlier. When he returned to the reservation Fisher was released to his father but fled civilization and in a few months was back among the Indians. Possibly because of his white background he was not included among the fifty or so Quahada runaways whom the army held at Fort Sill for nearly a year.

Although a natural yearning to return to their nomadic life motivated some of the escapees, the ration situation on the reservation helped make others desperate enough to risk Texas Rangers and U.S. cavalry. There were periodic shortages of key elements in the Indian ration. Time and time again the agents would report the situation and make dire prophecies of famine-inspired outbreaks if something were not done. The commanding officers at Fort Sill and their army superiors deplored the situation because they knew that if an outbreak did take place it would be their job to put it down. "It is unpleasant to be expected to make Indians behave themselves, who are unjustly dealt with," telegraphed Colonel Mackenzie from Fort Sill in August 1875.[8] Nine months later, confronted with another ration crisis, he abandoned the understated approach: "The position of a jailor for a vast band of half starving criminals can never be pleasant," he wrote, "no matter how bad you may consider the criminals."[9]

Colonel Mackenzie, Lieutenant Colonel J. K. Mizner, and Lieutenant Colonel J. W. Davidson, all of whom commanded Fort Sill during this period, urged that army rations at the post be made available to the Indian agent. After much correspondence up and down the chain of command in the War and Interior departments, and consultations between the departments, this was done on a few occasions.

But even with this help from the army the Indians often went hungry. The nonbeef components of the Indian ration were less than half of those of a soldier—and that is assuming that the Indians got the full authorized weekly rations of flour, coffee, sugar, and salt (which was seldom). Rarely were all components available in the specified quantity. The beef component always was short in late winter and early spring, when a steer might do well to provide 25 percent of his weight in actual meat. One such carcass was inspected by a member of the Board of Indian Commissioners and he concluded: "By scraping along each side of the backbone, a pound of meat could not be got."[10] For Comanches whose diet had featured large amounts of meat this was a disaster. Moreover, their stomachs had difficulty adjusting to the salt beef and bacon sometimes used to supplement their beef rations.

Aside from the fact that the ration simply was not large enough to support an individual, there continued to be problems in getting the nonbeef components to Fort Sill.

Tons of rations would sit for months at the depot at
Caddo, 165 miles from Fort Sill, while Indians were
going hungry on the reservation. Freighting contractors
pointed to the miserable condition of the roads and the
absence of bridges; there were four unbridged streams between Fort Sill and Caddo that were unfordable during
periods of high water. In February 1878 the contractor
reported that ox teams that had left the depot early in
December were still "floundering in the mud towards Fort
Sill."[11]

Stung by criticism from the army that came to him by
way of the president, Secretary of the Interior Delano in
September 1875 ordered Superintendent Hoag to personally visit western railheads to expedite shipment of
rations. There was little apparent improvement, but
Delano could report to President Grant that he had taken
action. He also criticized the "evident disposition [of army
personnel] to magnify and exaggerate the apparent short-
comings of the Indian Office."[12]

Ration shortages were not peculiar to Fort Sill. To some
degree the problem existed at each of the agencies for the
Plains Indians. None were becoming self-sufficient at a
rate satisfactory to Washington officials. Hard pressed to
justify to skeptical congressmen the need to feed Indians
several years after they presumably had settled on their
reservations, commissioners of Indian Affairs and secretaries of the interior pressed agents to increase farm production. In September 1875 Commissioner Edward P.
Smith protested Colonel Mackenzie's including sugar,
coffee, and cocoa—"luxuries"—in the supplies he was
turning over to the Indian agent at Fort Sill.[13] In February 1878 Smith's successor, Edward A. Hayt, ordered
the Comanche agent to require his Indians to work for
any rations of coffee, sugar, or tobacco they received.
At the time the agent received this directive he had no
bacon, sugar, coffee, or flour to issue under any circumstances.

Congress took a direct hand in ration matters by specifying frequency and method of issue, and labor to be performed for rations received. The labor requirement had been first legislated in 1874 and for several years was renewed with each appropriation bill. Faced with the impossibility of enforcing it for the Plains Indians, their agents routinely sought and received exemptions, although in February 1878 the order mentioned above required the Comanches, Kiowas, and Kiowa-Apaches to begin working for coffee, sugar, and tobacco. Since 1876 they had been scheduled to receive rations at no greater intervals than a week and to be present in person to draw them.

Designed to keep the potential runaways under surveillance, the legislation only worked against the efforts to break up camp life by locating each family on its own homestead, or at least reducing the size of the bands and scattering them. Indians living any distance from the agency now had little time to spend in the fields. The days spent en route to and from ration issues, and at the agency in company with friends, were no hardship to these nomands, but it did make a farce of their farming efforts.

The program to make farmers of the Comanches made little progress. Until the buffalo herds disappeared, many Indians refused to give up the hunting that had supported them so well. Those who attempted farming did not enjoy much success for several reasons. Even plowing a straight furrow was a major task for Comanches with no experience at farming, and if they had the competence their ponies were too weak to break the ground. Most of the small fields cultivated by the Indians had to be plowed by agency personnel. Moreover, the soil was not the best; the areas occupied by the Yamparikas and Quahadas were particularly poor.

The reliability of rainfall was a major obstacle. In the spring and summer of 1875 the rains did arrive when needed, and those Penetethka Comanches who had remained quietly on the reservation during the tumultuous months of 1874 and 1875 produced a good corn crop. Unfortunately, the 1876 and 1877 seasons were relative failures. A ratio of only one good season in three—which would have discouraged experienced farmers—made it doubly difficult to convince buffalo hunters that agriculture was a viable alternative. Nevertheless, authorities in the lush, well-watered Washington area held to the line that farming was the answer for these Indians.

For several years agents for the Comanches, and army officers stationed at Fort Sill, had been pointing out the impracticality of concentrating on crop production to make the Indians self-sustaining. The Comanches had an opportunity to experiment with caring for sheep as a result of a scheme devised by Colonel Mackenzie.

Of the 4,166 horses and mules the army seized from the Comanches and Kiowas in 1874 and 1875, 2,756 head had been sold for a total of $27,330.25.[14] This sum came to be known as the Pony Fund. On the recommendation of Colonel Mackenzie that the Kiowas and Comanches were more likely to become herdsmen than farmers, and that sheep were much less likely to be stolen than cattle, he was authorized to draw upon the Pony Fund to purchase sheep for distribution among the Indians. Late in 1875 Mackenzie arranged to have 3,600 sheep purchased in New Mexico and driven to Fort Sill. Ultimately 2,200 head were turned over to those Comanche bands that would accept them, and the Kiowas got 1,000. Three years later a Comanche held the 30 that had survived.[15] A flood on Cache Creek had killed 500 sheep, and coyotes, dogs, and disease had taken care of the rest. The Indians had exhibited virtually no interest in caring for the animals: mutton gained no converts and the wool clip proved disappointingly small.

A government housing program was equally unsuccessful. With the idea of encouraging those Indians willing to follow the white man's road, Secretary of the Interior Carl Schurz approved the construction of ten frame houses to be occupied by Comanche, Kiowa, and Kiowa-Apache Indians. They were completed in 1876, but owing to faulty fireplaces they proved uninhabitable until additional funds could be found to furnish them with stoves. A few

Mowaway's camp, circa 1873. (Fort Sill Museum)

On the left, Cheevers and his two wives; *center*, Tabananaka and wife; *on the right*, Frank Maltby, white interpreter. 1875. (Smithsonian Institution, National Anthropological Archives)

Wild Horse, 1880. (Smithsonian Institution, National Anthropological Archives)

Quanah in his bedroom with a portrait of his mother in the background, circa 1890. (Oklahoma Historical Society)

Indians contracted privately with white men to have log houses built and for these the agent provided doors, window sashes, and hardware. The overwhelming majority of Comanches clung to their tepees even if they had to cover them with canvas instead of buffalo hides.

Besides trying to make the Comanches self-sufficient and move them out of their tepees and into houses, the United States was continuing its efforts to break up the old band system, or at least replace the chiefs who proved uncooperative. The original band lines were blurring and Indian spokesmen were emerging more and more as Comanches rather than as Quahadas or Yamparikas. In councils with their agent, Tabananaka, Horse Back, Quanah, and Cheevers talked most frequently. Mowaway, a prominent chief for many years, abdicated his responsibilities in 1878. Other Comanche leaders died; they included Asatoyet and Esahabbe, who had remained at peace throughout the difficult years, and Red Food and Prairie Fire, who had been active in the 1874–75 hostilities.

One aspect of the civilization program that received little support from the chiefs was education. Nor did it receive the emphasis from the government that it deserved. Everyone who addressed himself to the Indian question emphasized the necessity for educating the children. There was general agreement that the proper vehicle was the manual labor boarding school where the child could be isolated from what one Indian commissioner called "the demoralization and degradation of an Indian home."[16] Both boys and girls were to be limited to the fundamentals of reading, writing, arithmetic, and geography. In addition, the boys should acquire a familiarity with those skills needed to operate a small farm or to fill positions on the agency staff, such as carpenter and stableman. The girls should become adept at managing a household, sewing, and working at the dairy. All instruction had to be in English except for the bare minimum needed to communicate with new students.

The Treaty of Medicine Lodge called for a teacher and

school for every thirty Comanche, Kiowa, and Kiowa-
Apache children. In 1872 Agent Tatum had managed to
enroll a handful of Comanche children for a few weeks.
Three years passed before any Comanche children again
were in the school. In February 1875 Agent Haworth
opened a term with twenty-seven students, almost half of
them Comanches.[17] His success stemmed from the military control of his Indians during the 1874–75 unrest. In
the next four years the figure gradually increased, Congress's failure to appropriate sufficient funds being the
main reason more were not in school. As the Indian commissioner pointed out in 1878 in a plea for more funds,
if the United States simply lived up to its treaty obligations to the Comanches, Kiowas, and Kiowa-Apaches it
would consume all the education funds allotted to the
entire population of Indian Territory exclusive of the Five
Civilized Tribes. Not that Indian parents were that eager
to enroll their children. Agent Haworth's creation of a
board of education with Cheevers and Quirtsquip as the
Comanche members was a quixotic move that apparently
achieved little. As late as 1879 only about 65 of a reservation population of 500 school-age children were enrolled.
   For the first few years the school was operated directly
by the agent. In 1875 a system was inaugurated under
which a contractor operated the school for a sum that
ranged from $4 to $6.50 per capita per month. The government would furnish the land and the building, beds and
some school supplies, and the students' shares of rations
and annuities. The contractor would supply the staff and
their subsistence, and any additional school supplies that
were required. During these years the school also received
gifts of clothing, school supplies, and a little cash from
Quaker groups. Quakers were also conspicuous among the
school staff. A. J. Standing, an English Friend, operated
the school for two terms. Some of the zeal with which the
Quakers approached their task is seen in the statement of
Sally Cowgill, who was employed at the school in 1875:
"I consider it a noble missionary work . . . and should it

be the will of Providence, I would be glad to go back to the work, and labour for the good of their precious immortal souls."[18]

It is easy to scoff at a system that had children fresh from camp life copying such phrases as "Angels are guardian spirits," and on an almost equally impractical level: "On demand I promise to pay to the order of Emerson E. White Nine Hundred and Eleven Dollars value received."[19] The physical plant also left much to be desired: the boys were stacked in double-deck bunks in a drafty shed attached to the main building. How can we today approve the compulsory Sunday service, even if led by Dr. O. G. Given, the agency physician, whom one inspector described as "a gentleman whose education fits him to acceptably fill a pulpit."[20] Nevertheless, it was a beginning and some of the young Comanche students, like Howard White Wolf, would emerge in the 1890s as Indian spokesman capable of meeting the whites on their own ground.

Certainly the Comanches had difficulty coping with the agents in the late 1870s, even when they were backed by the army, as was the case in the dispute over shifting the agency headquarters from Fort Sill north to the Washita River. This was first proposed by the commissioner of Indian Affairs in the summer of 1872 with the idea of merging the agency with that of the Wichita and affiliated tribes, thus enabling a reduction in staff and a savings to the taxpayer. Although proposals for consolidating agencies and reducing the acreage held by Indians were popular in the 1870s, Agent Haworth initially opposed it for fear that the Comanches and Kiowas would raise havoc among the peaceful tribes of the other agency. Six years later Haworth's successor would make the move to the Washita, and in the interim it became another issue exacerbating the already precarious relations between Fort Sill officers and Indian Service personnel.

Although all the commanding officers of Fort Sill in the period 1872–78 opposed transfer of the agency to the Washita, some were more vehement than others. One of

the most outspoken was Colonel Davidson, with whom
Haworth had had the dispute about the use of soldiers
as armed guards for the agency. The colonel, an officer
given to emotional outbursts, became extremely indignant
at a remark in one of Haworth's reports. The agent had
made a critical reference to the post trader maintaining an
open bar. Davidson responded in a flurry of letters denying
the charge and attacking Haworth for failure to follow
proper procedure in receiving supplies. One of his junior
officers wrote to the *New York World* assailing Quaker
policy generally and specifically questioning the veracity
of Haworth's overly optimistic first annual report.[21]

In contrast with Davidson, Colonel Mackenzie got along
quite well with Agent Haworth. Mackenzie came to Haworth's assistance when he ran short of rations and the
agent expressed his liking for the colonel. Their relationship was endangered once by the colonel's annoyance at a
letter appearing in the *New York Times,* apparently written by an agent of the Board of Indian Commissioners.
The author of the letter stated that Fort Sill was "a sort of
young Sodom, and the garrison is mostly made up of men
who neither fear God nor regard man." He pictured the
Indians as being in "great dread of being turned over to the
military."[22] Mackenzie's protest was endorsed by his
superiors and passed up the chain of command.

Meanwhile, Haworth had been converted to the advantages of shifting the agency to the Washita. The arguments
against the Fort Sill site were convincing. The agency was
located downstream from the fort and had real difficulty
getting uncontaminated water. Some of the buildings were
actually on the military reserve and there were not enough
wood and grass in the vicinity to accommodate large Indian camps. And since the post lay between the agency and
their usual haunts to the west, the Indians were discouraged
from visiting the agency freely. Most infuriating to the
army was the claim that soldiers from Fort Sill demoralized and debauched the Indians.

Haworth maintained that consolidating the two agencies

on the Washita would positively benefit the Indians. If drawn north to that location they would find better land and more wood. They also would be more than thirty miles farther from Texas and the post would be between them and the Red River. With a telegraph line connecting the agency and Fort Sill, the garrison could be alerted to intercept thieves raiding the Indian pony herds before they could get back to Texas.

The army officers countered these arguments by defending the morals of their men and emphasizing the expense of the shift. They also charged that moving the agency to the Washita would defeat the purpose for which Fort Sill had been built: to overawe the Comanches and Kiowas. One officer made a persuasive case for the future of the Indians in stock raising and for their present location being better for that than the valley of the Washita.[23] General Sheridan went so far as to charge that objection to the location of agencies near military installations "has for its main motive a desire to cheat and defraud the Indians, by avoiding the presence of officers who would naturally see and report it."[24]

In late 1877, in the midst of the acrimonious debate, Agent Haworth submitted his resignation. Together with virtually every other member of the agency staff he had developed malaria and he had not fully recovered. Haworth's tenure had been a tough experience for the gentle Quaker. At the height of his problems in December 1874, when he suffered the humiliation of seeing Colonel Davidson given greater responsibilities for the Indians of his agency, Haworth had declared that "in their elevation and welfare my heart is deeply interested and my faith stronger than it was a year ago."[25] While waiting to be relieved, however, Haworth confided to a fellow agent his judgment that the army "was the only honest branch of the Government."[26] Even while Haworth awaited his replacement the Central Superintendency was inactivated, easing the Quakers out of one of their most strategic Indian Service positions.

In the four months that he had to wait for his replacement, Haworth had much to reflect upon. Since Colonel Mackenzie had accepted the surrender of the Quahadas, United States policy had changed little, although the situation of the Comanches had altered radically. The disappearance of the buffalo had made them prisoners of the reservation, not so much by the threat of troops as by the promise of rations. The most commonly reported statement of the Fort Sill Indians in their many councils with agents, military personnel, and visiting Washington dignitaries was the piteous "Our children are hungry!" Recognition by Fort Sill officers and Indian Service personnel on the scene that it was futile to expect that the Indians would become farmers rapidly enough to compensate for the loss of the buffalo had led to efforts to introduce cattle and sheep. These failed because the Indians showed no interest in sheep and were driven by hunger to eat their stock cattle. Major outlays were required if the Indians were to become self-sufficient, but an impatient Congress was most receptive to proposals to reduce the expenses of the Indian Service. The inadequate budget for education and the enthusiasm for consolidating agencies reflected this. Clearly more was needed than a new agent.

7. "This Agency Is an Unhappy Failure"

P. B. Hunt served as agent for the Comanche and related tribes from the spring of 1878 until the summer of 1885. These were difficult years for the Indians: the buffalo disappeared, the United States attempted to coerce them into becoming self-supporting farmers and stock raisers, and white men encroached upon the reservation. For the first time, reasonably accurate census figures were available, revealing the Comanche population to be about 1,550, perhaps a 50 percent decline in the decade since the Treaty of Medicine Lodge.

Agent Hunt was a Kentuckian previously employed by the Bureau of Internal Revenue. During the Civil War he had reached the rank of lieutenant colonel in the Union army. His replacement of the Quaker Haworth had been eagerly awaited by Colonel Davidson, who assumed that as a former officer Hunt would see matters from Davidson's viewpoint. Indeed, the colonel offered post housing to Hunt in an effort to place him firmly within the army's orbit.

The Quaker policy inaugurated by President Grant in 1869 was quietly being shelved. The Friends were giving way to more conventional appointees like Hunt, usually Republicans with records of service in the Union army. The inactivation of the Central Superintendency in 1878 was recognized by the Quakers, "together with the general course of the Indian Department for the past few months," as evidence "that our co-operation instead of being heartily desired is a burden to the department."[1] For a time they continued to receive reports of schools, physicians, and other matters related to the civilization program, but the era of Quaker control of the three southwestern agencies had ended.

139

This, however, did not signify a general change in Indian policy. For example, the consolidation of agencies in the interest of economy continued to be advocated. Despite the protests of the army, the Indian Office proceeded with its plans to move the Kiowa and Comanche Agency from Fort Sill and consolidate it with the Wichita at new headquarters at Anadarko on the Washita River. In September 1878 P. B. Hunt moved to Anadarko and assumed his expanded responsibilities as head of the new Kiowa, Comanche, and Wichita Agency. The consolidation meant that two agencies whose combined payrolls had totaled $18,000 would now be administered for $10,000.[2]

For several years the army continued to protest the transfer from Fort Sill, arguing that it made more difficult the task of guarding the property and lives of agency personnel. Post commanders at Fort Sill sometimes threatened to ignore calls for assistance from Anadarko, but in emergencies they did respond. The army officers got some revenge by supporting the Comanches in their refusal to move closer to Anadarko. The Indian Office's hope had been to draw them to the vicinity of the Washita, where they would be more convenient for the ration issues and could find better farmland in the river valley. When Hunt left office seven years later the only Comanches near Anadarko were Penetethkas, who had been affiliated with the Washita Agency since its inception.

Not only consolidation, but the other key elements in United States Indian policy survived the ouster of the Quakers. Throughout Hunt's tenure as agent the government worked to make the Indians self-supporting farmers and stockmen. At least in the rhetoric of the Indian Office education continued to play a major role in the civilization program, and allotment in severalty was considered a necessary step before the tribesmen could be truly independent.

Despite the optimistic annual reports of the commissioner of Indian Affairs and the secretary of the interior, progress was painfully slow. The expense of administering the Indian Service steadily mounted. The number of employees on reservations continued to increase, the new Kiowa, Comanche, and Wichita Agency requiring a total of twenty-four in 1878.[3] Besides, contrary to expectations, the Plains Indians' dependence on rations did not lessen; in fact it grew in this period.

By the time Hunt became agent in 1878 buffalo had ceased to be a reliable source of support for the Comanches, and the antelope, deer, and other game populations also had declined precipitously. A hunt in June 1878 was permitted after the commissioner of Indian Affairs was informed that the Indians were desperate for food and tepee covers and well armed, "while the larger portion of the troops [at Fort Sill] are colored, and these the Indians have very little respect for and fear less."[4] The Indians did kill a few buffalo that June, but subsequent hunts were complete failures. In January 1879 hunting parties accompanied by cavalry escorts were in the Texas Panhandle, but game was so scarce that supplies had to be sent to them from the agency. When they proved insufficient, a local rancher let them have about twenty steers on credit.

Other Texas cattlemen had been complaining that Indian depredations had not ceased with the surrender of the Quahadas in 1875. Notwithstanding the 1876 law that Congressman Roger Q. Mills had authored specifically forbidding Fort Sill Indians from entering Texas under any circumstances, two years later Mills was denouncing the government's practice of permitting "large hunting parties of Indians under escort of a few soldiers . . . to go into Texas ostensibly to hunt Buffalo but really to steal our horses and murder our citizens."[5] Colonel Davidson denied that cavalry-escorted Indians had committed any depredations, while admitting that "some renegades from the reservations" were guilty.[6] The assignment of responsibility for such offenses was as difficult as ever and Texans responded by attacking any Indians they found south of Red River. In January 1879 a Kiowa who was a member of one of the parties hunting under cavalry escort was killed by Texas Rangers. The young Indian had borrowed a rifle and two shells from a cavalryman and had left the main party to hunt deer when he blundered into the Rangers, who scalped him.

The Texas legislature responded to inflammatory reports of "fully one thousand Indians from the Fort Sill reservation depredating" in the state with a joint resolution calling on its congressional delegation to get action from the federal government.[7] For their part the Indians in a council with their agent protested the killing of the young Kiowa. Shortly afterward a war party resorted to a more traditional type of protest by crossing into Texas and revenging their fellow tribesman by killing a young white man. Agent Hunt placed responsibility for the murder on the shoulders of the authorities, who had made no effort to punish the Texas Rangers for the death of the Kiowa. Texas won the last round with another law passed by Congress in May 1880, which forbade Indians to go into the state of Texas under any pretext whatever "without specific permission of the President of the United States."[8] Their exclusion from Texas and the disappearance of the buffalo signified the passing of an era for the Fort Sill Indians.

Another milestone was the last visit of the Comancheros to Comanche and Kiowa camps in 1880.[9] In contrast to the halcyon days of the 1860s, the Comancheros found little to barter for, no Texas cattle and horses, no buffalo hides and meat. In July 1881 the Kiowas did find two buffalo, a bull and a cow, and the bull's head was the focus of their summer ceremonial. Pautapety, a medicine man, promised to bring up from the earth all the buffalo the Indians needed if they used only bows and arrows to kill them, but his medicine failed.[10]

The vanishing of the buffalo adversely affected the Indians in several ways. Their spring and summer hunts had provided not only meat but tepee covers as well. Now they were forced to rely on canvas, which was an annuity item or had to be purchased from their traders. However, now the Indians had little to exchange for the canvas and other things—axes, kettles, ammunition, canned fruit—that had made their lives easier and more pleasant. For some families the only items they now had for barter were the hides from the cattle issued them for their beef ration.

Throughout Hunt's period as agent (1878-85), getting enough to eat was a problem for the Indians. Comanche males were warriors and hunters and, except for some of the Penetethkas living among the Wichitas, resisted any efforts to push them into agriculture and showed little more enthusiasm for raising cattle. The first two years Hunt was agent the rations were issued weekly in an effort to keep the Indians from wandering from the reservation. This also meant that they did little more than travel to and from the agency to draw rations. In 1880 Hunt was authorized to begin issuing rations at two-week intervals, which allowed more time in their fields for those Indians willing to work.[11] However, the agent could do nothing about the weather.

Agent Haworth had described the "principal obstacles to successful farming" as the "ignorance and idleness of the Indians and drought to which the country is subject."[12] P. B. Hunt had little cause to change that evaluation. Rainfall was insufficient nearly half of the farming seasons he was Comanche agent, and by the time he left office in 1885 he had concluded that the only hope of making the Indians self-supporting was to make them cattlemen.[13]

Agent Haworth had judged the potential of the Kiowa and Comanche reservations for stock raising as "almost unsurpassed. Fine nutritious grass in inexhaustible quantities, good and plenty of water, and good shelter."[14] P. B. Hunt agreed and two days after he assumed charge of the agency was urging the pruchase of stock cattle for the Indians. In 1879 the government did purchase 474 Texas heifers and several high-grade bulls for distribution among the Fort Sill Indians; the Cheyennes and Arapahos were issued cattle at the same time.[15] Three years later Hunt proposed taking for five years all the money that the 1867 treaty provided should be spent on the Fort Sill

Indians, a total of $263,500, and investing it in cattle for them.[16]

It was a good idea but too daring for the Washington officials. The most the secretary of the interior would consent to was the diversion in 1883 of $30,000 of Kiowa, Comanche, and Kiowa-Apache annuity funds from the purchase of the usual hardware and other "beneficial objects" to the purchase of stock cattle.[17] The 875 Texas cows and 31 graded bulls acquired in this fashion were the last stock cattle purchased during the administration of Hunt. Although far short of the numbers the agent had proposed, if held for five years their reproduction rate would have provided the Indians a substantial herd.

Unfortunately, this was not the case. Despite orders forbidding white men to purchase Indian cattle, they did. Cattle that had cost $37.50 a head were sold by the Indians for prices ranging from $8 to $20. Hunt attributed the selling to "the terrible mania of gambling"[18] and to hunger. In addition, roaming the open range of the reservation, the cattle were prey to the weather and to Indian and white thieves. Finally, of the graded bulls purchased for the Indians in 1883, twenty-six died of the tick-borne Texas fever. Regardless of the losses, a few Indians were building small herds, sometimes selling ponies to buy cattle. By 1884 Quanah had built his herd to the point that he could sell forty head to the government for distribution as part of the beef ration.

Comanche suffering from hunger reached a peak during Hunt's administration. In May 1879, four years after Eschiti had surrendered the last major Comanche band at Fort Sill, Hunt had no flour, sugar, or salt to issue, and only one-half the required amount of beef. The only ration component he had on hand in normal supply was coffee.

This crisis in the spring of 1879 was met by the secretary of the interior and an army officer. The secretary authorized an emergency expenditure of $3,000 for beef for the Fort Sill Indians. Captain Wirt Davis was in command of an escort accompanying Kiowa and Comanche Indians on a futile hunt in the western part of the reservation. "Hungry people whether mobs in cities, or savages on the prairies, are not scrupulous about procuring food," warned the captain. It was his opinion that the Indians wished "to do right" and were "entitled to food"—and Davis did something about it.[19] On his own authority he took twenty-four head from a herd crossing the reservation and personally guaranteed to their owners that the United States would pay.

The captain risked both his money and his commission by his action since he had no assurance his superiors would support him. The Indian Office could spend no more money for rations than Congress had appropriated, and Congress was slow to recognize that the Indians were more dependent than ever before. The matter came to a head in September 1879. Concluding that his ration funds were being expended at a rate that would result in their being exhausted before the fiscal year ended on June 30, the commissioner of Indian Affairs ordered a reduction in the already insufficient ration. However, Secretary of the Interior Carl Schurz decided after a conference at Muskogee with Indians from the southwestern agencies that the situation was so critical that he also would have to take some risks. He authorized the commissioner to issue those Indians full rations and the secretary then to go to Congress to ask for a supplemental appropriation.

When Congress convened in December 1879 Secretary Schurz had to ask for more rations not only for the two southwestern agencies but also for the Shoshones, Bannocks, Pawnees, and Joseph's Nez Percé band. For the two southwestern agencies alone Congress had to appropriate an additional $80,000, an increase of about 27 percent over the original appropriation. However, when the representatives and senators got around to voting the appropriations for the next fiscal year they provided not the $370,000 the rations had cost them for fiscal 1880, but only $305,000. By January 1881 the commissioner of Indian Affairs was estimating that at least $50,000 more would be required, and he ordered agents to reduce the beef ration to their Indians.[20]

Agent Hunt declined to do so until the commissioner had heard his case. Hunt predicted that if he imposed the reduction his Indians would begin to kill their own cattle and move from them to the herds of the beef contractors and the Texas ranchers. To emphasize the gravity of the situation he insisted that troops be assigned him for protection. The commissioner did not force Hunt to reduce the beef ration, but Congress failed to respond to the secretary's plea for a supplemental appropriation. This time President Benjamin Harrison resolved the crisis by approving the offer of the secretary of war to provide from army depots rations to the value of nearly $60,000.[21]

By January 1882 the secretary was again pleading with Congress for a supplemental appropriation. Beef prices had risen 30 percent the previous autumn and $100,000 was needed for the two southwestern agencies alone to carry them through the fiscal year. Congress's response in March was begrudging. The $100,000 requested for rations for the two southwestern agencies was reduced to $50,000. The commissioner had to inform Hunt he would have to reduce rations to his Indians by one-fourth.[22]

P. B. Hunt, knowing that "this could not be done and the white employees remain at the agency," improvised.[23] For two years herds, principally of Texas cattlemen, had been encroaching on the Kiowa, Comanche, and Kiowa-Apache Reservation. Unable to keep them off, Hunt now decided to take advantage of their presence. Backed by Fort Sill's Colonel G. V. Henry, the agent offered to condone the cattlemen's presence on the reservation until July 1 if they would supply beef to feed his hungry charges. Like Captain Davis, P. B. Hunt had been driven by circumstances to actions for which he had no authority. The cattlemen responded with 340 head, but before they could be delivered Hunt was informed that Congress had saved the situation by a further appropriation. Having already made the deal with the cattlemen, Hunt altered his levy to include only cows and distributed the 340 head to the Indians as breeding stock.

Meanwhile, the matter of the supplementary appropriation had been debated in Congress. Critics denounced it as an attempt to provide the Indians free of charge a standard of living white laborers could not afford. Kansan Preston B. Plumb reminded his fellow senators that there was no treaty obligation for rations for these Indians and that in his judgment

> the Indians will never do a thing for their self-support so long as we concede to them every single thing which their distended stomachs demand. . . . They are getting more from the Government today than they did five years ago, and the question of their independence of government support recedes every year.[24]

Despite the oratory Congress did vote the additional rations, and by 1884 the food crisis was easing. Contributing to the improvement was a higher level of support by Congress and the unofficial contributions of cattlemen in return for the privilege of grazing their herds on Indian grass. There is little evidence that most Comanches were contributing measurably more to their self-support.

P. B. Hunt had taken over the agency in the spring of 1878 to find a circular issued by the Indian commissioner that March stressing that "the chief duty of an agent is to induce his Indians to labor in civilized pursuits."[25] To promote this objective, Indians were to be employed in preference to whites where feasible, rations of coffee, sugar, tea, and tobacco were to be denied nonworking Indians, and the exchange of ponies for cattle, sheep, swine, or poultry was to be encouraged. Rations were to be refused visiting Indians to encourage them to remain on their own reservations and tend to their farms and cattle. Five months later the agents were reminded: "The practical test of improvement at your agency will be the decrease in the quantity of supplies which the Government will be called upon to furnish." In addition, they were warned they might be fired if results were not obtained.[26]

Such threats and exhortations achieved little. Four years later another circular informed the agents of a clause in the current Indian Service appropriation bill requiring that the secretary of the interior tell Indians being rationed by the government that this support was about to diminish, there was no treaty provision for rations, and they were "purely a gift." Moreover, the Indians were to be advised "that labor is not degrading, but on the contrary is ennobling, and that if they ever expect to become rich and powerful as the white races, they must learn the lessons of industry and economy."[27] Some clue to the paucity of results of such exhortation is to be seen in the necessity for the circular of May 31, 1883—five years after the original one denying sugar, tea, coffee, and tobacco to nonworking Indians—reaffirming the ban and now threatening to charge any unauthorized issues to the agents guilty.[28]

Despite the concept of Indian preference introduced into agency employment by Congress as early as 1875, few Comanches were on the payroll except as laborers, policemen, or freighters. Employing Indians as freighters had been successfully attempted elsewhere in 1877, and in July 1879 Hunt dispatched his first train. The Indians operated with their own ponies and were issued wagons and harness for which they paid from their earnings. Initially, at least, they hauled under the supervision of white wagon masters. The Indian freighters encountered some of the same problems that had plagued white freighters (bad roads and flooded streams). Merchants at the Caldwell, Kansas railhead introduced another complication by selling the Indians rifles and pistols. Nevertheless, freighting did provide the Comanches with income, and Indians as prominent as Eschiti, whose medicine had failed at Adobe Walls, were involved.

Indian employment as reservation policemen began in 1878.[29] Like other agents, those for the Comanches felt a need for a police force. James M. Haworth expressed it in January 1878 when he wrote the comissioner of Indian Affairs: "As the cold weather passes away, and the grass begins to grow the number of horse thieves increases."[30] Haworth proposed to organize a police force from among his Indians, and the commissioner assured him that a bill to accomplish this had been placed before Congress. In May it became law, but the organization of a force for the Kiowa, Comanche, and Wichita Agency was not completed until November. The chiefs had misgivings about permitting young men to arrest other Indians, and the Comanches were upset over the recent deaths of two of their fellow tribesmen at the hands of the soldiers. The agent finally got cooperation by threatening to withhold annuities and permission to hunt until a police force was organized.

Originally two officers and twenty-six men, the force reached a strength of thirty-seven early in 1882, dipped to half that later in the year, and stabilized at about thirty in 1885. Pay and equipment problems helped produce the fluctuations in size of the force. The 1878 appropriation bill set the pay at $8 a month for officers and $5 for privates. Agents protested their inability to recruit good men at salaries like that. Nevertheless, pay raises came slowly, and then only by cutting the number of police employed.

The same parsimony was apparent in arming the police. Not until the summer of 1880 were they issued rifles. Prior to that Hunt had had to depend upon the Fort Sill commanding officer to lend him weapons when the police needed them.

The Indian police were able to reduce the operations of white horse thieves, capturing several and killing one. However, most of their duties were more mundane: carrying messages, maintaining a night guard for the school, and arresting whiskey sellers such as the Creek Indians that visited the agency in 1883. A ready force of police was kept in camp near the agency and gave the agent a means of acquiring information and enforcing his will that was indispensable for his management of the two reservations.

By the fall of 1881 most of the police energies were being expended in an effort to keep cattle off the Kiowa, Comanche, and Kiowa-Apache Reservation. Drought conditions in north Texas had badly damaged rangeland, and cattlemen were driving their cattle onto the reservation from both the north and west. The 3-million acre tract the Comanches shared with the other tribes had attracted cattlemen for several years. Some of them had become acquainted with it while driving their herds north to Abilene or Dodge City. Individuals holding beef contracts for the agency also had maneuvered to pasture cattle on the reservation in excess of the number needed to fulfill their contracts. Licensed traders, squaw men, even Agent Hunt himself saw the advantages of holding cattle on the reservation, where they could fatten at bargain rates on Indian grass. The traders and Hunt were denied permission to graze cattle there, and the squaw men operated only on a relatively small scale. The Texans were running 75,000 head of cattle on the reservation by the time Hunt left office in 1885.[31]

In a period of three years the cattlemen progressed from being illegal intruders on the reservation to holders of a lease that had a degree of approval from the secretary of the interior. In March 1882 Agent Hunt was trying to contend with the presence of at least 50,000 head of cattle. He had sought and received aid from the small garrison at Fort Sill, but even with this help the Indian police could not cope with the task. Herds could be driven away, but in the absence of fences along the reservation's borders there were not enough troops and police to keep them from reentering at another point. The army regarded the task as impossible and suggested leasing the land. Hunt at first disagreed; however, the reduction in rations mandated in March 1882 led him to change his mind. As noted earlier, he worked out a deal with the cattlemen by which he would permit them to remain on the reservation until July in return for cattle to feed the Indians.

Late in the summer of 1882 the police, assisted by troops, began to move cattle off the reservation. Secretary Teller had decided that the proper policy was "to secure . . . cattle for the Indians, and to encourage them to raise stock themselves, instead of depending upon the small gains that will be realized by a tax on such herds."[32] Nevertheless, the cattlemen would be on the reservation until, twenty years later, it was divided under the allotment process.

While government officials were debating the desirability and legality of leasing, the cattlemen were making themselves at home, building corrals and fences and establishing camps. Obviously this could not have been done on such a scale without the cooperation of the agent and the Indians. Hunt had convinced himself that cattle could not completely be kept off, and under the circumstances the Indians might as well be paid. The cattlemen secured the cooperation of the Indians by placing on their payrolls influential chiefs and headmen such as Quanah, Eschiti, and Permansu (Comanche Jack).[33] Permansu was a nephew of the prominent chief Ten bears, and himself a former army scout and member of the Indian police. All three were Comanches because that tribe occupied the southern part of the reservation, the part nearest Texas and the one plagued by herds from that state. According to one rancher involved, Quanah was put on the payroll for $50 a month, with four other Comanches receiving $25 each. In addition, at one stage of the negotiations Quanah was promised 500 cattle. Squaw men on the reservation also had to be bought off, among them Thomas Woodward and George W. Conover.[34]

In the antileasing faction which developed were to be found most of the Kiowas, members of that tribe living too far north in the reservation to be wooed by the cattlemen, but also some Comanches. Prominent among the latter were Tabananaka and White Wolf, older chiefs of some standing.

Meanwhile, Secretary Teller faced a comparable situation on the Cheyenne and Arapaho Reservation and was having second thoughts about the issue, perhaps because he saw no possibility of Congress voting the funds to set the Indians up as cattlemen. Still not convinced that he had the authority to approve leases of reservation land, the secretary decided not to oppose the ranchers if they made provision for hiring Indians, thus enabling the tribesmen to learn the rudiments of the cattle business.

The Indians, however, still could not agree. Several councils were held, sometimes dominated by the proleasing faction, sometimes by the antileasing faction. All they confirmed was that most Comanches favored leasing and most Kiowas opposed it. At one council in May 1884 an imposing group of Comanches headed by Tabananaka, White Wolf, Cheevers, Howeah, and Mowaway demanded that Quanah and Permansu be stripped of all authority as tribal leaders.[35] Undeterred, Quanah and Permansu, accompanied by the Kiowas Big Bow, Howling Wolf, and Tohauson, were in Washington in August, probably traveling at the expense of the cattlemen. All the delegation got was a commitment that the commissioner of Indian Affairs would send someone to conduct an investigation.

Special Agent Paris H. Folsom spent more than a month on the reservation and concluded that a majority of the Indians opposed leasing.[36] He also thought he had detected signs of collusion between Hunt, his chief clerk, Quanah, and other Indians on the one hand, and on the other the cattlemen seeking a lease. He recommended strongly against a six-year lease that the cattlemen had drawn up calling for an annual rent of 6 cents an acre on 1.5 million acres, with the added provision that fifty-four Indian herders would be employed at salaries of $20 to $35 a month.

Agent Hunt had already forwarded a copy of the proposal with his endorsement to Washington. Quanah and

Permansu headed another Indian delegation to the capital, this time accompanied by two cattlemen, George W. Fox and E. C. Sugg. Early in February 1885 they conferred with a new secretary of the interior, Lucius Q. Lamar, who had at his side former agent James B. Haworth, currently serving as superintendent of Indian Schools. Secretary Lamar declined to ratify the lease, but neither did he direct Agent Hunt to ignore it. Like Teller, the new secretary was concerned about the legality of leasing and sought clarification from the attorney general. This official was of little help, holding that leasing could be done only by treaty or convention, subject to ratification by Congress. However, the attorney general concluded that although holders of leases approved by the Indians might be ejected from reservations, they could not be persecuted as trespassers.[37] The secretary's way out of the dilemma was to tacitly condone the six-cent-an-acre lease the cattlemen now claimed to have negotiated with the Kiowas, Comanches, and Kiowa-Apaches.

That summer the Comanches shared in the first "grass payment." The cattlemen distributed $9.50 each to the Indians as compensation for the first six months of the contract. It would have been far better for the Indians if the cattlemen had been barred from the reservation and the grass reserved for Indian herds. Congress certainly should have done more to help set the tribesmen up in the cattle business. But the Indians must also share the responsibility. With few exceptions they had done little with the stock cattle they had been issued. Nor could they overcome the divisiveness inherent in tribal society long enough to agree on acceptance of the grass money. At the first payment a few Comanches and most of the Kiowas refused to take it, which was indicative of a factionalism that plagued the reservation's inhabitants throughout the period.

The new issues fostered divisions that further eroded the old Comanche band groupings. During P. B. Hunt's seven years as agent the band chiefs gradually lost influence as a result of deliberate actions by the agent and also because of the altered life of the Indians. For the hunting existence on the plains the band had been the practical unit, large enough for protection from other Indians, small enough to make hunting possible. On the reservation, however, the Indians were pressured to break down into smaller groups and to open family farms. Hunt deliberately whittled away at obstreperous chiefs by singling out members of their bands and making them responsible for receiving rations and annuities for subdivisions of the band. Several actions of this nature could reduce the size of a chief's following from over a hundred to a mere twenty or thirty members.

Hunt then began to bypass all chiefs by issuing annuities and rations, other than beef, to individuals and heads of families. The chiefs protested the loss of their prerogative, for the ability to control the distribution of annuities and rations had been at the heart of their political power. For example, in 1878 a band of 93 received 2 axes, 2 ax handles, 18 bunches of beads, 8 thimbles, and 238 yards of ducking for tepee covers, and a long list of other items including dutch ovens, combs, and suspenders.[38] The chief of that band, after satisfying his own desires, was able to reward his supporters by determining just who got the annuity goods. When Hunt began distributing them to individuals and heads of families he also rewarded and punished. Those Indians who were cooperative and desired "emancipation from the domination and thralldom of their chiefs," as the agent phrased it, received favored treatment.[39]

When Hunt took office in 1878 the Comanches were divided into thirty-three bands for the issue of rations, not counting two Penetethka bands under Esahabbe and Toshaway on the Wichita Reservation. The thirty-three ranged in size from Cheever's with 115 members, to two bands with 10 each, the average having around 45. Eschiti was listed with 91 followers, which gave him the fourth largest band, and Quanah with 93 was in third place.[40]

Quanah's rise to prominence revealed the new elements at work in the Comanche hierarchy. He was about twenty years of age in 1875, the year he surrendered to Colonel Mackenzie. Despite his growing reputation as a warrior it probably would have been many years before he could have hoped to become a band leader had the Indians remained free nomads. However, in the new order he became a band chief in 1875, singled out for preferment by the agent and Colonel Mackenzie.

When Quanah had arrived at Fort Sill in advance of the main Quahada party he had informed the colonel of his white mother and sought help in locating her. Mackenzie addressed inquiries to several army installations in Texas.[41] One recipient shared it with a local editor, whose story was reprinted in other Texas papers. A Parker relative read it and informed Mackenzie that Cynthia Anne was dead.

Two years later Colonel Mackenzie was again writing at Quanah's request, seeking some evidence that the Indian would be welcome to visit his Texas relatives. As the colonel phrased it: "He certainly should not be held responsible for the sins of a former generation of comanches, and is a man whom it is worth trying to do something with."[42] This letter apparently elicited no response, but it was indicative of Quanah's standing with the military. He was not just another Comanche warrior; Quanah was an Indian who cherished the memory of his white mother and advertised in a Fort Worth newspaper for a picture of her. Quanah also was a man of some influence who was willing to use it to help lead his people down the white man's road. In the first few years after the Quahada surrender he helped track down Indian runaways and turned over to authorities a young white man captured about ten years earlier by Apaches.

The change in agents did no harm to Quanah's standing with the white establishment. P. B. Hunt also became interested in the young mixed-blood and sought unsuccessfully to secure for him a tract of Texas land reported to have been granted his mother by the state legislature. Even Charles Goodnight, the Palo Duro rancher, showed a special interest in Quanah by giving him a Durham bull to go with the cattle Quanah had been issued by the government.[43]

As ability to deal with the whites became the overriding qualification for a Comanche leader, Quanah's stock rose rapidly. As early as 1878, Colonel Davidson described him as "undoubtedly the most influential man among the Quahadoz, and one of the most influential among all the bands of the Comanches."[44] Such early eminence undoubtedly posed problems for Quanah with the older Comanche leaders. Some hint of the note of humility he struck with them was revealed in a general council of Indians held in 1881. Quanah was one of only three Comanche chiefs to speak, but he assumed a humble tone: "I am young and almost a boy, talking for assistance for my people." Citing his relationship with both "the white and the red people," the young Comanche continued. "For that reason I will not do anything bad, but looking for the good road, a suppliant for the red people, so when Washington hears he will help us."[45] The same ingratiating tone was to be seen in a note to Hunt someone wrote for Quanah from Wichita Falls: "Even though I am here with my friends yet there is but one council [sic] I listen to, and that is yours."[46]

As the leader of one of the largest bands on the reservation and a personal acquaintance of agents and Fort Sill commanding officers, Quanah held a position of authority that was well established by the time the cattlemen arrived on the scene. Just as P. B. Hunt and Colonel Davidson recognized the advantages of dealing with the Comanches through Quanah, so did the cattlemen. It was a mutually profitable relationship. Quanah led the proleasing faction while damning his opponents as "kind of old fogy on the wild road yet."[47] They charged that he had been "bought by the cattlemen."[48] But Quanah could afford the verbal abuse as long as the cattlemen provided him employment, junkets to Fort Worth, Dallas, and Washington, and thoughtful gifts such as engraved pearl-handled revolvers and diamond stickpins. The pin the Comanche chief could wear when he was attired in his "citizens's suit of black, neatly fitting" topped off by the "'tooth-pick' dude shoes, a watch and gold chain and black felt hat," observed a newspaper reporter in Fort Worth.[49] The only incongruous notes in Quanah's costume were the two long carefully braided plaits of hair, a style the Comanche maintained throughout his life.

It was on a junket to Fort Worth subsidized by the cattlemen that Quanah and a companion almost succumbed to illuminating gas. Blowing out the light when they retired to their hotel room after a night on the town, the companion was asphyxiated and Quanah narrowly escaped death. Reporting the incident, a Dallas paper observed: "He is thought a great deal of by the stockmen . . . as it was mainly through his influence that the leases were made and his peaceful talk that keeps the Indians on good terms with the leasers."[50] Quanah was a reporter's dream: a Comanche warrior with the romantic connection with the whites through Cynthia Anne, and distinguished enough to be singled out for praise by a congressman whose district encompassed areas once ravaged by the Comanches. Quanah also had learned enough of the white man's ways to recommend the appointment of his cousin, S. H. Parker, as agent at Anadarko.[51]

Quanah and his cattlemen connections were a complication for Agent Hunt, but there were other infringements on his authority as agent for the Comanches and the eight other tribes of the two reservations. Financial procedures had become increasingly restrictive as the Indian Office attempted to remove temptation from the agents. Hunt had to seek approval for expenditures for items as insignificant as two dozen bottles of sewing machine oil, or a $4.85 freight charge on a Christmas package for the school. And the approval of the commissioner of Indian Affairs was not sufficient; it had to come from the secretary of the interior. The secretary, or more likely someone in his office acting in his name, even scrutinized plans for a new residence for the agent and vetoed a bay window as an unnecessary extravagance.

Despite the rigor of this type of examination, an agent's superiors in Washington usually knew his operations only from what appeared in his reports and routine correspondence. The secretary's inspectors and the commissioner's special agents were too few to provide surveillance of an agent on a regular basis (months passed between their infrequent visits). In theory at least the agent was a little czar, dominating the Indians and employees of his agency. But it was a rare man who brought to the position the knowledge and energy to really master a complex assignment such as the consolidated Kiowa, Comanche, and Wichita Agency with its thousands of Indians from nine different tribes.

A shrewd agent learned very quickly that there were white men on the reservation with interests they were prepared to fight for and who could make his position untenable. These might be cattlemen such as E. C. Sugg, Samuel B. Burnett, and Daniel W. Waggoner, traders such as George W. Fox, Charles A. Cleveland, and Frank L. Fred, or squaw men such as Edward L. Clark, George W. Conover, and Emmett Cox. Many of these people had resided on the reservation for years and had seen agents come and go. Some had cultivated contacts in Congress, and in the Indian Office itself, and could sabotage an agent who crossed them. The squaw men could work through their Indian relatives to hamstring an agent who failed to perform to suit them.

To enforce his orders and curb dissent among the whites and Indians under his nominal control, the agent had only the inadequately trained and armed Indian police. The typical agent learned to avoid trouble by not pushing the civilization programs too hard and thus setting his Indians against him. He likewise learned to live with the traders, cattlemen, and squaw men, plus the staff he had inherited, permitting them to exploit the reservation's resources and Indian inhabitants so long as they did not become unduly greedy.

Some of the squaw men operated from particular positions of strength because they were both intermarried whites and long-time employees of the agency who had survived more than one agent.[52] Typical of this class was Edward L. Clark, whose enlistment in the army expired about 1870 while he was stationed at Fort Sill. Deciding to remain in the vicinity, Clark worked as an interpreter and in other capacities for both the Indian agent and local traders. A few years later Clark married the daughter of Moxie, a Mexican captured by the Comanches who had risen to the rank of band chief by the time Clark entered his family. Availing himself of his opportunities as the husband of a Comanche, Clark by the end of the century was farming nearly 100 acres with white labor he brought onto the reservation and grazing 12,000 acres on which he paid only a nominal rent.

However, there were frustrations associated with the role of squaw man. To marry an Indian woman was to take on responsibilities for her family and friends. On one occasion Clark sought the help of his agent in ridding himself of unwanted guests in the form of a visiting medicine man with a wife, two sons, and a herd of ponies. Clark also complained of another Comanche medicine man who apparently lived by dreams that foretold disaster for other Indians unless they presented him with a cow or something else of value.[53]

George W. Conover also had taken his discharge from the service at Fort Sill. After work around the agency comparable to Clark's, he married a young widow, Tomasa Chandler. Tomasa was a Mexican captive of the Comanches who had been sold by her warrior owner to William Chandler, a white man serving as agency interpreter, for $2 and a chicken. After his death Tomasa had married Conover, who by 1896 had 30,000 acres of the reservation under fence. In a letter to the agent in 1889 Conover revealed the social ties among whites that a squaw man could exploit. He invited the official to hunt deer and turkey with him, at the same time indicating his desire to get his share of barbed wire being issued the Indians.[54]

Unlike Clark and Conover, Emmett Cox came to the reservation as an employee of a cattleman, Daniel Waggoner. Like the other two squaw men, however, Cox married well. His first wife was the daughter of Chief Quirtsquip and after her death he married a daughter of Quanah. By the end of the century Cox was a licensed trader on the reservation and was grazing stock in a 14,302-acre pasture for which he paid Indian rates. He and the other squaw men profited in a variety of ways from their intermarriage. They farmed land and grazed their own cattle, boarded other men's cattle for a fee, and cut hay and timber from Indian land. Some squaw men were even charged with swindling the Indians out of cattle issued them as foundation stock.

Toward the end of his term as agent P. B. Hunt complained: "I had been nearly five years in office before I met the common experience of a United States Indian Agent's trouble with squaw men. . . . There are some good men among this class," he acknowledged, "but there are others whose character and influence are so bad that it is futile to expect peace as long as they are permitted to remain among the Indians."[55]

A government response to the problem was to reduce the number of bachelors on the reservation by giving married men preference for Indian Service positions. Few married men, however, found employment attractive at desolate, isolated agencies such as that at Anadarko in the 1870s and 1880s. Single men still comprised the majority of white employees recruited, and some persisted in finding love and financial security in the arms of Comanche girls.

The children who were the product of these unions were part of the regular population of the reservation schools. In the years Hunt served as agent the United States continued to stress the necessity of the Comanches educating their children, and Congress continued to fail to provide the

level of support for education that the Indian Office proposed. In 1882 Commissioner of Indian Affairs Hiram
Price reported that the government had fallen behind almost $2. million in meeting commitments on education
promised in the 1877-78 series of treaties.[56] A year later
Secretary Teller, in vain, described the commitments as
being "as sacred as the public debt."[57] When Hunt left
office in 1885 there were school facilities on the reservation for about one-fourth of the children of school age
among the Comanche, Kiowa, and Kiowa-Apache. But as
usual there was blame enough to go around. The Indian
parents still did not send their children in sufficient number to fill even the places available. The Comanches were
particularly lax in this respect, especially regarding the
young girls, who in that tribe could be betrothed by the
age of ten.

Some of the Comanche distaste for sending their children to school can be traced to its shift to Anadarko from
Fort Sill as part of the merger of the agencies. In addition,
the manual labor boarding school was less than a model
institution. The man who headed it was P. B. Hunt's brother
George. He remained in this position despite a circular issued in March 1879 that prohibited any relative except a
wife, daughter, or sister from being employed by an agent,
and then only as a schoolteacher. Moreover, a stepsister
of P. B. Hunt served as a matron in the school and her husband as agency storekeeper. Inspectors who detected these
relationships were critical of other aspects of the school.
It had no cows to furnish milk for the school table and to
enable the students to learn dairying. The manual labor
training program was weak, and one year the agent was
criticized because the school farm produced nothing but
weeds.

A problem with attendance at reservation schools was
their proximity to the Indian camps. Especially in the
spring the children played hooky in droves and their
parents condoned it. The first school term that Hunt was
agent he held up payment of annuities and denied permis-

sion to hunt until the Comanches filled their quota. He was reminded by the Indian Office on several occasions that he had the police and the power to deny rations as means of coercing uncooperative parents. An exasperated Commissioner Price pointed out in 1884 that although it was true that the United States had provided school facilities to accommodate only about one-fourth of the children of the three tribes, half of these seats were not occupied. He advised the agent that "if coaxing will not suffice, the ration argument must be applied" and alluded to the 1867 treaty, by which the Indians agreed to send their children to scoool. Authorizing the withholding of rations because they were "a gratuity, not demanded by treaty," the commissioner concluded:

> The Indians should be given to understand that the Government cares too much for their children to allow them to suffer from ignorance because their parents do not know the value of an education. If the parents are indifferent to the best good of the children then the Government must take the matter into its hands.[58]

If Comanche parents were reluctant to send their children to the reservation boarding school, it should have been easy to predict that they would not welcome the innovation in the Indian school system, the off-reservation boarding school or "training school." Nevertheless, the separation of the parents from their children was defended by the head of the Indian Service school as "kindly cruel surgery which hurts that it may save, and would in good time cure the Indian race of savagery."[59]

The first of the training schools, Carlisle, was the work of Captain R. H. Pratt, who had become interested in Indian education while in Florida in charge of prisoners from the southern Plains tribes. Opened in 1879 at an abandoned army post in the beautiful countryside of southeast Pennsylvania, the first class included children from the Kiowa, Comanche, and Wichita Agency. Captain Pratt proved to be an able administrator and Carlisle carried out very well what one official defined as the purpose of Indian schools: "teaching the Indian child to read and write, the Indian boy to till the soil, shove the plane, strike the anvil, and drive the peg, and the Indian girl to do the work of the good and skillful housewife."[60]

Pratt began by asking parents to surrender their children to him for three years, with no vacation trips home, and in 1882 the term was extended to five years. A typical directive from the commissioner of Indian Affairs in 1882 called on Hunt to provide for Carlisle twenty-five children between the ages of ten and sixteen, no fewer than twelve of them girls. "Their relationship to leading men of the tribe" was to be one of the criteria for selection. The injunctions that only children of "absolutely sound health" should be selected and that "special care must be taken to see that they have no taint of scrofula or tendency to lung troubles,"[61] had an ominous ring. There was a high mortality rate among the first children from Hunt's agency to attend Carlisle. By 1884 of sixty that had attended the school in Pennsylvania, at least eleven had died there or after returning home ill.[62]

Couple those statistics with the three- to five-year school term, and it is little wonder that the agent had trouble recruiting students. Regardless of his orders for the selection of healthy, intelligent children of chiefs and headmen, Hunt was reduced to sending anyone he could get. The Comanches particularly were very reluctant to let any of their girls go, and in the early years of Carlisle the recruits from the agency's tribes included a disproportionate number of orphans and children from families of little influence. For example, three of the earliest Kiowas and Comanches to attend Carlisle were Joshua Given, the son of the Kiowa chief Satank, who had died on the road to Texas in 1871, Lucius Aitson, son of a Mexican captive of the Kiowas, and Howard White Wolf, a Comanche who had lost both parents. In an effort to combat this opposition to Carlisle, delegations of leaders from the agency's tribes were taken East to view the institution. Nevertheless, in the period 1879-1900, a total of only forty-one Comanche children attended Carlisle.[63]

Notwithstanding the patent lack of enthusiasm of Indian parents for off-reservation boarding schools, others were established, including one at Chilocco in Indian Territory, about 140 miles from Anadarko. Opening in the fall of 1883, Chilocco received students from Hunt's agency but had difficulty keeping them. The school was badly mismanaged under its first superintendent; this and its proximity to the two southwestern agencies caused the students to slip away in large numbers. Some fathers even showed up in war paint and demanded their children. Hunt was ordered to return all runaways to Chilocco, and families harboring them were to be denied rations if they persisted. Several months later the Indian commissioner repeated the injunction:

> The Indians of your Agency have no treaty claims on the Government for the subsistence they are now receiving, and they must understand that as long as they are dependent upon the Government for support, the wishes of the Government in regard to the education of their children must be respected.[64]

The second pronouncement was to Hunt's successor, the agent having resigned from his position in August 1885.

P. B. Hunt had served as agent for seven years and four months, the longest time anyone served the Comanches and associated tribes in that capacity. His longevity is attributable to his having been relatively honest, reasonably successful in keeping his accounts straight, and a good Republican during years that party dominated the government. He had been reappointed in 1883, when his initial four-year term elapsed, but in 1884 Hunt was being pressured to resign.

Hunt's inadequacies had become increasingly apparent. Back in 1880 an inspector had criticized the agent for "a lack of system and tardiness of action."[65] Although his paperwork continued to be adequate, his books balanced, and his reports on time, the actual condition of the reservation was deplorable. The criticisms mounted. He had been unable, or unwilling, to keep the cattlemen off. Other white men, by the score, had found lodgement on the reservation. The schools were poorly attended and a "disgrace to the service."[66] The Indians seemed to be making little progress, and Hunt had no rapport with them. He was "petty, distant, and repelling."[67]

But getting rid of P. B. Hunt was not going to be easy. He declined an invitation to resign and a fellow Kentuckian, Senator J. R. Beck, arranged opportunities for Hunt to defend himself before the Senate Appropriations and Indian committees. Senator Beck also made clear that he would oppose the nomination of any new Kiowa, Comanche, and Wichita agent unless Hunt got a fair hearing. Beck described P. B. Hunt to the secretary of the interior as possessing qualities that richly merited political preferment in the early 1880s: "He was as good a soldier as fought for the Union, was crippled in the service, and is as ardent a Republican as you are."[68] However, in March 1885 the Democrat Grover Cleveland entered the White House and Hunt's qualifications were no longer so impressive. He gave up the struggle and resigned in August 1885. In terms of the government's plans for the Comanches and associated tribes, Hunt's agency had been, in the phrase of Commissioner Hiram Price, "an unhappy failure."[69]

8. Five Agents in Eight Years

In the years 1885-93, during which five men presided at Anadarko over the destinies of the approximately 1,550 Comanches, the United States' course in Indian affairs remained unchanged. In the words of Thomas J. Morgan, who served as commissioner of Indian Affairs under President Banjamin Harrison, "The Indians must conform to 'the white man's ways,' peaceably if they will, forcibly if they must." At least as Morgan saw it, "This civilization may not be the best possible, but it is the best the Indians can get."[1]

The pace of assimilation was accelerated by the implementation of the allotment in severalty program. Rationalizing, as one secretary of the interior did, that holding large areas of land which they were putting to no immediate use was a "bar to the Indians' progress, and our country's development,"[2] officials pushed the allotment program energetically. It was applied to the larger reservations by individual negotiations authorized by Congress, as these involved the purchase of the land remaining after each Indian had been allotted a farm. The funds from the sale of the remaining land were then credited to the Indians to be expended by them—under government supervision—on education, the purchase of stock cattle, and other useful objects. The passage of the Dawes Severalty Act on February 8, 1887 enshrined this as general policy.

While methodically stripping the Indians of their "surplus" land, the United States stepped up the education programs and continued to bombard the agents with threats and exhortations about increasing the Indian acreage under cultivation. Consistent with this a stronger line was taken against Indians joining traveling shows. As a commissioner of Indian Affairs declared in refusing to

166

permit an "opera company" to recruit ten Comanches, the Indians would be better off remaining on the reservation to cultivate their farms.[3]

If the general policy of the United States changed little in the years under consideration, the personnel administering the policy did. A principal factor was the alternation of Democratic and Republican administrations in Washington. In 1885 a Democrat, Grover Cleveland, entered the White House for the first time in a quarter of a century. After four years he was succeeded by the Republican Benjamin Harrison, only to return again to the presidency in 1893. Each change in administration brought a horde of office seekers to Washington. The prospect of the Republican return to power in 1889 could produce fifty applicants for a position as poor paying ($2,000) and as full of headaches as agent for the Kiowa, Comanche, and Wichita Agency.

Over the eight-year period under consideration the tendency was to concentrate appointive power in Washington. In 1886 the commissioner of Indian Affairs assumed full control of appointing clerks, physicians, and farmers. In addition he supplied traders for the reservations. For all these positions, backing from members of Congress was helpful with preference going to candidates from the locality of the agency—what was being referred to by 1890 as the "Home Rule Policy."

All agents, special agents, and inspectors were appointed by the secretary of the interior. Indeed, Commissioner of Indian Affairs Morgan claimed that he usually learned the identity of a new agent by reading it in a newspaper. Morgan, however, could have a hand in relieving an agent for poor performance. Removal of agents for strictly political reasons was in the hands of the secretary. The agents themselves nominated candidates for positions other than those of physician, clerk, and farmer. The net result of this patronage system was increased turnover in agency personnel, sabotaging the government's programs and strengthening the hands of those with whom the agent had to contend, such as the squaw men and the ranchers running cattle on the reservations.

Agent J. Lee Hall was a Democratic appointee who came to the Anadarko headquarters in 1885 with the blessings of the Texas delegation to Congress and the governor of North Carolina. The most colorful figure to serve as agent for the Comanches and associated tribes, Hall had been a city marshall, a deputy sheriff, and a Texas Ranger before entering the Indian Service. He also had tried ranching briefly. O. Henry, who knew him at this stage of his career, purportedly based one of his characters on Hall: "blond as a viking, quiet as a deacon, dangerous as a machine gun."[4] In contrast, a Methodist minister who knew him as agent remembered Hall as "a great man in ruins on account of drink."[5]

Hall gave an initial impression of great energy and devotion to duty. His impressive physique, generous hospitality, and frankness charmed a variety of visitors to the agency. To one representing the Indian Rights Association he confided that he had entered the Indian Service to become rich, which his visitor interpreted to mean that Hall wanted to be on the scene when the local reservations were opened for white settlement.[6] Investigations begun within two years of his assuming the agency suggested that Hall had taken some short cuts. Uncovered were fraudulent vouchers resulting in overcharges for goods and services. Misappropriation of lease money, intoxication, and lengthy absences without leave rounded out the grounds for relieving Hall of his position in October 1887. He subsequently was indicted by two grand juries, but the judge dismissed one case and a jury acquitted Hall in a second trial.

Hall was replaced at Anadarko by Special Agent E. E. White, who had participated in his investigation. During White's eleven-month tenure, he conducted himself much as other agents did. Although White later recorded his experiences in the Indian Service and reminisced at length about his association with the Kiowa, Comanche, and Wichita Agency, he failed to recall being forced to discharge his brother, whom he had put on the agency pay-roll contrary to policy.[7] Nor did White indicate that he later exploited his contacts at the agency to negotiate a grazing lease, which he then sublet to Texas cattlemen.

White had been a Democrat from Arkansas; Missouri furnished the next one to serve as agent, William D. Myers. His tenure was only slightly longer than White's: September 1888 to October 1889. Myers brought to the position some mining and business experience, most recently having managed a lumberyard in Cass County, Missouri. Considering his unfamiliarity with Indians, Myers seems to have done reasonably well, gaining the approval of a variety of Indians and missionaries, and even of the cantankerous Captain R. H. Pratt of Carlisle. Nevertheless, he was a Democrat. As a friend jocularly reminded Myers when the Republican Harrison entered the White House, "The only show you have is your religion. You and the President belong to the same church and that could help you out."[8] Party affiliation proved more important than church membership, and thirteen months after he took office Myers was replaced by a Republican. Apparently he found the Indians more exciting than shingles and two-by-fours because when Cleveland and the Democrats returned to power in 1893 Myers unsuccessfully sought reinstatement.

The Republicans had a pool of about thirty-five applicants from among whom they chose Myers's successor, Charles E. Adams. Myers had demonstrated that a Missouri lumberyard manager could find happiness among the Kiowas and Comanches; Adams did it with the background of a Baltimore grocer. A more valuable qualification was his membership in a "large family of Abolitionists and Republicans, who were faithful to the cause of the Union."[9] Although there is no evidence of his familiarity with Indians or the West, Adams sought first a position as inspector in the Indian Service, then lowered his sights to a Chippewa agency, and finally settled for Anadarko. He demonstrated his gratitude by restricting agency employment almost exclusively to Republicans. Adams could boast that even the physician and the baker were members of the Grand Old Party. In his twenty-six months at Anadarko, in addition to monitoring the political beliefs of his employees, Adams wooed and won a bride from the teaching staff of an agency school and allowed himself to be caught up in the constant wrangling of traders who held licenses at his agency. Forced to resign because of charges brought against him by one faction of traders, Adams was succeeded in December 1891 by fellow Republican George D. Day of Howard County, Maryland.

Day also was innocent of any prior experience with Indians or the West. However, he was acclaimed by one of his references as a "stalwart republican" who had held several public offices including that of sheriff and was "entirely free of bad habits (never drank liquor in his life)."[10] In the nineteen months that he served, Day pushed house construction for the Indians and played a key role in the negotiation of an agreement by which the Kiowas, Comanches, and Kiowa-Apaches were to accept 160-acre allotments of land and sell their remaining acreage to the United States. Despite his loyal cooperation with the commission sent out from Washington, Day was a casualty of the Democrats' return to power in 1893. Congress had authorized the president to fill vacancies at Indian agencies with army officers and Day was one of the agents Cleveland chose to replace. Like William D. Myers, Day hoped to be reinstated and predicted inaccurately that the next change in the occupancy of the White House would see him return to Anadarko.

Five agents in eight years did not make for a smoothly functioning agency when it could take an appointee two years to get a feeling for administering over 4,000 Indians from nine different tribes. In the absence of any continuity the special interests such as the cattlemen, the squaw men, and traders came close to having their own way. As observed previously, it was the traders who helped bring about the downfall of Agent Adams.

The practice of licensing traders to do business with Indians went back to the colonial period. The United States had found it wise to maintain the practice in order to exercise some control over their activities. The Comancheros had demonstrated how unlicensed traders could contribute to frontier unrest. Through a combination of licenses and bonds the number could be limited and their conduct guaranteed.

Whereas the number of white traders was controlled by licensing, Indians required no licenses. This was in accordance with the belief, as one official phrased it, that "it would seem to be the highest wisdom to open up mercantile careers to a people advancing from barbarism to civilization at as early a period as possible."[11] No Comanche, however, elected to enter the mercantile business during the reservation period. A society that stressed sharing did not nurture merchants.

During the first years Comanches were on the reservation the agent was responsible for the licensing of traders. But in 1876 Congress gave the commissioner of Indian Affairs sole authority for their appointment and regulation. Politics entered into the granting of licenses, as was particularly obvious in the first Cleveland administration. A chain of circumstantial evidence strongly suggested then that a resident of Tennessee obtained a license to trade at Anadarko as a result of pressure brought to bear by his brother, a United States senator from Tennessee, on a commissioner of Indian Affairs also from that state. The holder of the license then tried to make a deal with a trader who had just lost his license, by which the Tennessean would supply the license for a partnership in return for one-half the profits of the operation.[12] Although things that crude did not happen often, Indian traderships were considered political patronage in which members of Congress had a voice.

Regardless of how they secured their licenses, traders were expected to make available to the Indians useful articles at reasonable prices and pay a fair amount for any goods purchased from the Indians. In 1890 the commissioner of Indian Affairs ordered traders to cease handling playing cards: "The prevalence of gambling among Indians and its demoralizing effects upon them is such that the Office must discourage the habit in every respect."[13] Liquor always had been banned from traders' stores; however, the prohibition was difficult to enforce because of the variety of modes in which it appeared. Bottles with innocent labels such as "Florida Water" and "Stemons Iron Cordial" were ordered removed from Anadarko stores because of their high alcoholic content. Such vigilance was justified by the belief expressed in an Indian Office circular that "a drunken Indian is a condensed and intensified savage let loose on the community to commit crimes the blackest in the calendar."[14] One man applying for a license to trade with the Comanches and associated tribes was denied it when he was so naïve as to admit on his application form that he was a moderate drinker.

Ensuring that the traders did not take advantage of their Indian customers was no easy task. Indian Service personnel supposedly checked the invoices of goods that traders purchased from wholesalers and compared them with the prices the trader then charged his customer. In 1885 a circular even specified the markup the trader could impose on goods; it ranged from 20 percent on groceries to 35 percent on beads and twine.[15] Schedules of prices also were to be posted in conspicuous places in the store for the benefit of the literate Indians. The same concern was exhibited to see that the Indian received adequate compensation for those things he sold the trader. Hides from the beef cattle were the most common item in this category and on at least one occasion the Indian commissioner specified that 80 percent of the sum the trader could be expected to get for a hide on the St. Louis market was a fair price for the Indian.[16] But in the final analysis the regulations were only as effective as the personnel administering them. Agent Hunt was accused of paying his police in vouchers redeemable only at his nephew's store, and it is unlikely that the five agents who succeeded him in rapid succession became familiar enough with the agency scene to monitor adequately a trader's activities.

Even armed with the powers of an Indian agent, someone fresh from a lumberyard in Missouri or the grocery business in Maryland found it difficult to cope with the traders, of whom there were usually from two to four. In addition, prior to the consolidation of the agencies at Anadarko the post trader at Fort Sill frequently was licensed to trade with Indians. Although the firms went through various permutations, several of the traders were associated in one fashion or another with the Comanches and associated tribes for many years. Charles A. Cleveland first worked for his uncle J. S. Evans, who was a Fort Sill post trader and held an Indian trade license as well. In 1879 Cleveland branched out on his own with a partnership in a store at Anadarko. Frank L. Fred and Dudley P. Brown were also active traders in this period. Fred arrived in Anadarko in 1879 and remained at the agency as a trader for twenty years. P. B. Hunt once described his store as "the resort of all the disturbing elements . . . among whom are the dissatisfied squaw men and their allies whites and Indians."[17] Brown, Agent Hunt's nephew, was himself a thorn in the flesh of several agents after his uncle resigned.

Brown was given a job at the agency in 1878 by his uncle and obtained a license to trade in 1883. Before Brown and the Clevelands had a falling out he was in a firm that included the mother-in-law of W. H. Cleveland, a brother of C. A. Cleveland. Brown then went into business on his own and was at odds with the authorities constantly. The charges against him included buying from the Indians barbed wire the government had issued them and trying to run cattle on the reservation. Then Brown and the Clevelands joined forces against Frank L. Fred and Agent Adams. They charged Adams with trying to extort $1,000 from each trader in return for permitting a grass payment to the Indian.[18] Most of such grass payments promptly ended up in the tills of the traders. Brown also revealed collusion between the agent and Fred in the government purchase of an overpriced buggy and horses, an affair that probably contributed to the brevity of Adam's tenure at Anadarko. Alliances among traders and agents were constantly shifting and licenses were revoked and renewed in bewildering fashion.

Through it all traders like the Clevelands, Brown, and Fred maintained their positions, in part through employing squaw men such as Edward L. Clark, J. J. Sturm, and George W. Conover and exploiting their Indian connections. Conover, for example, once helped J. S. Evans corner the coveted hide trade of the Comanches.[19] In the early 1870s the traders competed for buffalo robes, but by 1880 the hides of the approximately 5,000 cattle issued every year to the Indians for their beef ration had become the traders' mainstay. The Indians also sold cattle, horses, hives of bees, furs, and skins.

When Hunt moved the agency to Anadarko in 1879 he required the traders to accompany him. For several years the Comanches were at the disadvantage of having their licensed traders located thirty to forty miles from their camps. This placed some Comanches closer to Texas merchants, who began to attract some Indian business.

The first Texan to profit from the situation was Judge J. Doan, who had established a store at Baldwin's Springs just across Red River from the Comanche-inhabited area of the reservation. Most of Doan's customers were area cattlemen or drovers taking herds north to Dodge City or Abilene. Occasionally, Indians would stop by with some furs or hides to barter.

It was rumored that Doan sold arms and ammunition to Indians, and at Agent Hunt's request a cavalry patrol from Fort Sill visited the judge. The officer commanding the patrol was Lieutenant Henry A. Flipper, the first black graduate of West Point who was later the subject of a celebrated court-martial. Lieutenant Flipper dismissed the rumors as planted by cattlemen trying to discourage settlement in the area.[20] Nonetheless, it was a reminder of the unpleasant possibilities of unregulated trade and an argument for reactivating an Indian tradership at Fort Sill to attract the Comanches. Not until 1886 did the government respond to the need by licensing the firm of Collier and Sneed to open near Fort Sill what became known as "the Red Store." This and the resumption of the issuing of rations in the vicinity of the military post signified the end of the Indian Office's efforts to move the Comanches north to the Washita River. By 1892 the department also had reconciled itself to recognizing the legality of pasture leases.

The six-year leases that had gone into effect in 1885 provided about $55,000 annual income for the Kiowas, Comanches, and Kiowa-Apaches[21] and a continuing source of controversy in Washington and on the reservation. Agent J. Lee Hall proposed using the grass money to purchase stock cattle for the Indians, an admirable plan that with good range management might have made them financially independent within a decade. However, the response of the commissioner of Indian Affairs was to shy away from any official recognition of the existence of leases, citing a recent opinion of the attorney general that there was no legal basis for leasing. The Indians supporting the current arrangements exerted no pressure on the government to accept Hall's plan, because they were happy to receive the cash. The antileasing faction, about one-third of the total reservation population in 1888, persisted in its opposition for several years, refusing to accept their per capita shares at the grass payments. By 1890 the unpaid balance of grass money being held had reached a total of $54,000.[22]

The subject of the renewal of the cattlemen's leases began to be debated in 1890. Quanah again led the proleasing faction and Tabananaka headed the opposition. For this round of leases Quanah proposed an eight-year term; Tabananaka preferred no lease but would settle for terms of no more than five years. They compromised at six years and this was ratified by an Indian council.

But meanwhile the United States was stiffening its stance against any leasing at all. There was a growing awareness among Washington officials that by condoning it they were creating more roadblocks in the way of allotment. Throughout the Southwest the prospect of losing the grass payments had made Indians more antagonistic to proposals to convert the huge pastures into hundreds of family farms. The result was that in March 1890 the United States ordered all non-Indian owned cattle off reservations in the Indian Territory by October 1, 1890.[23] Although the cattlemen on the Kiowa, Comanche, and Kiowa-Apache Reservation received a two-month extention and then went through the motions of dismantling their operations, in the spring of 1891 there were about 100,000 head of cattle devouring the reservation's grass. Indian police and Fort Sill cavalry cooperated in moving herds south of Red River, but they drifted back as soon as the police and soldiers went elsewhere. The Indians did not protest the presence of the cattle because some chiefs and headmen continued to accept bribes from the Texans. In addition, the agency staff was accused of being insufficiently vigorous in its dealings with the cattlemen. One clerk was revealed to have accepted a railroad pass from them.[24]

In June 1890 Quanah visited Washington to lobby for the leases and in March of the following year he was back on the same mission. This time he was accompanied by an attorney for cattlemen Daniel W. Waggoner and Samuel B. Burnett, and by a new ally in the cause, the Kiowa chief Lone Wolf. The foster-son of a celebrated raider of the same name, Lone Wolf apparently had been persuaded to abandon the antileasing faction by the prospect of sharing in the $54,000 that had accumulated when some Indians refused their grass payments. Together with White Man, who spoke for the Kiowa-Apaches, Quanah and Lone Wolf helped produce another change in United States policy on leasing.

Using a law passed in 1891 as his authority, the secretary of the interior approved a new series of leases. The "Big

White Wolf, 1890. (Fort Sill Museum)

Children of Quanah, 1892. *Front row,* Len and Baldwin; *back row,* Wanada, Werahre, and Harold. (Smithsonian Institution, National Anthropological Archives)

William Tivis on horseback, with his brother, circa 1893. (Smithsonian Institution, National Anthropological Archives)

In the morning after a peyote ceremony, 1893, Quanah is seated in the front, *second from left*, with, *at the left end of the back row*, two of his wives, Chony and Tonarcy. (Smithsonian Institution, National Anthropological Archives)

Five" (Burnett, Waggoner, E. C. Sugg, C. T. Herring, and
J. P. Addington) received preferential treatment because of
their long association with the reservation and were permitted to lease 1.3 million acres at six cents an acre without competitive bidding.[25] About 250,000 acres more
were advertised for bidding, but the response was disap-
pointing and the government ended up leasing that tract
at less than the six cents per acre obtained from the Big
Five. All leases were limited to one year, which served to
keep the issue constantly before the Indians. The government's decision to assume legal responsibility set the stage
for the distribution in the summer of 1892 of the accumu-
lated $54,000, plus $19,000 from an overdue grass payment on the first six-year lease.

Agent George Day presided over the $74,000 payment
and convinced many of the Indians to invest in farm wagons
and lumber for houses. Throughout the reservation government carpenters began building two- and three-room
houses with materials furnished by the Indians. Quanah
tried several times to get help in constructing a two-story,
ten-room house that he believed to be commensurate with
his status. The commissioner of Indian Affairs, however,
"did not deem it wise for the government to contribute
money to assist in building a house for an Indian who has
five wives."[26] Evidently Quanah then approached the
cattlemen, who assisted him in the $2,000 project. After
the basic structure had been completed, the Comanche
chief decided it needed a two-story porch to set it off and
did manage to secure the services of a government carpenter for this finishing touch on the imposing residence that
any rancher or trader in the area would have been proud to
own.

Quanah also was one of the leaders in the gradual expansion of farming among the Comanches, who on this
subject were relatively more progressive than the Kiowas
or Kiowa-Apaches. Every year saw a little more acreage
under cultivation despite drouth conditions in three of
the eight growing seasons from 1886 to 1893. Early in the

period the Indian Office again considered moving the Indians from the two southwestern agencies farther east in Indian Territory.[27] Security was not a factor this time but rather the hope of locating them where they would have a better chance to raise an annual crop.

Paucity of rainfall was not the only explanation for the failure of Indians to become farmers. They still lacked sufficient equipment, including horses strong enough to break the prairie sod for a first planting. The agent still had to hire white men at about $3 an acre to open new fields, and he seldom received enough money to break as much acreage as he would have liked. Nevertheless, a principal reason for the Indians' slow adaptation to farming was their unwillingness to apply themselves to it wholeheartedly. The Comanche male was still a raider and hunter at heart and found little pride or satisfaction in a well-hoed row of corn or a haystack capable of turning rain. Indeed, a close examination of the reservation scene from 1886 to 1893 reveals that most of the farming attributed to Comanches actually was being done by white farm laborers in their employ.

The squaw men had taken the lead in this as well. By 1886 George W. Conover had four fellow white men working on the 200 acres he had under cultivation. Other intermarried whites followed suit in starting farms on the best lands on the reservation. Quanah was quick to emulate them although he failed to seek out as good land. About 1888 David A. Grantham apparently began to work for the Comanche chief, presumably on shares. Industrious and moral, Grantham had the approval of the Indian agents and gradually expanded Quanah's farming operations while the chief was wheeling and dealing with agents, Texas cattlemen, and Washington officials. Barely literate himself, Grantham sometimes wrote letters for Quanah. Evidence that he regarded himself as something more than a hired hand or sharecropper is to be gleaned from a bragging letter he wrote the agent:

I am very sorry that I was not at home when were out
to us. I like to know how you like Quanah House how
his women's cooking and the country out hear. I want
you to come out hear and stay with us 3 or 4 days and
see what white People such as Myself can Do among
Indians.[28]

Grantham remained with Quanah until his own adoption
by the Comanches enabled the white man to claim 160
acres of reservation land.

Neither Grantham nor any other white man could work
for an Indian without authorization from the Indian Department for fear that he would "attempt . . . settlement
on the reservation or ask to acquire, directly or indirectly
. . . color of ownership of livestock or land by lease or
otherwise."[29] Nor was any Indian to be permitted to hire
a white laborer unless he were incapable of caring for the
land himself. The government also reserved the right to review the terms under which the white man worked on the
Indian's farm. Nevertheless it became a routine matter for
the agent to apply through the Indian commissioner to the
secretary of the interior for permission for older men such
as Cheevers or Mowaway, or even younger Comanches, to
hire white men. By 1893 there were several hundred working as hired hands or sharecroppers on the two reservations
of the Kiowa, Comanche, and Wichita Agency. Many of
them were inhabiting the houses built for Indian families
while the Indians lived in, by their standards, the more
comfortable tepees. Indeed, it is likely that much of the
interest in house building manifested by the Comanches
around 1892 stemmed from their desire to provide quarters
for tenants. In other respects the Indians made clear their
attachment to the old ways.

Visitors to Anadarko and Fort Sill in this period were
impressed by the persistence of old practices. Indians still
wrapped themselves in blanket or sheet and wore long hair.
On occasion they painted their faces. Although most fami-

lies now had wagons, Agent Adams declared that as late as 1890 one could still see

> now and then . . . wandering through the hills a pony train which furnishes the conveyance for family and household property. One pony will drag the tent poles and carry the canvas, another jingling with bells will be ridden by the baby not long released from its stiff-backed cradle, sitting erect and proud in the consciousness of independence.[30]

Newcomers to the reservation also were struck by the time the Indians spent racing their horses in the summer and card playing the year round. J. Lee Hall claimed that when he came to the agency in 1885 the gambling was carried on openly around the traders' stores and in arbors erected for the purpose—the games sometimes continuing through the night. The ex-Texas Ranger put a halt to public gambling, but it remained a private diversion no agent could eradicate. The Indians expressed perplexity that a white man would try to stop an activity which the Indians had learned from other whites.

Tribal customs survived both the introduction of Indian police and, in 1883, Secretary Henry M. Teller's contribution, the Court of Indian Offenses. Tribesmen coped with an elopement not by a call to the Indian police but by the brother of the girl involved seizing some of the best ponies of the brother of her paramour. Nor did they readily abandon their traditional views on proper disposition of the property of a dead man. One Indian commissioner overreacted to the news that instead of a Kiowa widow inheriting all her husband's property it had either been burned or taken away by members of the family:

> Let all your Indians plainly understand, that the superstitious, savage and abominable custom of destroying the property of a deceased Indian, or depriving his family or estate of any portion of the same, will not be tolerated by the Government, and that any Indian

hereafter attempting to practice the same, will be regarded as no better than a common criminal, who disregards the plainest principles of justice, decency, and humanity, and such action will be taken towards him as the enormity of the offense, and the welfare of the Indians demand.[31]

Comanche squaw man Edward L. Clark suffered similar cultural shock when his father-in-law's will, which assigned Clark's wife some of her father's horses and cattle, was flouted by her brother, who seized all his father's livestock. It also worried Clark, understandably, that by Comanche custom when a wife died her brother inherited her property.[32]

Indian methods of killing the cattle issued them for their beef ration created as much concern among white officials as their property customs. A cow fleeing across the priarie pursued by a gang of young Indians riddling her with arrows and pistol shots was a revolting sight to many whites. They found even more shocking the butchering of the animal when it finally collapsed. One inspector complained that at Anadarko "it is not an uncommon sight to see them begin to skin an animal before it is dead, nor to see an Indian mother cut a piece of raw liver, dip it in the warm blood, and give it to her child."[33]

Reports of this nature inspired Commissioner of Indian Affairs T. J. Morgan in 1890 to order Indian agents to erect slaughterhouses where the cattle could be killed and butchered, with the provision that "during the killing women and children [be] specially prohibited from being present." Morgan also forbade the "savage and filthy practice" by which the Indians consumed the "fifth quarter" of the animal—its blood and intestines—in the belief that such practice "serves to nourish brutal instincts" and was a "fruitful source of disease."[34] Despite the order, when the commissioner visited Anadarko that fall he found "this bit of barbarism" still flourishing.[35] To build and operate slaughterhouses required funds that only gradually became available. In the interim the cattle would continue to be killed to the accompaniment of all the sights and sounds of a buffalo hunt, and even Morgan would be brought to condone the use of the fifth quarter "under proper sanitary precautions to be prescribed by the Agency physician."[36]

That whites were not always repelled by the sight of Indians in paint and feathers and the gory scenes at the beef issue pens was demonstrated July 4, 1893. Anadarko's celebration of Independence Day opened with a parade of Indians featuring "all of the old war relics and costumes." There were Indian foot and horse races and the climax was the release of beef cattle from the pens for "a buffalo hunt in primitive style."[37] Apparently the several thousand whites attracted to Anadarko by notices in nearby papers were not disappointed. As one woman described it:

> They have turned the cows, four of them loose. The whole crowd has gone perfectly wild. I am standing with a party of ladies on the top of the high fence. The sun is scorching hot, the wind is blowing a regular gale and the dust coming in clouds. Oh my stars! The Indians have guns—no arrows about it! There! One cow has fallen. The dogs are tearing at it and there go a crowd of women to dress it.[38]

Commissioner Morgan would not have been pleased at the sight of Indians slaughtering cattle and parading in their native costumes for the entertainment of whites. He not only opposed it at Anadarko but refused to countenance the recruitment of Indians for the popular Wild West shows. The former professor of church history also took a dim view of another vestige of Indian culture, polygamy, as Quanah found to his chagrin.

In the summer of 1890 Commissioner Morgan was informed that Quanah had six wives and was wooing a seventh. The commissioner responded by ordering Quanah stripped of his chieftainship and his judgeship of the agency's Court of Indian Offenses and denied further rations.[39] This was a severe blow to Quanah, who clearly enjoyed his chiefly status and the perquisites that accompanied it and even had his own stationery with the heading "Quanah Parker: Principal Chief of the Comanche Indians."

Quanah's removal also was disturbing to Agent Charles E. Adams, who had no desire to see the Comanche leader alienated. Compared with the Kiowas and Kiowa-Apaches, the Comanches were reasonably cooperative and Quanah deserved much of the credit. Even before Morgan's ultimatum, Adams had acknowledged that Quanah "has his faults" and that "he is no white man and has never been treated as such." Indeed, as the agent was writing Commissioner Morgan, the Comanche was in his office "dressed in buckskin and blanket."[40] When the order to fire Quanah came down, Adams offered the rather limp defense of his ally that he had only five wives, not six as the commissioner had charged, and that none of them had been married in the last year. The agent promised to investigate and report, obviously hoping that events at some of the other sixty or so agencies would divert Morgan's attention.[41] But the issue refused to go away. Adams decided to try to reorganize the agency's Court of Indian Offenses, and if it were to be effective he needed three judges capable of commanding the respect of the Indians and yet willing to cooperate with the government's programs. Among the Comanches none was better suited for a judgeship than Quanah.

In the fall of 1890 Agent Adams composed a letter to Commissioner Morgan in the hope of winning his consent to the appointment of Quanah to the court. He acknowledged the Comanche's wives as "five undisputed facts." Nevertheless, as Adams pointed out, Quanah had been very cooperative, even supporting Agent Hall on one occasion when he was threatened by the Kiowas. "He is ambitious and shrewd enough," said Adams, "to know that any real progress for himself or people must be by the white man's way." The agent expressed the hope that

Quanah would "find his much married position untenable, and will find some way out of his matrimonial entanglements before long." He concluded on a pessimistic note: "If Quanah is ineledgible [sic], any other Comanche whom I select would be ineledgible for the same reason; the men of influence being, without exception, men of family."[42] The commissioner was not won over and at least for a time the Court of Indian Offenses would have to function without Quanah.

In proposing the Court of Indian Offenses, Secretary Teller had intended it to help do away with plural marriages, the influence of medicine men, and what he referred to as "certain of the old heathenish dances; such as the sun-dance, scalp-dance, &c."[43] Of the three associated tribes, the Kiowas were most attached to their religious ceremonies. In April 1887 Quanah reported to Agent Hall, by way of a letter written for him by squaw man Emmett Cox, that he has been solicited by the Kiowas to join them that summer in an attack on Fort Sill. He told of a medicine man who was agitating the Kiowas but reassured his agent: "Me and my people have quit fighting long ago and we have no desire to join anyone in war again."[44] Together with other reports of Kiowas withdrawing their children from school and refusing to plant crops, killing cattle and quirting whites they met on the reservation, Quanah's information sufficiently alarmed the agent for him to call for troops. With them he intimidated the Kiowas and levied fines of ponies and cattle on some of the ringleaders of the unrest.

The buffalo whose head and hide had been featured by the Kiowas in their sun dance in the summer of 1887 had been obtained by them from the rancher Charles Goodnight. A year later he was still trying to get $50 for it.[45] Apparently the Kiowas did not hold a dance in the summer of 1888 and were denied permission to hold one in 1889 by Agent William D. Myers on specific instructions from the Indian commissioner, who authorized calling for troops to prevent it. But Myers was replaced by Adams in the fall of 1889 and, illustrating the discontinuity that could occur with the change of agents, the following summer Adams was writing Charles Goodnight to convey a Kiowa offer of $100 for a buffalo so that they might hold their sun dance.[46]

Quanah already had alerted Agent Adams to a development that would be more alarming to the whites than the Kiowa sun dance. In the middle of May 1890 he had David Grantham write a letter for him that laboriously communicated some disturbing news:

> I hear that the koway and Shianis Say that there are Indian come from heaven and want me to take My People and go to see them. But I tell them that I want My People to work and pay no attention to that that we Depend on the Government to help us and no them.[47]

The Ghost Dance had arrived on the southern plains.

The movement had originated with Wovoka (Jack Wilson), a Paiute Indian who purportedly had died, gone to heaven, and returned with a message for all Indians. In true messianic fashion he promised them a return to the glorious days of their past when the buffalo defied counting and no white men intruded on Indian land. To regain this halcyon age the Indians need only follow a code of conduct prescribed by Wovoka, a code which included a ceremony that came to be known as the Ghost Dance. Unlike the Sioux version of Wovoka's message, that of the southern Plains Indians was essentially pacific—no Ghost Dance shirts capable of turning bullets appeared among them.

The Indians of the Kiowa, Comanche, and Wichita Agency first learned of Wovoka's message from their Cheyenne and Arapaho neighbors. Poor Buffalo, a Kiowa, was the first convert and by the summer of 1890 was disseminating the doctrine. During the fall and winter of 1890 Sitting Bull, a Southern Arapaho who had lived for many years among the Northern Arapahos and become a disciple of Wovoka, visited the Anadarko agency on three occasions.[48] Each time he gained more converts for the new faith.

The Ghost Dancers chose remote parts of the agency for their ceremonies and constantly shifted the location. This behavior and rumors of threatening overtones to the new doctrine alarmed the military and civilian officials. While on a tour of reservations Commissioner Morgan stopped at both Anadarko and Darlington (headquarters of the Cheyenne and Arapaho Agency) in November 1890. He discussed the messiah's message with the Indians and concluded there was no immediate danger. However, Agent Adams sought and received authorization to recruit up to fifty additional Indian policemen if an emergency developed.[49]

Meanwhile, both the agent and the Fort Sill commanding officer kept the Ghost Dancers under close surveillance. Major Wirt Davis and Lieutenant Hugh L. Scott attended one dance in December 1890, as did two celebrated interpreters, Horace P. Jones and Ben Clark. Lieutenant Scott, who commanded the troop of Indian cavalry at Fort Sill, made several visits to dance encampments that winter. Neither he nor Major Davis found the Indian attitude threatening. Major Davis concluded: "The wagons, buggies, well arranged tepees, the abundance of food, and the solemn songs of supplication combined to form a scene very similar to an old-fashioned Methodist or Baptist camp-meeting."[50] Both he and Lieutenant Scott were of the opinion that it was the social opportunities the dances offered which attracted most of the Indians. Scott strongly opposed banning the dances:

> The forcible stopping . . . would seem to be a violation of those rights common to every human being, viz: the right to the pursuit of happiness to personal liberty under the law and the right of each person without contravening the law to worship God according to the dictates of his own conscience.[51]

After further exposure to Sitting Bull, Lieutenant Scott

expressed admiration for the Arapaho and admitted he may have misjudged him initially;

> There is possibility that he is largely sincere in his teachings, there is this to be said in his favor, that he has given these people a better religion than they ever had before, taught them precepts which if faithfully carried out will bring them into better accord with their white neighbors and has prepared the way for their final Christianization, and for this he is entitled to no little credit.[52]

Agent Adams denounced such views as "sentimental or theoretic,"[53] but like Scott and Davis he refrained from any overt action that would produce a confrontation with Sitting Bull's followers. That and the absence of the belligerence the Sioux infused into Wovoka's doctrines saved the Indians of the Southwest from the type of tragedy that occurred at Wounded Knee.

Agent Adams and the two army officers also agreed on attributing to Quanah much credit for the Comanche apathy toward the Ghost Dance. Only the Penetethkas appeared to be much involved. Some of them still lived among the Indians north of the Washita River, the Caddos, Wichitas, and others to whom the doctrines of Wovoka proved even more appealing than to the Kiowas. While the Penetethkas were dancing for the return of the buffalo, Quanah had a letter written to a Fort Worth newspaper replying to the paper's statement that he was agitating the Indians with the new doctrine. "But few of the Comanches pay any attention to the Messiah craze, and those who do are crazy," Quanah declared. He went on to describe his own material progress and to defend his people: "We have been accused of most everything imaginable except being fools, and people who know the Comanches have never credited them with that."[54]

By the spring of 1891 the interest in the Ghost Dance was subsiding. That the Comanches had been so little involved, even at its height, was attributed by his contemporaries to Quanah. Two other explanations have been offered. One stresses a Comanche reputation for religious skepticism; the other theory argues that they were unreceptive to Wovoka's doctrine because they already had found comfort and satisfaction in another movement, the peyote cult.

Although the Comanches had used peyote throughout their residence on the reservation, it did not become an issue between them and their agents until the late 1880s. Squaw man Edward L. Clark had described its use by a Comanche medicine man as early as 1883:

> This man has in his possession some of those poison roots which Quanah and Black Beard used to be so crazy to get hold of. He calls several of the Indians together and has them eat those roots which acts directly upon the brain and throws them into sort of a dream, and after recovery they conclude that they have had a divine revelation, and the secret of their sickness is then imparted to each of them by him.[55]

Agent Hall expressed concern about it in 1886,[56] and Special Agent White undertook to forbid its use. White's order in June 1888 banned the consumption of peyote in any form on pain of the Indians losing their annuities, rations, and grass money. Because the Comanches were the major offenders he lectured them in council at Fort Sill on the evils of the practice. The Indians first resisted White, saying they would die rather than give up their peyote. However, perhaps to humor the agent, they finally agreed to limit its use to one night at each full moon until they exhausted their supply, which they promised not to renew.[57] Despite the pledge peyote use spread among the Comanches and from them to their neighbors. When it was called to the attention of Commissioner Morgan the same summer the Ghost Dance appeared in the Southwest, he ordered Agent Adams to employ his police and Court of Indian Offenses to eliminate it from the agency.

Although they were in agreement that it was bad for the

Indians, the white men differed as to peyote's effect. Agent Hall, whose weakness was alcohol, compared it to opium and claimed it put the Indians to sleep for as much as twenty-four hours. Special Agent White described peyote buttons as "destructive to both the health and mental faculties of these Indians, and will soon greatly decimate them, if their use is not checked." He also spoke of the "strange hallucinations" it produced.[58] Agent Myers feared that peyote would "not only retard their progress for many years, but finally make slaves and kill them with the same certainty that the morphine, opium, or alcohol habit kills the white man."[59]

Agents deplored the Comanche use of peyote and attempted to ban it, but the Ghost Dance movement undoubtedly aroused more concern among the white settlers. As long as Quanah, upon whom the agents leaned in this period, participated in peyote ceremonies it tended to blunt the zeal with which the agents moved against the drug. It is significant that the period's skimpy records from the Court of Indian Offenses, on which Quanah served, reveal no cases involving peyote, in spite of Commissioner Morgan's injunction to use the court to combat the cult.

Commissioner Morgan had been inspired to move against peyote by the missionaries who became active at the Kiowa, Comanche, and Wichita Agency for the first time since the Quakers had left the scene. Although several denominations were represented in this period, the Comanches failed to attract a full-time missionary. It was not because the United States did not encourage missionaries. As E. E. White expressed it while serving as agent: "I recognize in them potent auxiliaries of the Government in the great and important work of civilizing and Christianizing the Indians."[60] However, missionaries tended to gather around the agency headquarters at Anadarko, and the Comanches, except for some Penetethkas, lived thirty to forty miles away. Toward the end of the period the Methodist-Episcopal (South) mission near Anadarko under the leadership of J. J. Methvin did extend its work to the Fort Sill area, especially the district east of the military reserve, occupied in large part by Mexican captives of the Comanches. The Reformed Presbyterian Church also established a mission among the Kiowa-Apaches that attracted an occasional Comanche. The schools that the Methodists and Reformed Presbyterians supported recruited a few Comanche children and contributed to the slight missionary impact on those Indians in the years 1885–93.

Neither in the mission schools nor in the regular Indian Service establishments did the emphasis on substituting white culture for Indian culture waver. Instruction was to be conducted exclusively in English, although religious services could be performed in the native languages. Commissioner of Indian Affairs J. D. C. Atkins in 1887 made the case for English:

> The intention is to prevent the waste of valuable time by Indian children in schools, in learning a barbarous tongue which is not comprehensive enough to embrace civilization or to comprehend it, and to utilize that time in school in learning the language of the country of which they are to become citizens—a language in which not only the scriptures can be read, but all the extensive literature of the civilized world.[61]

"Rules for Indian Schools" not only provided for instruction in English, they also mandated the teaching of "sports and games enjoyed by white youth, such as baseball, hopscotch, croquet, marbles, bean bags, dominoes, checkers, logomachy, and the use of dissected maps, etc."[62]

To help prepare the Indian child for the rights and responsibilities of United States citizenship, patriotism was to be inculcated by display of the flag and celebration of national holidays. The study of history also would contribute to this end, but here some care was to be taken:

> While in such study the wrongs of their ancestors can not be ignored, the injustice which their race has suf-

fered can be contrasted with the large future open to
them, and their duties and opportunities rather than
their wrongs will most profitably engage their attention.[63]

Or as another circular directed: "The Indian heroes . . .
need not be disparaged, but gradually and unobtrusively
the heroes of American homes and history may be sub-
stituted as models and ideals."[64] Instruction in civics,
acquaintance with manuals of rules of order, and participation in debating societies would help prepare the young
Indian for the day he would assume a citizen's role.

Poor attendance still plagued Indian schools, and the
government continued to authorize the withholding of
rations and annuities from uncooperative parents and the
use of agency police to round up truants. In 1893 Congress
wrote such practices into law. Coercion was not supposed
to be used to supply students for off-reservation boarding
schools such as Carlisle and Haskell. Congress required
parental consent for children recruited for these schools.

All the problems that could afflict an Indian school
were manifested at the Kiowa, Comanche, and Wichita
Agency. For most of the period 1885-93 there were two
schools: the Wichita School, which served the tribes north
of the Washita River, and the Kiowa School on the south
bank. It was to the latter that Kiowa, Comanche, and
Kiowa-Apache parents were supposed to send their children.

About the time that J. Lee Hall succeeded P. B. Hunt as
agent in the late summer of 1885, the agency's schools
were described by an inspector as "an asylum for relatives
and friends who cannot earn a support elsewhere."[65]
Personnel problems haunted the Kiowa School for several
years. Turnover was frequent and the quality of the appointees generally low. Between 1885 and 1889 four men
served as superintendent of the Kiowa School. The first
was judged by C. C. Painter, an investigator for the Indian
Rights Association, to be "a nice well-meaning man; industrious, honest, and all that, and would make a good

farmer, but has no faculty for managing a school."[66] His successor, Charles H. Carr, was fired by Agent Myers for being drunk, the superintendent having imbibed too heavily of Hostetter's Bitters, a concoction based on medicinal alcohol provided by its maker, the agency physician. Carr was reinstated on orders from Washington. However, when Indian parents threatened to withdraw their children from the Kiowa School because Carr abused them, the superintendent was finally dismissed. The third man to head the school in this period lasted only a few months, during which he was charged with using "objectionable and profane language to such an extent as to shock the female employees of the school."[67] In September 1889 G. P. Gregory, a twenty-five year old from Kansas, was appointed superintendent and performed satisfactorily until his removal in 1891 after the death by freezing of two Kiowa boys who had fled school after being whipped by a teacher.

Personnel problems were not confined to the position of superintendent. C. C. Painter in his visit to the Kiowa School in 1887 found two of the three teachers to be incompetent. One of them Painter described as "a little mite of a man, sallow, spiritless . . . looked as if he had gotten out of his grave to find 'a chaw of terbacker' and had lost his way." When told that the teacher was a distinguished Texas lawyer, Painter's reaction was that "it is well that he has achieved distinction in some field of labor. He wd. certainly never achieve it in the field of pedagogy." The agent of the Indian Rights Association was equally unimpressed by the superintendent's wife, who held a teaching position. This unfortunate lady was portrayed as "scrawny and yellow" wearing under her thin cotton dress "either the cast away framework of an old buggy top, or of an umbrella, which did service for a bustle." A third teacher won Painter's approval; she and the matron and the seamstresses were, in his judgment, "the grains of salt which save this school from absolute stench."[68]

Forced by the shortage of housing in Anadarko to live in

the main school building, the school's staff suffered from the jealousies and petty bickering such close proximity inevitably produced. Agent Myers finally concluded after the drawnout controversy involving Superintendent Carr that only an entirely new set of teachers could restore harmony to the Kiowa School. When his advice was followed and all the incumbents were discharged or transferred at the end of the 1888-89 academic year, it was almost November 1889 before a new staff had been assembled and the school could be reopened.

The new staff should have been harmonious, judging from the network of family relationships among them. The superintendent and one of the teachers were husband and wife. Another teacher was the cousin of the superintendent's wife. The industrial teacher and the assistant matron were married, and the matron and the cook were sisters. Situations such as this became less frequent after school positions were brought under civil service in 1891.

Housing male and female staff members in the same building produced another type of problem. An industrial teacher and a matron were asked to resign when he was seen in his stocking feet leaving her room at night. There was a scandal involving a young Kiowa widow employed at the school as an assistant matron and a Methodist minister newly come to the agency and housed at the school. When they were found in bed together, Agent Myers ordered "the wretch" from the reservation, and when he was detected later near the school with a buggy the missionary was lodged a day and night in the agency lockup before being escorted to the Texas boundary by policemen. The minister wished to marry the Kiowa girl, but Myers refused to consent, denouncing him for his "lustful soul and the cloak of righteousness around his hypocritical form." The agent concluded:

> A villain who would under the cloak of religion accomplish the ruin of a woman, was unfit in every sense of the word for a father to her orphan boy, and a husband

for herself, or a citizen among the Indians, and especially did I lose confidence in his adaptability for the mission work.[69]

The building that housed all this intrigue was a three-story affair in dilapidated condition. There were no bathtubs, and water had to be hauled from the river in the absence of a cistern or windmill. When it rained, plenty of water did come through the roof, however. For the four years preceding its renovation, these and other deficiencies were noted by agents and inspectors, who used such terms as "badly out of repair," "in a wretched condition," and "a disgrace to the Government that owns it and the reservation upon which it stands."[70] Aside from structural faults in the building, the dirt and general disorder that inspectors found at the school reflected the bad morale and inefficiency of the staff.

The use of barbed wire to cover transoms, a tactic to keep the boys out of the girls' rooms, suggested another problem at the school. The Comanches explained their failure to enroll their children as stemming from their reluctance to have them associated with the Kiowas, whom they charged with poor morals.[71] Certainly relations between the two tribes in this period were not good, and Comanche pupils did tend to segregate themselves in the classrooms and dormitories. Yet by persuasion and coercion the agent managed to keep about forty Comanche children enrolled. Fortunately, the girls had been transferred to the new institution near Fort Sill when measles struck the agency in the spring and summer of 1892. Over 200 deaths resulted at the agency, most of them among the Kiowa and Kiowa-Apache children. The superintendent of the Kiowa School was criticized severely for sending sick pupils back to their parents' camps, where they not only did not receive proper care but also helped spread the infection.

The capacity of the Kiowa School was about 100. In addition, the agency's children were welcomed at the off-reservation boarding schools such as Carlisle and Chilocco.

Usually about a dozen Comanches would be attending them. The law requiring parental approval before children were sent to such institutions was interpreted narrowly by Commissioner T. J. Morgan. He directed Agent Day to ignore the Indian practice of uncles, aunts, and grandparents assuming responsibility for children and to send orphans qualified academically to the off-reservation schools regardless of opposition from their relatives.[72]

During this period six religious groups were granted the use of 160 acres of Indian land each for the purpose of establishing missions and schools. In 1890 Reverend J. J. Methvin began the operation of his Methodist boarding school under contract with the government, and in the spring term of 1891 he had enrolled sixteen Kiowas and five Comanches.[73] Reverend W. W. Carithers opened a Presbyterian school among the Kiowa-Apaches in 1891 on a comparably modest scale.

But what the Comanches sought for years and finally obtained was their own school at Fort Sill. Beginning with J. Lee Hall, the agents supported the Comanche request, as did a long string of inspectors and the Indian Rights Association's C. C. Painter. Agent Hall and Painter once rode together over the grounds near Fort Sill and picked out a good site. The Indian Office first approved the renovation of a building at the old agency and then shifted to the more practical idea of a new structure. Unfortunately, just as the project was beginning to get serious consideration Congress limited expenditures on new boarding schools, including furnishings, to $10,000. Plans for a brick building were actually drafted, but it obviously could not be built under the ceiling set by Congress. For three years nothing was done despite unanimous support from agents and inspectors.

Finally in 1890 construction on a two-story frame building, with outbuildings, got under way about four miles south of Fort Sill. The site chosen by Agent Adams overlooked the valley of Cache Creek, which was about a mile from the school. Not until October 1892 did the school open, and even then all the buildings had not been completed, forcing a limitation of the first class to 33 Comanche girls aged six to ten.[76] By the spring of 1893 the plant was finished and filled to capacity with the 100 or so students about equally divided between boys and girls (the addition of the boys raising the average age by two or three years). Ironically, the opening of the Comanche school, a victory for Comanche unity, had coincided with the negotiation of an agreement providing for allotment in severalty for the Comanches, presumably the last step in the dissolution of their old way of life.

9. Negotiating the Jerome Agreement

In January 1890 Commissioner of Indian Affairs T. J. Morgam made an announcement to all agents:

> The 8th of February, the day upon which the "Dawes bill" signed by the President and became a law, is worthy of being observed in all Indian schools as the possible turning point in Indian history, the point at which the Indians may strike out from tribal and reservation life and enter American citizenship and nationality.[1]

The agents were informed that Franchise Day might be fittingly observed in the schools by "songs, recitations, tableaux, etc." to convey to the Indian youth "clear ideas of what the allotment law does for them."[2] The circular illustrated how important the United States believed it was for the Indians to give up holding land in common.

The Indians of the Kiowa, Comanche, and Wichita Agency already had given notice that they hoped to postpone the application of the law to them. Within a week of the bill becoming law, Lone Wolf was telling Commissioner J. D. C. Atkins of his opposition to allotment. The Kiowa warned that he could not control his young men and that war might result if allotment were forced upon them. Atkins assured Lone Wolf that there were no immediate plans for allotting the Indians of his agency but advised against listening to critics of the Dawes Act.[3] The commissioner was alluding to Dr. T. A. Bland's National Indian Defense Association, which, alone among organizations working for Indian welfare, was opposing allotment.

Copies of Dr. Bland's publication *Council Fire* soon appeared at Anadarko and Lone Wolf began to agitate for a fund to hire lawyers to oppose the Dawes Act. Meanwhile,

201

the commissioner ordered Agent Hall to "exert your influence to induce the Indians to take their lands in severalty and do all in your power to prepare them for this action."[4] The stage was being set for a struggle that would last more than a decade.

The first Comanche of consequence to ally himself with Lone Wolf in the fight against allotment was White Wolf. Hall had notified the Indian Department that about 150 Comanches, Kiowas, and Kiowa-Apaches wished land allotted them. How Hall could have made such a report is beyond comprehension. Undoubtedly most Comanches would have lined up with White Wolf in opposing allotment; certainly practically all the Kiowas agreed with Lone Wolf on the issue. Nevertheless, the commissioner accepted the agent's optimistic estimate and obtained the president's approval for extending the provisions of the Dawes Act to those Indians of Hall's agency "as may be found ready, competent and qualified therefor."[5]

But there was a problem in applying the Dawes Act to a reservation such as that occupied by the Comanches and associated tribes. The law provided that surplus reservation land remaining after each Indian had been allotted should be purchased by the United States to be made available to white farmers. However, the statute did not create a fund for such purchases. The prospect of acquiring the surplus land aroused more enthusiasm in Congress than the vision of Indians acquiring individual title. Allowing homesteads of 160 acres for every Indian on the larger reservations would still leave thousands of homesteads for clamorous white settlers, citizens already enfranchised and aware of how to reward or punish members of Congress. These same members of Congress, particularly those from areas adjoining large reservations, began to be pressured to appropriate funds for negotiations that would lead to the purchase of the surplus lands.

Throughout the 1880s there was agitation for the settlement of unassigned public lands in what would become Oklahoma. Those most active in colonization schemes came to be known as "boomers." Their first success was the opening in April 1889 of a 2-million-acre tract northeast of the Kiowa, Comanche, and Wichita Agency and touching it at one point. This would be followed a year later by the organization of Oklahoma Territory and the opening of the Oklahoma Panhandle. Meanwhile, the area between the North Fork of Red River and the Texas Panhandle had been claimed by Texas and opened for settlement as Greer County. By 1889 the county that bordered the Comanches to the west claimed more than 5,000 inhabitants. They added their voices to the chorus calling for the allotment of reservation land as a prelude to opening more acreage for white settlers.

Another result of the incessant clamor was the creation by Congress in March 1889 of a three-man commission to negotiate with the Cherokees and other tribes claiming lands west of the ninety-sixth degree of latitude in the Indian Territory. Known as the Cherokee Commission, in its four-year life it negotiated ten agreements, which when ratified would extend the blessings of allotment to twenty tribes and open to white settlement over 15 million acres. The commission's three members were David H. Jerome, who served as chairman, Alfred M. Wilson, and Warren G. Sayre. Jerome was a former governor of Michigan and had served five years on the Board of Indian Commissioners. Of the three he was the best acquainted with Indian affairs.

The Kiowas, Comanches, and Kiowa-Apaches were not long in letting the Indian Office know of their unwillingness to negotiate with the newly formed commission. In September 1889 Quanah tried to visit Washington to forestall an anticipated trip to Anadarko by Jerome and his colleagues.[6] The Comanche chief would take the position in the next few years that he did not oppose allotment per se. Nevertheless, he did want the Indians to hold on to their surplus lands so that they might continue to receive grass money from the cattlemen; the money was to go toward the purchase of lumber and furnishings for houses and other items to equip their homesteads. This increasingly was the Indian line. They did not oppose allotment; they merely wanted to delay any sale of their land until they were in a better position to strike out as independent homesteaders. Their delaying tactics were warmly supported by the cattlemen, who had their own contacts in Washington. The boomers recognized the existence of the coalition and resented it. Thus early in 1892 they protested Quanah's visit to Washington accompanied by an attorney of the cattlemen: "They are there in the interest of a few cowmen and do not represent the people of northwest Texas or the nation."[7]

The Comanches and associated tribes were the last Indians of the two southwestern agencies to be confronted by the Cherokee Commission. The Cheyennes and Arapahos came to terms with the commission in October 1890 and their reservation was thrown open to settlement in April 1892. In June 1891 Jerome and his colleagues met with the Wichitas and affiliated tribes, who occupied one of the two reservations comprising the Kiowa, Comanche, and Wichita Agency. However, not until 1895 would Congress ratify the Wichita Agreement and the president sign it.

The Cheyennes and Arapahos received about $0.50 an acre for 3 million acres of land they sold the United States. The Cherokee Commission made the same kind of offer to the Wichitas and affiliated tribes for 574,000 acres and they refused it. The agreement they signed provided that the final price would be set by Congress, which more than doubled it to $1.25 an acre. Complicating both negotiations was the possibility that the Choctaws and Chickasaws would ask for compensation based on their claims to the Leased District, from which the United States had carved the three reservations of the two southwestern agencies. To quiet the Choctaw and Chickasaw claims to the Cheyenne and Arapaho Reservation, Congress paid them nearly $3 million, which meant that they received about twice as much per acre as the Cheyennes and Arapahos did. This precedent had been established by the time the Cherokee Commission began to negotiate with the Kiowas, Comanches, and Kiowa-Apaches and could not be ignored by the commissioners in setting the price the United States would pay them.

The Cherokee Commission arrived at Fort Sill about September 20, 1892. In the next month it would hold numerous meetings with the members of the three tribes; a journal was kept of the proceedings of eleven of these sessions.[8] Eight of the meetings were held in the vicinity of Fort Sill and the last three at Anadarko. Official interpreters for the commission were Emsy J. Smith, Edward L. Clark, and Joshua Given. Emsy Smith had come to Fort Sill as a child about twenty years earlier and had attended Indian Service schools in the area and learned Comanche from her schoolmates. Clark was the well-known Comanche squaw man, and Given was the brilliant young Kiowa educated at Carlisle and Lincoln Institute.

The first formal session took place September 28 and the differences between the three commissioners and the Indians quickly became apparent. The white men opened by talking in generalities about the advantages the Indians would derive from the sale of the land they held in excess of their needs. The Indians were told that they no longer required so large a reservation: "Now you have an opportunity to sell to the Great Father all the land you can not use for homes for his white children."[9] The commissioners very early made reference to the Dawes Act of 1887, which authorized the president to "make an order whenever he pleases requiring the Comanches, Kiowas and Apaches to take allotments on this reservation."[10]

The Indians just as early made it known that they did not want to be rushed into anything. Quanah was the principal Comanche spokesman, although Tabananaka, Eschiti, Cheevers, and Howeah also spoke for that tribe. In his first presentation to the commission Quanah repeated his advice against haste: "Do not go at this thing like you were riding a swift horse, but hold up a little." The Comanche said that on a recent trip to Washington he had been told that the Cherokee Commission would not actually have the money to buy the Indian land but would "want to buy it with mouth-shoot." Quanah then got down to specifics: "How much will be paid for one acre, what the terms will be, and when it will be paid."[11]

Thus opened, negotiations went on for the next week and a half. The commissioners spelled out their offer of 160 acres for every Indian, half in grazing land and half in cropland. They compared this favorably with the Dawes Act, which provided only 80 acres for those not the heads of families. For the land remaining after each Indian got his homestead the commissioners offered not a price per acre, but $2 million for the total, a blatant effort to confuse the issue. Again they drew a comparison with the Dawes Act, pointing out that they were offering 5 percent interest in contrast to 3 percent and permitting the Indians some cash in hand whereas the Dawes Act placed all the Indian proceeds in the U.S. Treasury, from which only Congress could appropriate it for the benefit of the tribesmen.

It was clear from the beginning that the Indians did not want to sell. If they had to sell, they wished to delay it for three or four years, preferably until 1898, when the annuity provision of the 1867 treaty would have lapsed. They also wanted more for the land than the United States was offering. In response to repeated requests for a price per acre, the commissioners finally estimated their offer at around $1.00 to $1.10 per acre, pleading that they could not be more specific because of their inability to predict exactly how many Indians there would be to receive allotments. However, after the agreement had been completed the commissioners estimated that they had offered not $1.00 or $1.10 but about $0.80 per acre for the Indian land.[12]

The tribesmen arguing for a three- or four-year delay, Quanah most prominently, were trying to hold on to the grass money from the cattlemen as long as possible. Those who spoke in terms of the Treaty of Medicine Lodge believed erroneously that if they accepted allotment before the treaty expired they would lose the annuities and services it provided. On the price per acre Quanah observed that the commissioners had paid tribes rates that varied from $0.50 to $1.25. He asked for the latter, which according to the commissioner's own figures would raise the purchase price from $2 million to $2.5 million.[13]

The commissioner's response was to stress the amount of interest the Indians would lose if the sales were delayed for three years. David Jerome tried to make his point with the Indians by describing the $725,000 the Indians would lose in per capita payments and interest if the agreement were delayed three years, as a quantity of silver dollars it would require eight wagons each pulled by a six-mule team to transport.[14] Jerome also maintained that under any cirsumstances the agreement's implementation would be delayed two to three years by a provision recognizing pasture leases already in effect and by Congress not receiving the agreement until December.

To other arguments against the agreement the commissioners had less effective responses. Iseeo, a Kiowa in a troop of Indian cavalry stationed at Fort Sill, cited the poverty of the Cheyennes and Arapahos, who had recently negotiated the sale of their surplus land to the United States. The commissioners responded that those tribes exaggerated their poverty in order to beg ponies and cattle from the Kiowas and that if they were hungry it was because of their own improvidence. The commissioners chose to ignore Komalty's much more telling argument against the offer. This Kiowa predicted that with only 160 acres the Indians could not feed their ponies and cattle.[15] Fifteen years' experience on the reservation had demonstrated that very few Indians could hope to live by farming the 80 acres of cropland that they would receive in an area where the average annual rainfall was only about twenty inches. Because it required at least 15 acres to support one cow, neither was there any way that the Indians could become self-supporting by stock raising on their entire allotment of 160 acres.

During one break between negotiating sessions the commissioners stayed overnight at Quanah's home. When they
reconvened they praised its furnishings, his 100 acres
under cultivation, and his herd of 400 or 500 cattle and
"great drove of hogs."[16] They chose to ignore that Quanah
had additional income from grateful cattlemen and had
sequestered for his own use not 160 acres, but many times
that amount.

In the October 3 negotiating session Quanah sprang a
surprise. He announced that he would like a recess of two
months during which the Indians could consult with a lawyer he had sent for. The Kiowas at the session indicated
they were willing to go along with the proposal. The commissioners manifested no great surprise or chagrin at the
announcement that the lawyer would arrive at the reservation that night. It is possible that they had been apprised
of this development by John T. Hill, a white man with a
mysterious role in the negotiations.

Hill somehow had insinuated himself into the position of
adviser to the Indians. That he had some connection with
the commissioners is demonstrable. When they had dealt
with the Kickapoos he had aided those Indians in their
negotiation of what was for them a poor bargain and then
had filed a claim against the tribe for $5,000. When he
appeared at Fort Sill in the company of the commissioners
they permitted him the use of one of the government's
interpreters, Emsy Smith. The lawyer whom Quanah
brought to Fort Sill was an acquaintance of Hill's from
Guthrie with the intriguing name of Asp. To represent
them, Asp proposed to charge the Indians 7 percent of any
payment made them for their surplus land. Rumors circulated that others were to be cut in on the fee of at least
$140,000, including Quanah, Lone Wolf, Tabananaka, and
the interpreter Joshua Given.[17] John T. Hill undoubtedly
would have been compensated royally for having put the
Indians in touch with Asp.

Lieutenant Hugh L. Scott subsequently claimed credit
for alerting Kiowas to the shady deal, who then squelched

it. Whether or not this was the whole story, when the Cherokee Commission and the Indians met again in formal council on October 5, Quanah announced that the lawyer had concluded he could do nothing for them at this stage of the negotiations. The Comanche chief, for reasons he knew best, had decided on another tack. He now proposed that the commissioners take back to Washington an agreement that left unsettled the price for the surplus land. The commissioners could tell Congress of their offer of $2 million and of the Indian demand of $2.5 million and leave it to Congress. To assist that body in its deliberations the Indians would send a delegation accompanied by a lawyer.[18] Possibly Quanah was influenced in this by the example set by the Wichitas and affilaited tribes, who refused the offer made them by the Cherokee Commission and left it to Congress to arrive at a fair price.

The next day the commissioners announced they would accept Quanah's proposition, which now carried the endorsement of Lone Wolf and the Kiowa-Apache spokesman, White Man. But it would differ from the Wichita agreement in one salient particular. The commissioners' original offer of $2 million would be written into the Kiowa, Comanche, and Kiowa-Apache agreement and all the Indians would get would be "an opportunity to be heard for the other half million dollars."[19] The Indians actually were getting nothing that had not previously been offered. Nor would there be any further debate on the matter. When Tohauson, a Kiowa chief, informed the commissioners that he would not sign the agreement nor would half of the other Indians, David Jerome informed the council that "all that do not want to trade under any circumstances need not weary us with their talk."[20] The commissioners intended to stifle the opposition to the extent that they could.

Jerome and his colleagues were still a long way from completion of their mission. The Treaty of Medicine Lodge provided that any sale of land by the three tribes would have to be approved by three-fourths of the adult males. This meant that they had to get at least 422 signatures, and very few Indians had indicated a willingness to sell their land.

But the United States had learned something from a century's experience in buying Indian land. A frequently employed device for assuring a deal was to include in it provisions for individuals who might favorably dispose the Indians toward it. The Jerome Agreement, as it would come to be known, was written to include, presumably at the request of the Indians, two such clauses. One stipulated that eighteen whites "be entitled to all the benefits of land and money conferred by this agreement." Among them were the wife of interpreter Joshua Given, interpreter Edward L. Clark, and Quanah's son-in-law Emmett Cox. Clark and Cox were also Comanche squaw men, as were George W. Conover and William Deitrick, who were included in the eighteen.

The other clause granted "the benefits, in land only" to seven other "friends of said Indians, who have rendered to said Indians valuable services." They also were a significant assortment, among them Emsy J. Smith, the third of the three interpreters for the negotiations. The mysterious John T. Hill appeared among the beneficiaries, as did David Grantham, who had been sharecropping Quanah's farm for ten years. J. J. Methvin, a Methodist minister among the Indians since 1887, made the list along with Zonee Adams, the year-old daughter of former agent Charles E. Adams, and his missionary wife. Agent George D. Day and Lieutenant Hugh L. Scott completed the roll call of the seven. Agent Day faithfully performed the services required of him by the government, doing his utmost to expedite the work of the Cherokee Commission. After telling the Indians that their only choice was between the commission's offer and the Dawes Act, he advised the former.[21] The minutes of the commissioners' journal reveal Hugh Scott speaking but one time, and then he affected neutrality. He later claimed to have encouraged opposition to the Cherokee Commission's offer. Nevertheless, he did not insist that his name be dropped from the list of those who stood to benefit by the agreement.

That all the official interpreters—the agent, the former agent, and an army officer under whose command a number of Kiowas served—should be beneficiaries of the agreement either directly or through close relatives clearly raised questions of conflict of interest. Because the commissioners were unable to communicate in the Indian languages and only a very few tribesmen spoke English, the interpreters were in especially sensitive positions since all the exchanges had to pass through them. The inter-married whites, besides Clark, who was an interpreter, could not directly participate in the negotiations, but they now had ample incentive to work behind the scenes through their network of relatives.

With Quanah, Tabananaka, Lone Wolf, and White Man behind the agreement and the twenty-five whites who were to be beneficiaries of the agreement using their influence, the commissioners began to collect signatures for the document. Within two days they had nearly half the total that would be required under the Treaty of Medicine Lodge. With few exceptions the Comanches were willing to sign, as were the Kiowa headmen who had participated in the negotiations. But the council had met at Fort Sill, which was in the area occupied by the Comanches, the Kiowas being farther north and west. Rumblings from those areas of the reservation suggested that the commissioners would have difficulty collecting the remaining number of signatures required.

At a meeting at Fort Sill with Kiowas belonging to Lieutenant Scott's troop of cavalry, the commissioners got some idea of the trouble yet facing them. Iseeo did finally sign it, although other Kiowas refused because they feared the displeasure of their fellow tribesmen. A report circulated that a clause calling for a three-year delay in the implementation of the agreement had been omitted from it. Jerome went through his routine that such a stipulation was unnecessary because it was unlikely that it could possibly be implemented in that time anyhow, but the Kiowas obviously were not reassured. Jerome then announced that the commission was moving to Anadarko at the request of the Kiowa headmen.[22]

The final week of the Cherokee Commission's work would be a hectic one. When they met the Kiowas in council at Anadarko October 14, the depth of the opposition of those Indians became apparent very quickly. It was led by Apiatan, who had been dispatched by his people the previous year to report on the Paiute messiah. At one point Apiatan asked for a standing vote of those Kiowas who opposed the agreement and "are with me on the Medicine Lodge road." Most of the Indians present rose to their feet.[23]

At the opening of the next day's session of the council, David Jerome acknowledged the persistence of rumors that Joshua Given was not interpreting accurately for the Kiowas in an effort to expedite their acceptance of the agreement. The commissioner flatly denied this, declining to discharge Joshua on the grounds that firing one of the official interpreters might invalidate the proceedings. Jerome did agree to accept the services of two additional interpreters proposed by the Kiowas, and all three were sworn in to work with the council. The Indians were not satisfied by this gesture and continued to vigorously oppose ratification of the agreement. Jerome, who did most of the talking for the commissioners, reported to his ultimate weapon, the Dawes Act:

> Now Congress has full control of you, it can do as it is a mind to with you. . . . Congress has determined to open this country and settle with these Indians. . . . If this fails, and we tell Congress and the Great Father that we can't trade with the Indians, the President may order you to take allotments under the Dawes law.[24]

The third and last formal session at Anadarko took place October 17. The Indians present were Kiowas with a scattering of Comanches. It was a stormy affair. Big Tree accused Jerome of trying to monopolize the floor, and Apiatan when he was able to speak upbraided the commissioners for fraud. On hearing that, Jerome ordered the Indians out and they left in an uproar, only a few Comanches remaining. That virtually ended the formal negotiating sessions; the commissioners took the attitude that the agreement had been offered to the Indians and it only remained for them to sign or not.

Before they left the reservation the commissioners had obtained the signatures of 456 of the 562 adult males in the Kiowa, Comanche, and Kiowa-Apache tribes. Even if the names of squaw men Edward Clark and Thomas Woodward—Clark had used his Indian name—were left out of the document, a clear three-fourths majority had signed. Some of the Kiowas, however, claimed later that they had asked to retract their signatures and had been denied permission to do so. There also were repeated declarations that the interpreters, particularly Joshua Given, had misled the Indians. A Kiowa medicine man placed a curse on Joshua, and the returned model student and Presbyterian minister began hemorrhaging on the date and in the fashion the medicine man had predicted. Agent Day tried to console Joshua; nevertheless, the young Kiowa who had been expected to head a new generation of leaders for the agency's Indians went into decline and died shortly afterward.

It is unlikely that Joshua deliberately misled the Kiowas or that the commissioners openly lied to them and to the Comanches and Kiowa-Apaches. That the commissioners threatened the Indians with the Dawes Act is patent. Jerome and his colleagues, and behind them the Indian Office and Congress, had set purchasing the Indians' surplus land for homesteads for whites as their first priority. Even if one accepted the conventional wisdom of the day that only if the Indians obtained individual title to their land could they progress, it did not excuse limiting them to 160-acre allotments. This action doomed the Comanches and associated tribes to the poverty that Iseeo, Apiatan, and others had foreseen.

The threat of the Dawes Act could not have done it alone. The influence of the twenty-five whites proposed as beneficiaries of the treaty must have had a considerable impact. Even more crucial was the lack of unity among the Indians. Apparently none wanted an agreement providing for an immediate opening of the reservation; however, that was the only thing on which they agreed. Quanah's role was a key one, but he was inconsistent. The Comanche could be a shrewd bargainer and he asked some important questions about unit price and mineral rights. Yet he seemed to have fallen under the sway of John T. Hill, who at best was out to make what he could from the role of middleman, and at worst was a plant by Jerome and his colleagues. Quanah permitted the commissioners to get his essential backing in their drive for signatures on an agreement that did not include the one provision the Comanche had held out for: the ultimate price for the land to be established by Congress after consultation with an Indian delegation. Perhaps Quanah was convinced the Cherokee Commission would have its way anyhow and was willing to settle for the safeguarding of the cattlemen's leases then in force. Certainly they had been his primary interest and a dependable source of income for several years.

It is hard to avoid the conclusion that Quanah was an architect of the Comanche surrender to the Cherokee Commission. By 1892, although he had competition for influence among the Comanches, Quanah came close to being the "Principal Chief" that he claimed to be. Eschiti remarked of him during the deliberations at Fort Sill: "What he learns from the Government he writes on his tongue, and we learn from him."[25] And when Eschiti became persistent about delaying the signing of an agreement for four years, Quanah cooly assured the commissioners, "I think there will be no trouble in controlling him."[26] If Quanah had chosen to use his power against the commissioners, there was no way enough signatures could have been obtained to legitimatize the agreement.

In defense of the $2 million offer the commissioners made for the land remaining after the Indians received their allotments, it should be remembered that the Choctaw and Chickasaw claims were still very much alive. The commissioner of Indian Affairs predicted that the land being surrendered by the Kiowas, Comanches, and Kiowa-Apaches, based on the settlement for the Cheyenne and Arapaho Reservation, would cost the United States an additional $3,086,116.25 to quiet the Choctaw and Chickasaw title to the tract.[27] As it turned out, the Jerome Agreement would take eight years to be ratified, and along the way the Choctaws and Chickasaws would fail to realize on their claims.

David Jerome and his colleagues were hardly away from Anadarko with their controversial agreement when J. E. Prindle of Perryville, Arkansas, wrote Washington to inquire as to when land on the Kiowa, Comanche, and Kiowa-Apache Reservation would be opened to white settlers.[28] The pressure was already beginning to build; the miracle is that the Indians managed to hold on to their land for another eight years.

10. Eight Years of Sooners and Boomers and Tribal Factionalism

The members of the Cherokee Commission had estimated that it would take about two years for Congress to ratify the agreement it had reached with the Kiowas, Comanches, and Kiowa-Apaches. During the negotiations Quanah had pled for at least four years, and others had wished to postpone the sale of their land until the annuity provisions of the Medicine Lodge Treaty expired in 1898. As it developed, it was not until June 1900 that Congress ratified the Jerome Agreement, and then in an altered form.

Throughout this period the United States never wavered in its general objective of assimilation. As a commissioner of Indian Affairs informed an agent seeking permission for the Kiowas to adopt a white woman:

> The policy of this office is to make citizens of the Indian—not to increase the role of Indians by admitting to membership white persons who gain the good will of Indians and then apply for adoption into their tribe—and so fast as possible to change the relations of Indians from that of wards to citizens, which means the utter destruction of tribal relations.[1]

To implement this policy six individuals held the position of agent at Anadarko during the eight years from negotiation of the agreement to its ratification. Agent George D. Day, a Republican who had used his office to assist the Cherokee Commission, did not survive the return of the Democrats to power under Grover Cleveland in 1893. The previous year Congress had enacted a law authorizing the president to appoint army officers as agents if he chose. Cleveland in the first six months of his second term placed more than half the agencies, including the one at Anadarko, under military men.

The substitution of officers for civilians was neither the disaster its critics had predicted nor the overwhelming success its proponents had promised. As in the earlier experiment with agents appointed by church groups, there was mixed performance. Surely, three of the four military men to serve at Anadarko from 1893 to 1900 displayed commendable zeal and a willingness to take on all comers to fight for what they judged to be the best interests of the Indian.

The first officer to serve as agent for the Comanches and associated tribes was Captain Hugh G. Brown, who succeeded Agent Day in July 1893 and finished out the year. A veteran of the Civil War, Captain Brown was in his late fifties when he assumed one of the more difficult assignments in the Indian Service. An editor in a neighboring town observed sourly, "Captain Brown . . . has taken charge . . . and the work of turning over to him the usual amount of tongueless wagons, dismantled reapers, brainless mules, sorebacked horses, and scattered cattle goes bravely on."[2] In his brief tenure at Anadarko Brown addressed himself to the problem of administration by subdividing the agency into farming districts, each with its supervisor. Each farming district then was assigned an Arbitration Committee of six Indians to settle minor disputes brought to their attention. Brown also sought guidance from Washington in determining what was the proper amount of land a squaw man or Indian could hold free of charge. But before the captain could get into this thorny issue he was relieved by Lieutenant Maury Nichols. What lay behind the change in assignments is not clear, although Brown must have sought it. Rumors did circulate that he was transferred because he had been too rigorous with some of the agency's suppliers or because he had aligned himself with the cattlemen leasing Indian pastures.

Lieutenant Nichols took responsibility for the agency on

January 1, 1894. He asked to be relieved in September on the grounds he was suffering from malaria; however, it is doubtful that he would have remained much longer, because of adverse reports on his performance. An inspector had found him unsuitable for the position and specifically charged him with employing whites under Indian names, acting as a bill collector for the traders, and permitting Indians to engage in ghost and war dances within sight of the agency.[3] In the ten months the young lieutenant served as agent he primarily occupied himself by drilling the Indian police force as a troop of cavalry.

The short tenures of Brown and Nichols, and the poor performance of at least the latter, made the task of Major Frank D. Baldwin even more difficult when he assumed charge of the agency in November 1894. He found administrative chaos—vital records missing and letter press books being used as toilet paper. Like High Brown a veteran of the Civil War, Baldwin had won a Medal of Honor in that conflict. In his decade of service on the plains he won another and inspired generations of screenwriters when he charged a Cheyenne village with his infantry blazing away from mule-drawn wagons. Although in his early fifties when he succeeded Nichols at Anadarko, Baldwin was still vigorous (as assorted squaw men, traders, and conservative Indians learned to their discomfiture). But these elements could frustrate an agent on his home territory and undercut him in Washington. Major Baldwin became so involved in controversy that he lost his effectiveness. Perhaps his being recalled to army duty by the outbreak of the Spanish-American War saved him from being relieved of his position under a barrage of charges.

For a year after the departure of Major Baldwin the position of agent was occupied by an Oklahoma newspaperman, William T. Walker. Throughout much of that period, however, Special Agent Gilbert B. Pray was stationed at the agency on the orders of Commissioner of Indian Affairs W. A. Jones. Supposedly, Special Agent Pray's mission was to bring some order out of the confusion of leases, but his obvious influence with Commissioner Jones prevented Agent Walker from ever establishing himself as the real authority at Anadarko. On July 1, 1899 Walker surrendered the office to Lieutenant Colonel James F. Randlett.

Colonel Randlett was one of those Civil War veterans who had reentered the army after a brief interlude of civilian life. Following service with cavalry regiments on the plains he was detailed in 1893 as agent for the Utes. Randlett served in that capacity until 1897, in the meantime being retired from the army. Despite his advanced years (he was nearly 70) he was offered the Kiowa, Comanche, and Wichita Agency in 1899 because of the fine record he had compiled as Ute agent. In the six years he held the position at Anadarko, Colonel Randlett demonstrated what one observer termed "stern integrity."[4] He also proved himself an able administrator and effective in the infighting that such a position demanded of anyone intent on safeguarding Indian interests.

For the Comanches the eight years between the negotiation and the ratification of the Jerome Agreement saw them at their most prosperous. Although there was a reduction after 1898 in the amount of rations they received from the United States and the annuities ceased completely, they had more income from other sources. The cattlemen's grass payments to the Comanches and associated tribes had reached $232,000 by 1900.[5] In addition, some of the Comanches had opened farms and most of them owned cattle, a few holding herds that ran into the hundreds. Hunger was no longer the problem it had been throughout most of the 1880s.

The improved economic condition of the Indians was not reflected in an increase in population. In 1892 the Comanche population was 1,531 and by 1900 it had dropped slightly to 1,499. In the same period the Kiowa population rose from 1,014 to 1,136, and the Kiowa-Apaches decreased from 241 to 173.[6] The Indian infant mortality rate apparently was quite high, although this can only be surmised because many died before appearing on tribal rolls. Malaria was endemic on the reservation, and bronchial and venereal diseases took a heavy toll, as did measles and smallpox.

The Treaty of Medicine Lodge had provided that the United States would supply the Indians the services of a physician for at least ten years. The government did not withdraw the service in 1878, although it was not easy to recruit an able man, given the top salary of $1,200 a year and the remote location. The turnover of physicians was as high as it was for agents. Dr. Obadiah G. Given was one who lasted longer than usual, serving from 1873 to 1877. He not only ministered to the sick but on occasion preached the sermon on Sunday morning. The tenure of Dr. W. W. Graves, who served almost as long, ran from 1886 to 1889. He evidently was more proficient at concocting Hostetter's Bitters from the medicinal alcohol in his possession than he was at preaching sermons, and the agent had to sequester fifty-eight quarts of the raw material to put him out of business.[7] The record for longevity as agency physician was set by Dr. C. R. Hume, who served at Anadarko for most of the 1890s. Although physicians had been placed under civil service in 1891, Dr. Hume was a sufficiently partisan Republican to arouse the ire of a Democratic inspector. The latter accused the physician of anticipating a Republican victory in 1896 and chiding his Democratic associates with predictions that "there would be no more Indian school children named after Grover Cleveland or Stevenson and other little attempts at wit."[8]

Dr. Hume should have had little time for such bantering. The consolidation of the agencies at Anadarko in 1878 made the physician responsible for the medical care of more than 4,000 Indians scattered over 5,800 square miles. It is likely that only the white population at the agency received much medical attention under the circumstances; surely, very few Comanches did since they were located thirty to forty miles from the dispensary at Anadarko.

P. B. Hunt began to call for additional medical personnel

shortly after the consolidation of the agencies. Indeed, at one point he was willing to settle for a man whose chief qualification for a position as assistant physician was that he had served as an assistant surgeon in the British navy during the Crimean War! This arrangement did not work out, possibly fortunately for the Indians, and in 1884 authorization was granted for a dual appointment of farmer and physician, which would carry a salary of $75 a month. It is doubtful that the regular physician received much assistance from this unusual hybrid. Commissioner T. J. Morgan could have had Anadarko in mind—he had visited it—when in 1890 he described the "utter inadequacy" of the government medical programs for Indians.[9]

Some relief seemed on the way in 1892, when a physician was authorized for the Fort Sill School and the agent proposed that he also treat the Comanches in that part of the reservation. Not only did Washington refuse this, but the agent was informed that the physician was supposed to divide his time between the Comanche children at the Fort Sill School and Kiowa youngsters at the Rainy Mountain School forty miles away! This job description further complicated recruiting, and the government finally gave in and assigned a full-time physician at each school. Nevertheless, the positions still proved unattractive. In 1896 three men held the post at the Fort Sill School in rapid succession, the first man going into shock after arriving from Vermont and seeing the facilities. "Is there no redress for such indignities?" he complained, "Must the medical profession become so belittled?"[10]

With no hospital facilities at the agency and very little access for Indians to a physician, it is small wonder that medicine men continued to flourish. One agent suggested that the physician faced odds of 200 to 1 in his efforts to counteract the influence of the native practitioners.[11] Meanwhile the Comanche death rate generally kept pace with the birth rate.

The Treaty of Medicine Lodge provision for education called for the government to offer that service not the minimum of ten years as in the case of medicine but for at least twenty. Again the time limitation was ignored and in the 1890s the United States was still operating schools for the Comanches and associated tribes but never facilities capable of accommodating all the students, as was promised in the treaty. The commissioner of Indian Affairs and the secretary of the interior continued to place great importance on education in their public statements, but Congress failed to vote the necessary funding. Under the circumstances administrators began to find merit in the cheaper day schools, one being opened at Anadarko in the late 1890s. There was a corresponding decrease of enthusiasm for off-reservation boarding schools that involved expensive transportation.

One interesting innovation was the field matron. First authorized by Congress in 1891 on an experimental basis, the matrons were employed to circulate among the Indians, instructing women and girls in the household arts. As Congress gradually expanded the program two were assigned to Anadarko. A returned Carlisle student, Laura Doanmore Pedrick, a Kiowa, served in this capacity in the late 1890s.

The opening of the Fort Sill School for Comanche children in 1893 had resulted in a much greater percentage of them attending than ever before. However, even with at least 125 packed into that school, approximately 75 Comanche children could not be accommodated on the reservation because the other two government boarding schools were also overpopulated and the four mission schools filled to capacity. Agent Baldwin persuaded the Indians to set aside $25,000 of their grass money with the expectation that the United States would add to it at least $40,000 for the construction of a new boarding school at Mt. Scott.[12]

Comanche parents could choose among the local government and mission schools for their children. They continued to resist pressure to send them to off-reservation schools. Some authorities charged that parents condoned early marriage for girls, in part to prevent their being sent away to school.[13] The law mandating parental approval for sending a child out of the state or territory cut into the enrollments of Carlisle and Haskell. One agent tried unsuccessfully to meet his Carlisle quota of nineteen Comanche children by subdividing it among seven chiefs, with Quanah saddled with producing seven of the students.

Parents were only relatively less resistant to Chilocco, which was in Indian Territory. All the techniques of withholding rations and annuities and threatening arrest in order to send Comanche children there persisted. Agent Baldwin, in the process of forcing children off to Chilocco, made the discovery that had been made by so many whites before him: "I never saw a people as devoted to their offspring as the Indians are."[14] The superintendent at the Fort Sill School was troubled by the same phenomenon. His regulations permitted Comanche parents to visit their children only once a month, although every weekend some of them showed up laden with more goodies than he believed were good for the students.

Another source of dissension was the rivalry among the different schools. Presumably, students who had completed the curriculum at the local schools or had reached the age of fourteen were eligible for transfer to off-reservation boarding schools. Superintendents of the local government and mission schools were accused of not complying with this policy. They also squabbled among themselves, and with parents, over the transfer of students among the reservation's schools. Agent Baldwin tried to promote some feeling of common purpose by holding annual conventions in which all the schools participated, the children performing for an audience of parents and visitors.

The Fort Sill School was a considerable improvement over the old Kiowa School, which was finally abandoned in this period. Inspectors generally gave the Fort Sill School good marks and spoke approvingly of its 100-acre farming operation, its orchards, and livestock. There was some consternation in 1898 when the main school building was declared unsafe and hastily condemned.[15] This forced a temporary reduction in enrollment and even more crowding in a school already criticized for having two children to a bed in its dormitories.

Quanah symbolized the more cordial attitude toward education found among Comanches in this period. For the first time he set the desired example by sending his own children to school, four of them being among the few Comanches to attend Carlisle in this period. Quanah and Pohocsucut were chosen to represent the Comanches on a five-man Board of Visitors set up in 1894 in a vain attempt to bring a little Indian participation into school management.

The education system, inadequate though it was, began to pay dividends for the Indians by the 1890s. Young Comanches and Kiowas were replacing squaw men and old army scouts as interpreters. A council held in 1898 even saw Lucius Aitson, a Kiowa, and Howard White Wolf, a Comanche, both alumni of Carlisle, selected as president and secretary of that meeting.

Such honors would not come often to young people in societies that associated wisdom with the experience of years. A more practical concern was simply finding employment for the returned students, who represented the best-educated class among the young Indians. Congress mandated employment of Indians "as herders, teamsters, and laborers, and where practicable in all other employments in connection with the agencies and the Indian service."[16] Agent Baldwin made a real effort to find them positions on the agency and school payrolls and engaged in a controversial project to open farms for them. While the students were still away at school he would select quarter-sections for them, erect houses there, and arrange for white farmers to work the farms until the youths finished school. When they did they would return, in Baldwin's words, "to a real home instead of being turned loose on the wild plain to shift for themselves."[17] However, some people denounced Baldwin for flooding the reservation with whites in pursuit of the policy. There were also

Big Looking Glass, 1894. (Smithsonian Institution, National Anthropological Archives)

Eschiti, *on the right in the back.* The others are probably members of his family, circa 1895. (Panhandle Plains Historical Society)

Seated, *left to right,* are Quanah, Hugh L. Scott, Big Looking Glass, and Apiatan. The two standing are unidentified. (Smithsonian Institution, National Anthropological Archives)

Delegation to Washington, 1897. *On the left,* standing, is Quanah. Seated, *from left to right,* are Tonarcy (a wife of Quanah), Apiatan, Apache John, and Big Looking Glass. *On the right, at the end of the middle row,* is William Tivis. (Smithsonian Institution, National Anthropological Archives)

questions about activities of the missionaries during this
period.

A sharp upturn in missionary activity among the Comanches and associated tribes marked the years 1893–
1900. In addition to the staffs of the mission schools,
there were fifteen missionaries working on the reservation
by the end of the century,[18] although without much success in proselytizing. Their greatest contribution was still
in education.

The mission school that attracted the most Comanches
was the one on Cache Creek about twenty-five miles southwest of Anadarko. In the 1890s it was an operation
requiring a staff of five to house and educate the school's
population of about forty students. It was costing the
Reformed Presbyterian Church several thousand dollars
a year to operate it. The Reverend W. W. Carithers, the
superintendent, was an aggressive young man who dreamed
of locating his ex-students in the vicinity and developing
the nucleus of a Christian community.[19] He expanded his
grazing operations to cover 640 acres in order to raise
enough cattle to give his students a few head when they
were ready to branch out on their own. This and his effort
to locate his ex-students' allotments nearby brought him
into conflict with cattlemen leasing in the area.

Jesse G. Forester pastored the little Methodist church
near Fort Sill as a substation of J. J. Methvin's mission.
He was more typical of the missionaries the Comanches encountered. Reverend Forester preached in his church three
Sundays out of four; the other service was presented near
Mt. Scott. The three services near Fort Sill attracted students and staff from the nearby Comanche school, some
members of the Fort Sill garrison, and a few older Indians
to whom Reverend Jesse Forester spoke through an interpreter. The service at Mt. Scott was attended almost exclusively by Indians.

Like Carithers, Methvin had expanded his operations. In
1897 his church held 160 acres near Anadarko, another
quarter-section on the Little Washita, 40 acres near Mount

Scott, and two smaller tracts, one of them in Anadarko and the other near Fort Sill. In spite of these holdings he sought another 160 acres in one of the best farming areas in the agency, where he proposed to open a day school and maintain an encampment as "a sort of Indian Chautauqua."[20] Agent Baldwin was not impressed and managed to stop the project. Later, however, the Methodists did get 80 acres in the same vicinity. In addition, Methvin had applied within months of the signing of the Jerome Agreement for the 160 acres that would become his personal property once the agreement was ratified.[21] The missionaries sometimes seemed to exhibit an unholy interest in land.

The permission of the Indians was supposed to be obtained for any use of reservation land by a church group. Competition was developing for good farm acreage by the 1890s and sometimes the Indians showed their displeasure at the missionaries appropriating another tract. When the Reverend W. W. Carithers sought to open a new mission station among the Comanches the land he wanted for it was already occupied by an Indian. Carithers offered him $100 to move on, but the Comanche refused, saying he would not sell the land if the reverend gave him enough money to fill his tepee up to the smoke hole.[22]

Comanches also gave a cool reception to the Reverend E. C. Deyo's efforts to establish a Baptist mission among them. He came to the agency in the winter of 1893–94 and started construction of a church at three or four locations before he found one acceptable to the Indians. Moreover, they did not flock to it once established. In the first four years of its operation the mission gained only eight members although services might attract others on an irregular basis.

Letters to a newspaper published in Marlow, a town near the western boundary of the reservation, reveal that the Reverend E. C. Deyo saw himself as both a missionary to the Indians and the vanguard of white settlement. Writing the first spring he was on the reservation, Deyo enthused about "the blessing of having some of our own race with us" and extended an invitation to other whites to worship at the mission. In the columns of a newspaper devoted to hastening the day Congress would open the reservation to whites, Deyo not only referred to his labors "to prepare the Comanche to meet his God, and dwell with him in heaven forever," the reverend also anticipated the time when "these broad prairies may be settled by industrious Christian whites, who will help to roll onward the Grand Old Gospel car."[23]

In a subsequent letter Deyo gave his readers a tour of the eastern part of the reservation in terms designed to activate the salivary glands of a land-hungry white. Under the reverend's glowing pen the Wichita Mountains, classified by the Cherokee Commission as worthless, were reputed "to be very rich in mineral ore." Fort Sill was transformed into a superb townsite, and the area to the east of the fort appeared as "broad green prairies" watered by "numerous creeks."[24] The Reverend E. C. Deyo was an authentic specimen of the Oklahoma "boomer."

Boomers had raised their voices before the negotiation of the Jerome Agreement, and during the eight years its ratification was pending they kept up a drumfire of hyperbolic descriptions of the "Fort Sill Country" coupled with demands that its opening be expedited. The opening of the Cheyenne and Arapaho Reservation in 1892 had left the two reservations of the Kiowa, Comanche, and Wichita Agency as the boomers' principal target in the recently organized Oklahoma Territory. In the decade of the 1890s the territory's population grew from 60,000 to 400,000. One line of the Rock Island Railroad was constructed across the northern part of the Kiowa, Comanche, and Kiowa-Apache Reservation, and another branch of the same railroad bordered its western boundary.

Each of the small towns that sprang up along the Rock Island envisioned itself as a future metropolis if only settlers were permitted to develop the Fort Sill area. And most of the towns seemed to have newspapers with editors of unfettered imagination and boundless hostility for those they blamed for delaying the opening, usually the cattlemen with leases on pasture land. The Indians opposing the opening were usually dismissed as the pawns and tools of the cattlemen.

The *Minco Minstrel* denounced the "boodlers and schemers" delaying ratification and suggested the time had come for "forcible settlement by the deceived, wearied and exasperated white."[25] Equally inflammatory was the editor of the *Marlow Magnet,* who liked to describe his town as the "Gateway to the Fort Sill Country," connected by a twenty-three-mile dirt trail that emerged from his overheated pen as a "simply magnificent" road. But this was no embarrassment to an editor who could describe the Fort Sill area as having "some of the richest virgin soil in the world."[26]

In reporting gold discoveries in the Wichita Mountains the Marlow editor compared the situation with that in Dakota Territory fifteen years earlier: "It might be a repetition of the rush to the Black Hills when the government vainly tried to keep out the miners."[27] At a mass meeting in October 1893 citizens of Marlow drew up resolutions that included one pointing with alarm to the "barrier between this country and Texas . . . depriving this country of western trade, thus clogging the wheels of commerce and paralyzing trade."[28]

Texans who were settling communities along the south bank of the Red River were equally vehement about the necessity of opening the Fort Sill country. People in Wichita Falls called the Indian reservations "a wall of fire between Texas and her future development."[29] In a letter to President Cleveland a citizen of Fort Worth preferred the term "Chinese wall" but expressed the same idea.[30] His local chamber of commerce also had conveyed its "very earnest feeling for the opening of the country."[31]

The growth of settlement in the Southwest meant that the boomers could make their voice heard in Congress. Delegate Dennis Flynn from Oklahoma Territory lacked a vote in the House, although he could participate in debate and introduce measures. Congressmen in neighboring states that had organizations of boomers found it wise to show an interest in their proposals. Texas congressmen clearly were torn between the importuning of the cattlemen, who opposed opening in order to hold on to their grass leases, and the settlers, who knew how to talk votes to a candidate. Joseph Bailey stayed with the cattlemen, but some of his colleagues sided with the boomers.

The arguments the boomers employed were heard at one of their public meetings in Chickasha, one of the towns near Anadarko. The principal speaker attacked "the cattlemen and their paid boodle gang which has from time to time controlled with money the committees of the National Congress." The resolutions at this public meeting included one emphasizing the benefits that opening would bring to the Indians by exposing them to the example of the hard-working white settler, who would "stimulate him in his effort at self-support, and would surely have the effect to encourage him to put his children in school."[32]

A colorful figure at many of the "On to Fort Sill" meetings in the early 1890s was J. S. Works, better known as Buckskin Joe. He was the editor of the *Iowa Park Texan* and headed a boomers' organization operating under the title Texas–Oklahoma Union Colony. Even before the Cherokee Commission visited the Comanches, Buckskin Joe was exposing the ties between Quanah and the cattlemen and thus trying to diminish the impact of the Comanche chief's opposition to an opening.

After the negotiation of the Jerome Agreement, Works threw himself into the fight for ratification. In October 1893 he gave a speech in Duncan, a town on the Rock Island Railroad only a few miles from the western border of the reservation. According to the editor of the *Minco Minstrel*, Buckskin Joe's speech was in fine form:

> full of meat and well seasoned with red hot sauce for the cattle syndicates, interspersed with a goodly

amount of salt rubbed into the putrid areas found here and there on our Uncle Samuel's anatomy. . . . The speech was received with applause and cheering . . . [and] the Duncan Silver Cornet Band played their famous piece, "On to Fort Sill."[33]

Six months later Buckskin Joe rode into Marlow in a covered wagon whose canvas sported a painting of the Wichita Mountains and the slogan "On to Fort Sill." He announced that he hoped to lead a vanguard of "sooners," as were designated those who declined to wait for an official opening, into the Fort Sill country. He predicted that within a matter of months gold would be produced by the ton from the Wichitas, and 19,000 sooners would be located in the area. Buckskin Joe declared that the United States would then be confronted with another Black Hills dilemma and would have to choose "between the man and the steer, the babies and the calves."[34]

Whether or not in response to Buckskin Joe's fervent appeal, sooners were infiltrating the reservation. Some undoubtedly were drawn by the reports of mineral wealth that had circulated since the 1870s. Others simply used this as a pretext. In either case entering the area was not difficult. The government guaranteed access to the several public highways crossing Indian reservations. One ran from Chickasha to Greer County; others traversed the reservation north and south connecting Texas and Oklahoma Territory. In addition to legitimate travelers there were whites who left the roads to steal horses and other property of Indians, to cut timber and stone, or to prospect in the mountains.

If the United States had ever weakened its stand against the prospectors the reservation would have been overrun by whites in a matter of weeks. As it was, there was a steady trickle of them in and out of the Wichita Mountains and the Indian police force was too small to stop it. All inquiries to Washington about mining privileges on the reservation (and they were numerous) were met with a firm negative and sometimes a reminder that a $1,000 fine could be levied on those who returned after having been removed. Nevertheless, reports persisted of fantastic discoveries. One Texan asked his congressman to intercede in his behalf after he claimed to have been guided to an old Spanish gold mine by a Comanche chief.[35] A resident of the Chickasaw Nation maintained that he had found both gold and silver in the Wichitas and, as he assured the secretary of the interior, he had discovered mines before and knew a good one when he saw it.[36] Unquestionably some of the prospectors were victims of gold fever. Most, however, were sooners hoping on any pretext to be inside the reservation when the opening came.

The timber and stone cutters were not waiting for the opening. As towns like Chickasha sprang up, builders invaded the Indian reservation for materials. On the western border the thousands of settlers in Greer County were desperate for timber for fuel, homes, and fencing and entered the reservation in increasing numbers to steal it. When apprehended and remanded to local courts they were usually released by sympathetic judges. A common rationalization was that as long as the cattlemen leasing pastures were permitted to cut fence posts by the thousands, the law could wink at a struggling homesteader taking out a load of down and dead timber. The next step was for the homesteader to slip in and cut what he wanted and then return openly in a few days and haul out the "down and dead" timber.

Timber cutting was one of the lesser offenses charged against white squatters who located on what was locally called "the strip," a tract in a bend of the Washita River on the northern boundary of the reservation. In 1894 they moved in and when Agent Baldwin had eviction notices served on them they threatened to kill him on sight and held their ground.[37] The whites permitted their cattle and hogs to invade Indian fields and gardens, physically assaulted Indians, robbed an Indian's home while he was in church, and stole siding off another Indian's house.[38]

When Baldwin persisted in his efforts to move the squatters from tribal land they were backed by a memorial from the Oklahoma Territory legislature. Emboldened, the whites then got an injunction against Agent Baldwin.[39]

The unsettled conditions provided rich opportunities for the unscrupulous, such as the confidence man selling certificates for $3.10 each that authorized the purchaser to file a homestead claim in the Fort Sill country. Another opportunist was William Kinman, whom Agent Baldwin stigmatized as "one of the worst of the border men that I have had to deal with for the past three years."[40] Kinman had been a principal boomer of the mineral wealth of the Wichita Mountains. For some time he had been operating a small smelter with which he pretended to refine ore from the reservation. Kinman also was trying to sell lots in an alleged townsite, again on Indian land, and was suspected of being the author of erroneous reports about the opening of the reservation that kept both Indians and whites on edge. Agent Baldwin managed to have the sooner removed from the reservation in 1898, and Kinman promptly had the Oklahoma delegate to Congress intercede for him. The very responsiveness of the United States government to its citizens made it very difficult to safeguard the rights and property of the noncitizen Indian.

The boomers and sooners did drive the Indians into the arms of the cattlemen. By the mid-1890s Indian opposition to leasing had evaporated with a growing recognition that in the cattlemen they had allies in the fight against the Jerome Agreement. And the grass money, of course, was increasingly important to the tribesmen.

Not that grass money was the only form in which Indians collected from cattlemen. In 1896 White Wolf, a conservative Comanche frequently aligned against Quanah, was on the payroll of holders of one lease for $35 a month.[41] A chief of influence such as White Wolf or Lone Wolf, who was drawing $25 a month in the early 1890s from a rancher with a 23,000-acre pasture,[42] could guarantee the cattleman relative immunity from the intrusions of other Indians.

Less prominent tribesmen discovered another technique for sharing in the bonanza. They would claim 160 acres in leased pasture, go through the motions of planting a crop, and then collect from the cattleman when his stock invaded their "farm." Such individuals could be bought off by a payment of $15 or $20 or an occasional steer. All these operators were pikers compared with Quanah. It is impossible to determine how much he received from the cattlemen, although his style of living suggests it certainly was more than the $25 or $35 a month Lone Wolf and White Wolf rated. The cattlemen offered as one excuse for their being unable to pay more than six cents an acre for pasture, that they had to pay large sums to Quanah to lobby for them in Washington and with the Indians. Quanah admitted this to the commissioner of Indian Affairs but insisted guilelessly that "the money I got was from the cow men and not out of the lease fund."[43]

In the 1890s the southern part of the reservation, which was Comanche country, remained the site of a few very large pastures totaling about 1.3 million acres. The cattlemen leasing them during most of the decade were still members of the Big Five (see p. 181). In any given year fifteen or twenty other individuals, including squaw men such as Edward Clark and Emmett Cox, might hold leases to an additional 300,000 or 400,000 acres. A significant difference between the Big Five and the other leasers was that the former, in addition to having much more extensive holdings, ran their own cattle in their pastures year after year and had a stake in maintaining good fences, cattle tanks, and corrals. In contrast, most of the smaller leasers would sublet their pastures or take in the cattle of other ranchers. The agents and the Indians found the Big Five to be more dependable and preferred to lease to them.

Over the years the amount of grass money steadily rose,

in part due to more land being offered for lease. The initiative for this came from Cyrus Beede, the Quaker who in the 1870s had been on the staff of the central superintendent and who was now an inspector for the secretary of the interior. The elderly Beede believed that the Indians profited more from leasing land to cattlemen such as the Big Five than renting their farms to whites who had failed elsewhere and were just seeking a way of becoming sooners.[44]

Another cause for an increase in grass money was the action taken to limit the amount of pasture any Indian or squaw man could claim. Something did need to be done. George W. Conover in the mid-1890s was in control of 36,640 acres, which he sublet to a cattleman for $2,600 while paying into the tribal coffers only $300.[45] Other squaw men had more modest holdings, but every dollar they made in this fashion was money that did not go into the common fund. Of the tribesmen themselves, Quanah seems to have been the only one operating in a fashion comparable to some of the squaw men. The Comanche chief had his own 44,000-acre pasture that he leased to cattlemen and pocketed the proceeds.[46]

Agent Baldwin fought hard to reduce the holdings of the squaw men and eliminate the petty take of Indians such as Lone Wolf and White Wolf. In the process he made some bitter enemies; nevertheless he managed to reduce individual holdings to no more than 10 acres per head of stock actually owned by the individual, with the maximum number of acres set at 5,000. Baldwin did not disturb Quanah in his possession of the 44,000 acres because the agent needed the chief's support against the opponents he made among the squaw men, the traders, and the other Indians. However, Special Agent Gilbert B. Pray, who was at Anadarko investigating leases for several months in 1898, allied himself with a faction opposed to Baldwin and Quanah and reduced the chief's free pasture rights to the 5,000-acre ceiling.[47]

A final source of additional grass money was an increase

in the rental per acre from six cents to ten cents. As early as 1894 a jump to nine cents an acre had been suggested by William C. Shelley, an attorney whom the Comanche and associated tribes employed the year before to protect them against depredations claims. This did not make him popular with the cattlemen or with Quanah, who represented their interests among the Indians. Between 1893 and 1898 every year saw the enactment of a new one-year lease at six cents per acre. About November or December the agent would remind the Indian commissioner that the current leases would lapse April 1. Around February Quanah, at government expense if he could get authorization, or lacking that, traveling on the cattlemen, would lead a delegation to Washington to make the case for renewing for a year the leases of the Big Five at six cents per acre.

The cattlemen would have liked longer leases and early in 1894 attempted to achieve this by working through Colonel J. D. Cobb of Georgia, who just happened to be a cousin of Secretary of the Interior Hoke Smith. Samuel B. Burnett and others signed contracts with Colonel Cobb to pay him one cent an acre if he could get their six-cent-an-acre contracts renegotiated for three-year terms.[48] Apparently the colonel could not produce, but for obvious reasons the cattlemen were prepared to go to some lengths to be spared the inconvenience of negotiating annual contracts.

The cattlemen finally got their wish, although in other respects they were unhappy with the contract. In January 1898 the Indian Office advertised that it would be accepting bids on the pastures for a three-year period, but at a minimum of ten cents an acre. Burnett, Waggoner, and Sugg, who were the surviving members of the Big Five, ignored the advertisement and submitted their routine six-cent-an-acre bids. These the secretary of the interior summarily rejected. In a last ditch effort to avoid paying the higher rate Burnett wrote the secretary a long letter on the economics of running cattle on the reservation. Meanwhile, Quanah had collected $400 in "wages" from Burnett and Waggoner.[49] Together with Apiatan, representing the Kiowas, and Apache John of the Kiowa-Apaches, he headed for Washington. In a conference with Commissioner Jones, Quanah spent most of the time responding to charges that he was on the payroll of the cattlemen. The secretary of the interior held firm to the ten-cent-an-acre minimum and the cattlemen capitulated.

Agent Baldwin did not take an active role in the fight over increasing the rent per acre, because he was too immersed in several fights of his own. In his three years on the reservation Baldwin demonstrated all that was good and much that was bad in having a professional military man serve as Indian agent. He was completely honest and his formula for administering an agency, as might be expected, stressed control: "Govern them with kindness but firmness, compelling those who are disinclined to work to do so; allow no idleness; punish the wrong doers under their own laws."[50]

Baldwin not only tried to discourage loitering around the agency headquarters, more to the point he tried to find employment for Indians on the government payroll and urged the traders to hire them. The agent wholeheartedly supported the program to locate the tribesmen on their own homesteads and tried to ensure that they remained on them to cultivate their crops and care for their livestock rather than visit around the reservation as was their want. To this end he encouraged the Indians to buy farm wagons instead of the buggies they preferred, and the agency blacksmith was directed not to repair buggies if any wagons required attention. Because rough usage and poor maintenance made the Indians frequently resort to the blacksmith's facilities, Baldwin soon had most of them at least riding in farm wagons.

Although he pushed the opening of farms by Indians, the agent was not reluctant to permit them to employ white farmers if agency employment, absence at school, or bad health prevented the Indian from working his own land.

Baldwin also attempted to ensure that there was some reasonable distribution of the farm equipment issued to the Indians. Too often the chiefs, headmen, and squaw men had received a disproportionate share. In some cases it was purely a status matter since the equipment would not be used. In his inspection trips (he left Anadarko more than most agents) Baldwin found "stacked up, often in the brush, plows (as many as six in one place), harrows, rakes, forks, shovels, cooking stoves, and everything that had ever been issued to an Indian."[51] Some of the equipment issued the tribesmen found its way into the hands of whites. One estimate was that at least half the barbed wire issued in one three-year period to Indians to fence their farms was sold by them for a fraction of its real value.[52] In an effort to educate the Indians that "everything they have . . . is of some value, and it is not right for them to give things away for nothing," Baldwin insisted on paying for his food and lodging as he traveled around the agency.[53] He left no clue as to how this sat with his charges, for whom hospitality was a virtue.

Other whites were happy to take advantage of the Indians' lack of a highly developed sense of property values. Indeed, Baldwin declared, "Half the problem of advancing these Indians lies in protecting them against the avarice of the white man."[54] He had in mind the trader who encouraged the Indians to go deeply into debt for unnecessary purchases and the white man who prevailed upon the improvident Indian to sell him a steer for a fraction of what the Indian could get if he held it for a few months and sold it to the government.

As the grass payments became larger, these semiannual affairs drew a sordid crowd intent on getting as much of the money as they could wheedle, cajole, or threaten from the Indians. Baldwin recalled one such group:

> One sold lumber . . . one a patent medicine peddler, one an Eye Dr., one a mescal [peyote] seller, water melon, green apple and peach peddler, some who had

partly built Dugouts, some who had made fruitless
attempts at putting up fences for breaking an acre or
two of ground. Divine Healers, men bringing stolen or
strayed Indian stock, with demands that they be paid
for their services. . . . Grocers and other merchants . . .
and last but not least the sewing machine peddler and
horse thieves.[55]

After seeing this flight of vultures descend on the Indians
at one grass payment, Baldwin had his Indian police arrest
fifteen or twenty of them and escort the whites from the
reservation. He topped off this performance by lecturing
the bemused Indians on the economics of the marketplace.
Baldwin believed that the only solution for the moment
was a greater degree of government paternalism until the
Indians could learn to fend for themselves.

This agent was not afraid to disturb special interests in
his campaign to protect the Indians. As previously noted
he alienated the squaw men by depriving them of more
free pasture than their per capita share. Baldwin also
forced the beef contractor to pay for pasture rights for the
thousands of cattle he had been grazing on the reservation
in excess of the number needed to fulfill his contract. The
agent upset the traders by recommending the licensing of
more competitors and by trying to curtail their use of
credit to reduce the Indians to what he called "positive
peonage."[56] Baldwin likewise instituted a new method for
disposition of hides: hides the traders had been paying the
Indians only $1.00 each for in 1895 were earning the
Indians $4.05 by 1898.

This reform did not endear him to the traders; nor were
they happy with his success in persuading the tribesmen to
invest $50,000 of grass money in stock cattle after he al-
ready had convinced them to set aside $25,000 for a new
school. At this time the Indians were in debt to the traders
about $40,000. The whites reacted to the stock cattle
purchase and the plans for the new school as if the agent
had taken the money right out of their pockets, as indeed

he had. From their standpoint the final indignity was Baldwin's permitting, if not encouraging, the Indians to leave the reservation to shop at nearby towns. The agent argued that his charges would benefit from the lower prices to be found off the reservation,[57] but it is little wonder that the traders were out for Baldwin's scalp.

The efforts of the squaw men and traders to get Baldwin were under way late in 1895 and continued unabated until his recall to active duty with the outbreak of the Spanish-American War. It was a no-holds barred contest. Four of the squaw men, including George W. Conover and William A. Deitrick, who were married to Comanches, retained Attorney William C. Shelley, who was also the lawyer for the three tribes in depredations cases. As a former Indian Service employee based in Washington, Shelley had contacts that enabled him—according to reservation rumor—to read all correspondence relating to the Anadarko agency. Exploiting their extensive connections on the reservation and the factionalism endemic among the tribesmen, the anti-Baldwin squaw men and traders developed a base of support among the Indians. Anti-Baldwin councils began to be held and petitions prepared attacking the agent. Indian leaders in this movement included the Comanches Eschiti and Big Looking Glass and the Kiowas Lone Wolf and his brother Chaddlekaungky.

The attacks were not only on Baldwin but also on any supporters he might have on the reservation. The agent himslef was charged with excessive drinking, corruption in connection with the purchase of stock cattle for the Indians, and harassment of his opponents. Quanah and Apiatan were accused of polygamy, which led to their removal from the Court of Indian Offenses. A trader who had been permitted to open a store near Quanah's ranch, to the displeasure of Samuel Strauss, who operated the Red Store near Fort Sill, was accused of allowing Indians to gamble on his property and temporarily lost his license.

Baldwin was a fighter, as his service record demonstrated, and he struck back. He inspired counterpetitions and coun-

cils that passed resolutions in his behalf. He solicited affidavits from cattlemen on "corrupt transactions" involving
ten of his enemies, including Samuel Strauss, the Cleveland
brothers, and former Special Agent E. E. White.[58] The
agent dismissed the charges of corruption against himself
as originating with individuals who opposed him for trying
to prevent them from fleecing the Indians. He denounced
Shelley for a conflict of interest in representing both the
three tribes and the squaw men.

Samuel Strauss was accused by Baldwin of employing a
clerk who was having an affair with one of the Comanche
girls from the Fort Sill School, and of opposing every effort by the agent to promote the Indians' welfare. The
agent condemned squaw men as "generally speaking . . .
the worst type of white man on the frontier, and a curse
and menace to the advancement and welfare of the Indians."[59] The two Indian judges, Chaddlekaungky and Frank
Moetah, with whom the Indian commissioner had replaced
Apiatan and Quanah, also felt the agent's wrath. He described Moetah as a "worthless, good-for-nothing Indian"
and Chaddlekaungky as a bribe taker in a previous unsuccessful tour of duty on the court.[60]

Defending Quanah of Polygamy charges proved more
difficult for Baldwin than smearing his opponents. Back
in 1890 the Comanche chief had aroused official wrath by
courting a prospective seventh wife. During Lieutenant
Nichols's brief tenure as agent, Quanah actually acquired
her from another Indian for a team of horses, a buggy, and
$100.[61] Topay was an attractive young woman of about
twenty and Quanah was reluctant to give her up despite
the demands of Commissioner of Indian Affairs Daniel M.
Browning, who had been tipped off by some of the chief's
enemies. Facing dismissal from the Court of Indian Offenses, Quanah signed a pledge to surrender Topay. In a
trip to Washington a few weeks later, however, the chief
discussed the matter with Commissioner Browning and
heard what he thought was permission to retain Topay. As
Quanah later liked to tell the story, he had informed

Browning that he loved all his wives, had children by all of them, and would leave it to the commissioner to select the ones he should give up. Faced with this task Browning stayed his efforts to turn Quanah into a monogamist. Nevertheless, three years later Commissioner Jones summarily deposed the chief from the court for polygamy. Baldwin staged an election in which Quanah and Apiatan handily whipped Big Looking Glass and Frank Moetah, but Jones was not impressed.

As the struggle intensified, more parties were drawn in and it became even more confusing. Dudley P. Brown, the trader with whom Agent Adams had had trouble, was a close associate of Baldwin during his early months as agent. Some said that Brown helped supply the liquor that the agent was rumored to be imbibing to excess.[62] Then for reasons unknown, the agent and his former drinking buddy became bitter enemies, and Baldwin recommended against the renewal of Brown's trading license. The agent then seized some cattle Brown was running on the reservation illegally and the trader responded with a suit against Baldwin in which he was awarded a judgment.[63] Commissioner Jones settled this skirmish by relicensing Brown on the understanding that he would cancel his legal proceedings against Baldwin and pay all the court costs. The trader was slow to do this and capped his campaign against the agent with an attempt to get the secretary of war to court-martial him![64] Although Brown failed at that, Baldwin also was unsuccessful in a second effort to have Brown's trading license canceled.

Commissioner W. A. Jones played a strange role in events at the Kiowa, Comanche, and Wichita Agency in Baldwin's years. Although regarded by contemporaries as honest and reasonably efficient, the commissioner allowed himself to become a partisan of the Shelley-trader-squaw man coalition against Baldwin. The explanation may be that he was too much under the influence of one of his subordinates, Special Agent Gilbert B. Pray. Late in 1897 both the Indian commissioner and Special Agent Pray visited Anadarko, as did Attorney Shelley. Within a few weeks Quanah and Apiatan had been discharged as judges, the trader near Quanah's ranch had lost his license, and Pray was filing charges in Washington against Agent Baldwin. The outraged agent responded with a letter to Commissioner Jones blaming him for the mess that had developed:

> It is very evident to me that you are fully under control of that gang of people who have heretofore defrauded and cheated the Indians and you must bear in mind that I am not going to be a party to it.
>
> Ever since you have been here there has been more disturbance and more trouble among the Indians than has existed here for the past three years, and it has all been brought about by the influence which you left.[65]

Only an agent who was also an army officer could risk writing such a letter to his administrative superior in the Indian Service. The day before he wrote it, Baldwin asked Hugh L. Scott, then in Washington, to plead his case with the secretary of the interior and General Nelson A. Miles, the ranking officer of the army. The same day Baldwin told off Jones, he wrote the secretary informing him that Scott would be delivering to him several papers that the agent feared might not be passed up through the regular channels.

Agent Baldwin had another ally in the East, the Indian Rights Association. Its Washington agent had gone to bat for him early in 1897, when there had been a move in progress to return Baldwin to army duty to make way for George D. Day, who wanted to resume the post at Anadarko he had vacated in 1893.[66] Early in 1898, when Special Agent Pray and his allies on the reservation were making it difficult for Agent Baldwin, the association again intervened at the War Department in his behalf.[67] But the beginning of the Spanish-American War ended the controversy as the army officers serving as Indian agents were recalled from those assignments. Before he left Anadarko Baldwin had the satisfaction of seeing the Comanches and associated tribes vote not to renew their contract with W. C. Shelley and to shift their legal business to Charles P. Lincoln.

Even with Frank Baldwin out of the picture the struggle among the factions sputtered on. Special Agent Pray returned to Anadarko and did his best to persuade the Indians to continue with Shelley, as he made clear in a revealing letter to Commissioner Jones:

> The war between the factions of these Indians is still on. . . . The old crowd of Baldwin adherents, are bound to force the fight, and find out which shall be master, and the issue is on the employment of an Attorney. All of the men who have been known as your friends and mine; the men who were against Baldwin and his plans are for Mr. Shelley. . . . I cannot yield to the [Apiatan] and Quanah Parker element.[68]

Nevertheless, Shelley did lose out. At a second council called by the new agent, William T. Walker, the Indians again voted by a substantial margin to employ Lincoln.

Shelley continued to represent the squaw men and Pray had some subsequent successes. When Inspector Cyrus Beede was on the reservation in September 1898 he tended to support Pray's criticisms of Quanah and Apiatan as polygamists and leaders in the peyote cult. However, the Indian Rights Association had a representative there about the same time who sided with Quanah and Apiatan, or at least he was very suspicious of Gilbert Pray and questioned a grazing lease held by Dudley P. Brown. As a result the association asked for another investigation of the reservation. Further checking by the association revealed that Dudley Brown's partner in the grazing lease was the son-in-law of Utah Senator Frank J. Cannon,[69] which may go a long way toward explaining the ability of Brown to remain on the reservation regardless the many charges against him.

The inspection requested by the Indian Rights Association was carried out by James McLaughlin, an Indian Service veteran of unimpeachable character. Inspector McLaughlin concluded that the association was unduly alarmist, but he did confirm that Agent Walker had been unable to escape the shadow of Special Agent Pray and probably should be replaced by a stronger man. McLaughlin also confirmed reports that Pray and Shelley were partners in a mining company set up to seek gold in the Wichita Mountains, a highly dubious enterprise for one of the commissioner's special agents. McLaughlin's report also included a sorry commentary on the impact of the intense factionalism: "I found that there was no difficulty in procuring affidavits for or against on any question."[70] Obviously what was needed was a change in personnel in the hope that a new agent could make a fresh start and avoid being caught up in the clash of factions. To make the attempt the government brought out of retirement Lieutenant Colonel James F. Randlett.

In his first year in office Randlett managed to damp the fires of factionalism on the reservation, but not without getting singed. He made an obvious effort to avoid prejudging anyone. Taking office July 1, 1899, Randlett set as one of his tasks reconciliation of the chiefs who headed opposing factions. Commissioner Jones, because of Special Agent Pray's influence, had favored the Eschiti–Big Looking Glass–Chaddlekaungky group over the Quanah–Apiatan combination. By the time Randlett became agent, Big Looking Glass had died and Chaddlekaungky would do so in 1900. The agent persuaded the commissioner to replace Chaddlekaungky on the Court of Indian Offenses with Apiatan and to recognize the latter as chief of the Kiowas.

Clarifying the leadership among the Comanches was a more difficult matter. Quanah was upset because Eschiti had a commission making him "a principal chief." Randlett recognized quickly that of the two Indians Quanah was the stronger personality and persuaded Commissioner Jones to issue him a new commission.[71] This one read "chief of the Comanches"—satisfying Quanah—and the agent could go on to other problems.

Dudley P. Brown rapidly exhausted the new agent's

patience and forbearance. Randlett began his administration by assisting Brown in getting a refund on a pasture lease, reasoning that his predecessor perhaps had failed to give Brown an even break. However, within less than a year of his arrival at Anadarko, Agent Randlett had come to see Brown for what he was, a grasping, conniving troublemaker. The ex-trader was up to his old tactics. He had managed to lease a pasture that was listed as containing 5,000 acres when it was actually closer to 15,000.[72] Months after subletting the pasture to other parties he still had not supplied the bond required by his contract. Randlett then demanded Brown's expulsion from the reservation because he no longer required residence as a licensed trader. An acting Indian commissioner consented to Brown's ouster. Incidentally, Frank Cannon was no longer representing Utah in the Senate.

Dudley Brown's eviction came at the end of an era for the Comanches. Since the negotiation of the Jerome Agreement in 1892 their income had increased to the point that they no longer went hungry, despite the tapering off of government support. Quanah had had his role as chief confirmed, but a new generation of educated Comanches was beginning to edge into power. They had had a crash course in reservation politics in the constant maneuvering of the coalitions that had formed around the special interest groups on the reservation—the traders, the squaw men, and the cattlemen.

Thirty years had elapsed since the Treaty of Medicine Lodge, but the Comanches had not been transformed into the self-sufficient homesteaders envisioned by the architects of United States Indian policy. Indian farms there were, but most were tilled by white sharecroppers while the Indian proprietor was content to lead a marginal existence on the income from his farm and his per capita share of the grass payments. Unfortunately, the blow the Indians had been dreading was about to fall. Pressured by the boomers and sooners, Congress finally was ready to ratify the Jerome Agreement, which would wreck reservation life as the Comanches had known it since the 1870s.

11. Ratifying the Jerome Agreement

For eight years the possible ratification of the Jerome Agreement had hung over the heads of the Comanches, Kiowas, and Kiowa-Apaches. They brought it up at every council regardless of the agenda—evidence of how it prayed on their minds.

The agreement had been examined by both Commissioner T. J. Morgan and Secretary John W. Noble before being transmitted to Congress by President Harrison. With reference to the compensation provided the Indians, Morgan observed: "The price paid, while considerable in excess of that paid to the Cheyennes and Arapahoes seems to be fair and reasonable." He endorsed the adoption of the eighteen intermarried whites listed in the agreement but opposed the clause granting 160 acres to seven "friends of the Indian," including Lieutenant Scott and Agent Day. "If this is allowed," he declared, "we may expect that hereafter the success of negotiations looking to cession of Indian lands, will depend upon benefits conferred upon officers of the government stationed among the Indians."[1]

Secretary Noble limited his objections to the inclusion of Agent Day and Lieutenant Scott in the list of beneficiaries. However, he proposed a clause be added to the agreement to protect the Indians against any claims arising out of depredations cases.[2]

President Harrison sent the agreement to the Senate in January 1893. The Fifty-second Congress ended before any action could be taken on it, but each succeeding Congress saw at least one bill introduced calling for the ratification of a version of the agreement. The first was submitted by Delegate Dennis T. Flynn of Oklahoma Territory in September 1893.

The Indians and their allies mobilized their forces to

postpone ratification as long as possible, or barring that, to secure revisions in the agreement that would increase the size of their allotments and hike the price per acre the United States would pay for the surplus land.

Although Reverend J. J. Methvin was scheduled to be one of the beneficiaries of the agreement, his church was the scene of two gatherings to protest the negotiations. One of them had occurred on October 17, 1892, while the Cherokee Commission was still collecting signatures. At that meeting more than 400 Indians signed a memorial against agreement, but the original never reached Washington. Eight years later Reverend Methvin recalled that he had turned it over to Agent Day to send through channels. Early in January 1900 Methvin gave a copy of it to Agent Randlett, who sent it on to the Indian commissioner, who in turn forwarded it to the secretary of the interior. It was Randlett's opinion that Agent Day, a possible beneficiary of the agreement, had deliberately suppressed the memorial.[3]

The second Indian council at Reverend Methvin's to protest the agreement came in May 1893 and followed by a week one at Fort Sill held under the auspices of Hugh Scott. The council at Methvin's went on record in favor of delaying ratification until 1898, when the annuity provisions of the Treaty of Medicine Lodge would expire. The Fort Sill meeting produced a document alleging that Joshua Given had obtained signatures for the agreement by misleading Kiowas into believing that it would not be ratified until 1898. Moreover, when they had learned that such a delay was not guaranteed, some Kiowas had asked that their names be removed from the agreement, thus reducing the number of signatures below the three-fourths required. Their request had been refused by the Cherokee Commission.

The Fort Sill document was sent to the president of the United States through military channels. In an accompanying letter, Lieutenant Scott called for postponement of ratification, reasoning that "many of these Indians believe they were tricked into signing." Hugh Scott predicted that "if these lands are opened to settlement any time in the immediate future, these Indians will be converted from a people having the prospect of a useful and happy future into a band of miserable and degraded beggars."[4] The Fort Sill commandant endorsed Scott's statement, and General Nelson A. Miles added his recommendation for an investigation and the annulment of the agreement if the lieutenant's charges were substantiated.

When the Indian commissioner finally received the material, he dispatched a copy of it to Agent Brown, who had just relieved Day, with orders that Brown conduct an investigation. Hugh Brown's report in August 1893 revealed that during the negotiation of the agreement the Indians indeed had been threatened with the Dawes Act and that Joshua Given had misled them as to the date the reservation would be opened. Agent Brown concluded his report with the observation: "The Kiowas, Comanches, and Apaches are almost without exception, now that they understand it, earnestly opposed to the agreement."[5]

Nevertheless, the following month Delegate Flynn introduced his bill for ratification, inspiring additional protests from the Indians and their supporters. James Mooney of the Bureau of Ethnology, who had done field work among the Kiowas and Kiowa-Apaches, called upon the Indian Rights Association to help block the agreement. "I believe," stated Mooney, "it can be proven that this agreement was procured by threats, bribery and deception . . . and that if consummated it will work [the Indians'] speedy destruction."[6] Mooney proposed that the association contact Lieutenant Scott and Captain J. M. Lee, a former agent of the Cheyennes and Arapahos, for additional information. In response to a query from Herbert Welsh, the corresponding secretary and one of the founders of the Indian Rights Association, Captain Lee claimed no personal knowledge of the negotiation of the Jerome Agreement. He did, however, express confidence in James

Mooney and in the belief of Lieutenant Scott and other witnesses that the agreement "was accomplished through threats, cajolery, misrepresentation, and possibly bribery."[7]

Meanwhile, Herbert Welsh was directing C. C. Painter, the association's Washington lobbyist, to look into the entire matter, and the Indians were preparing another memorial to Congress. Containing the usual charges of deception and misrepresentation, this memorial was signed by Quanah, Lone Wolf, and 321 other Indians. Painter twice took his protest, including Mooney's letter, directly to Indian Commissioner Daniel M. Browning. When a congressman asked for the Interior Department's reaction to the ratification bill, Commissioner Browning passed on to the secretary, without comment, a bundle of material including letters from Painter, Lee, and Mooney, Agent Hugh G. Brown's report of August 1893, and Scott's memorial of May 1893.

When the Indians asked permission to send a delegation to Washington to meet with members of Congress about the Jerome Agreement, Commissioner Browning refused. However, Quanah was in Washington in January, apparently traveling at the expense of the cattlemen, and again in March. The latter visit followed a trip to Carlisle by Quanah and Lone Wolf. Richard H. Pratt, Carlisle's superintendent and founder, interceded for them with Commissioner Browning and they were permitted to go on to Washington to appear before committees considering the Flynn bill. There they were joined by a delegation from Anadarko escorted by Lieutenant Scott and headed by Apiatan and Apache John. Before a subcommittee of the House Indian Affairs Committee, Quanah and Lone Wolf recited their by now familiar story of fraud and deception. A few days later C. C. Painter was reporting to Welsh that the Flynn bill was dead and that he believed that the Jerome Agreement would never be ratified. Painter was willing to take much of the credit for stopping the bill, but the cattlemen also were entitled to a share of the credit. Texas Congressman Joseph W. Bailey was representing their interest in postponement of ratification, although he maintained that he was concerned only for the condition of the United States Treasury.[8]

During the next three years Painter's optimism seemed justified. The Fifty-third Congress expired without taking further action, and although the Fifty-fourth saw two bills introduced, neither of them got out of committee. In January 1896 Commissioner Browning assured a delegation including Quanah and Eschiti, the latter making his first trip east, that "I cannot tell what Congress will do but we are trying very hard not to have ratification."[9] But pressure was mounting in Oklahoma Territory and the surrounding states for access to the Fort Sill Country, as the boomers liked to call it.

The Fifty-fifth Congress, which opened in March 1897, reflected the growing demand for ratification. Early in the first session the House Committee on Indian Affairs received a communication from Agent Baldwin referring to the possibility of ratification as "a most ill-advised act."[10] The agent stressed the concern of the Indians and proposed that a delegation be permitted to go to Washington to testify against the agreement. Late in April, Quanah headed east with Apiatan, Apache John, Big Looking Glass, and two interpreters. One of the latter was William Tivis, a Comanche who had returned to the reservation in 1890 after nine years at Carlisle and had become active in reservation politics. Agent Baldwin entrusted Quanah with a petition the agent had circulated among the Indians, and he arranged to have Hugh L. Scott, now a captain stationed in Washington, keep an eye on the delegation.

Captain Scott accompanied the delegation to a conference with Commissioner Jones. The captain opened the session with an impassioned plea for justice for the Indians: "To plunge them at this time into the midst of the hostile population of Oklahoma would as surely work their destruction as the abandonment of a baby to a pack of hungry wolves." Scott charged that the Cherokee Commission "by threats, coercion and deceit practised upon these unsuspecting people who trusted in the honor of the representatives of the Government, obtained a fraudulent agreement." Quanah and Apiatan seconded what the eloquent Scott had said. Commissioner Jones responded that if they succeeded in having the agreement recalled from Congress and it were referred to him, he would "do all in my power to right the wrongs that seem to me [to] have been done in the past."[11]

In an effort to stave off the opening of the reservation and the introduction among the Indians of what Agent Baldwin called "that class of white people who are ever ready in their greed to pounce down upon them,"[12] the Indians considered ceding land to other tribes. At a council in July 1897 the Kiowas, Comanches, and Kiowa-Apaches discussed selling 160 acres to each of 206 Wyandots who were seeking a new home. Quanah as usual spoke often and well, expressing his approval of the idea and raising the possibility of persuading Congress to scrap the agreement and substitute for it a law that would authorize opening the reservation to purchases by other tribes. At this time also the Comanches and associated tribes were considering making available 50,000 acres of their land to the Geronimo band of Apaches who were assigned to Fort Sill. Agent Baldwin strongly endorsed this approach to opening the reservation, pointing out that it represented "an opportunity to these people to develop a policy of their own without being under restraint or compulsion, as was undoubtedly the case . . . in 1892."[13] But Congress was a better vehicle for the development of policies in the interest of white settlers, and the Wyandot and Apache proposals were heard of no more.

Before the Fifty-fifth Congress closed, despite a recommendation of Secretary of Interior C. N. Bliss that the government shelve the Jerome Agreement and negotiate anew with the Indians, the House passed a bill to ratify the agreement. This version was less desirable to the Indians than the original because it would have made payment to the Indians contingent on sale of the surplus land to settlers and on the adjudication of the Chickasaw and Choctaw claims.

The Indian Rights Association, which supported the general principle of allotment and disagreed with the government only on the size of the allotments and the price to be paid for the surplus land, rushed a circular into print. It advised 480-acre allotments and introduced testimony by employees of the United States Geological Survey on the inadequacy of 160-acre farms in view of the quality of the soil and the paucity of rainfall in that part of the country. The circular set $1.25 an acre, about 50 percent more than the Jerome Agreement provided, as a fair price for the surplus land. The publication was aimed at the senators, who now had to consider the bill passed by the House. Senator O. H. Platt of Connecticut, who was friendly to Indian Rights Association causes, assured its Washington representative that he was confident the bill would fail in the Senate.[14]

The Fifty-fifth Congress was in recess from July until December 1898. During this period S. M. Brosius, now representing the association in Washington, made his first visit to Anadarko and concluded that the 160-acre allotments should not be tripled, but quadrupled to 640 if the Indians were to have a fair chance of self-support. When Congress reconvened, however, Brosius had to admit that the chances of increasing the allotments to even 480 acres were not good. The Rock Island Railroad with lines adjoining and crossing the reservation had a big stake in seeing it opened to white settlers. The railroad had its own friends in Congress. Prominent among them was Representative Charles Curtis of Kansas, whose modicum of Indian blood was widely publicized years later when he served as Herbert Hoover's vice-president. In the Senate, Arkansas's James K. Jones favored the ratification bill, presumably because he was an adviser to the Choctaws and Chickasaws, who stood a good chance of getting whatever money was raised by the sale of the surplus land. Democratic senators generally were favorable to the legislation because it would promote statehood for Oklahoma, which could be expected to send a Democratic delegation to Congress. With these various forces working in its behalf, the bill was reported favorably by the Senate Committee on Indian Affairs.[15]

Alarmed, the Indian Rights Association put out another circular in February 1899 repeating the demand for allotments of at least 480 acres. Reflecting the controversy growing out of the territory acquired from Spain the previous year, the circular spoke of the dangers of domestic colonialism:

> It seems especially important that Congress should refuse to sanction so gross an act of injustice . . . at the very moment when we are assuming responsibility for the elevation and protection of millions of island wards. The enactment of this measure will create an additional bad precedent in the treatment of our dependent races.[16]

The senators received copies of the circular, and Welsh also sent it to several eastern newspapers and magazines with the request that they publish all or portions of it. One of the editors receiving the circular was Lyman Abbott of *The Outlook*. He replied that he would be happy to publish the material if Welsh could indicate how Indians could be placed on the same footing as other citizens while retaining government protection for their land.[17] This was the common dilemma of the white reformer who took the Indian as his cause. In the late nineteenth century assimilation was the almost universally accepted panacea for the Indian's problems, but it was a two-edged sword. If he received the rights and privileges of the citizen, he received complete title to his allotment and risked losing what little land remained to him.

Perhaps some of the senators were impressed by the arguments advanced by the Indian Rights Association against ratification. The bill did fail of passage in the usual rush that accompanied the closing of the Fifty-fifth Congress, with Senator Platt getting credit from the association for a vigorous rearguard action. However, the Jerome Agreement had come close to ratification and its opponents could not have been optimistic as the Fifty-sixth Congress was gaveled to order for the first time in December 1899.

The opposition to the Jerome Agreement had done what they could to prepare for the expected onslaught. The new agent, James Randlett, had called an Indian council in October to draw up yet another petition against ratification. For once the factions ceased their bickering and Randlett, who had been warned of their contentiousness before he took office, was pleasantly surprised to see their unanimity on the issue. Quanah in attacking the agreement referred to his much traveled state:

> I have been in Washington 16 times and 5 since we signed that treaty, and have told all the officials of the Government every time that we were misled when we gave our names to that treaty, and I have told . . . that if anything was done to open up our country for settlement, the Government should see to it that more land per capita be given us because our country is not a good farming country and we would have to get our supplies from raising cattle.[18]

Senator Platt, acting on the advice of the Indian Rights Association, also had moved in October to buttress the argument that the Indians needed more than 160 acres to be independent of government support. He asked the Interior Department to conduct an investigation as to the condition of the Indians and the productivity of their land. In November, Special Agent Gilbert Pray was again sent to Anadarko and together with Agent Randlett prepared a report based on the testimony of squaw men, missionaries, and other whites thoroughly familiar with the region.

Their report was ready when the Senate in December passed a Platt-inspired resolution calling for information on the Kiowa, Comanche, and Kiowa-Apache Reservation. Pray and Randlett concluded, according to Indian Commissioner Jones's version of their report, that owing to frequent drought and hot winds, farming was "a very precarious business on the best of lands and an absolute failure on the uplands," and that the Indians could not "reasonably be expected to gain [self-support] from the lands of the reservation if allowed to them . . . in tracts of less than 1,000 acres per family."[19]

Commissioner Jones was at last prepared to go all out in trying to persuade Congress to reject the agreement. In January he forwarded the petition Agent Randlett had originated back in October. In his accompanying letter he observed: "Although this office has not hitherto definitely opposed the ratification . . . the result of the investigation by Special Agent Pray and Agent Randlett is such as to lead it to conclude that the Agreement ought not to be ratified."[20] Two weeks later the commissioner transmitted the copy of the long-lost memorial of October 17, 1892, which Reverend Methvin had turned over to Randlett.

Meanwhile the proponents of the agreement in the House had attempted to shortcut the normal process by attaching it to the Indian Service appropriation bill. This maneuver was blocked by Representative Marriott Brosius of Pennsylvania on a point of order. But the agreement's supporters were successful in producing testimony challenging the Pray-Randlett report. Several Oklahomans, including the chief justice of the Supreme Court of Oklahoma and one of his associates on the bench, submitted statements to the effect that the reservation was much more productive than had been described. As a newspaper reported it, these Oklahomans maintained that if Congress learned "the real facts," "the cattlemen who had controlled the Indians, Indian Agents and Special Agents, would be compelled to move their herds and give way to higher civilization."[21]

The next three months would see a compromise worked out behind the scenes and the Jerome Agreement, or at least a version of it, become law. The House passed a bill early in March 1900 that limited the Indians to 160 acres each and, like earlier bills, would not have guaranteed them a cent for the remainder of the reservation, payment being conditional on sales to settlers and adjudication of the Choctaw and Chickasaw claims. The Indian Rights Association dispatched letters to editors and senators demouncing the bill, one of them damning it as "utterly destructive of that honor and good faith which should characterize our dealings with any people, and especially with one too weak to enforce their rights as against us by any other means than an appeal to our sense of justice."[22]

The final bill, which was attached to another piece of Indian legislation for passage, was the result of bargaining between Senator Platt, who was the spokesman for the Indians' interests as interpreted by the Indian Rights Association, and the lobbyist of the Rock Island Railroad.[23] The railroad had resisted previous efforts to give the Indians allotments of more than 160 acres of land. Now its lobbyist agreed to go along with setting aside an additional 480,000 acres, which amounted to about another 167 acres per Indian, to be held in common by the three tribes. The House bill was further improved by a provision that the Indians would be guaranteed at least $500,000 of the $2 million purchase price of the surplus land, with the remainder also to be theirs if the Choctaw and Chickasaw claims were disposed of.

While the fate of the Indians was being determined in Washington, they were dissuaded from sending a delegation to testify in their own behalf. The Indian Office reasoned that because both the Indian commissioner and the secretary of the interior had opposed the Jerome Agreement everything had been done that could be done. Quanah and Apiatan accepted this argument, but Lone Wolf and Big Tree did not and raised money and went to Washington, only to arrive too late to affect the outcome.

Undoubtedly, the final version of the Jerome Agreement was a better one for the Indians than some of its predecessors. They were able to retain 480,000 acres and were assured at least $500,000 for the land that the United

States was taking. S. M. Brosius, although quite aware that the agreement was being "railroaded" through Congress, believed that it was as good as the Indians could hope for given the strength of the opposition. Brosius found comfort in the contemporary myth that with intensive cultivation the lands of the region would improve in quality and the annual rainfall would increase.[24]

Nevertheless, Congress had made changes in the Jerome Agreement that the Indians were not permitted to pass upon, despite the Medicine Lodge Treaty requiring consent of three-fourths of the adult males to any land cession. Nor were the Indians directly involved in the final framing of the legislation. While they were dissuaded from sending an official delegation to Washington, a lobbyist for a railroad and a senator who took his lead from an association headed by a white man who had never seen the Kiowa, Comanche, and Kiowa-Apache Reservation determined their fate. A clause in the bill as it finally was passed was a clue as to who could get justice. It granted preference in filing land claims on the reservation to the white squatters who had occupied illegally the strip in the bend of the Washita River since the early 1890s, notwithstanding Agent Baldwin's best efforts to remove them. They now had been rewarded for their persistence by legislation that otherwise clearly violated the United States pledge to the Comanches and associated tribes in the Treaty of Medicine Lodge.

12. Adjusting to the Opening

Six years elapsed between Congress's ratification of a version of the Jerome Agreement in 1900 and the dissolution of the 480,000-acre tract that was the last land the Comanches and associated tribes held in common. During this period the Comanches suffered heavily from a smallpox epidemic as well as from the temptations and persecutions attendant upon the introduction among them of several thousand whites. Comanche unity, never a strong feature of tribal life, was damaged by another bitter controversy when some Comanches sided with Lone Wolf's Kiowa faction in a last ditch fight to stop the opening of their reservation.

In June 1900 Agent James F. Randlett broke the news to the Indians of Congress's action on the Jerome Agreement, presenting it as the best deal they could get under the circumstances. Speaking for the Comanches, Quanah and Eschiti accepted it. However, at a meeting a month later there were rumblings of discontent from Eschiti. The agent decided that it would be best if the Indians sent a delegation, at their own expense, to Washington to have what he had said confirmed by higher authority. The delegation included Eschiti, Quanah, and William Tivis; representing the Kiowas were Apiatan and Delos Lone Wolf. Delos, the Carlisle-educated nephew of Lone Wolf, was on the agency payroll as a district farmer, the best job held on the reservation by an Indian.

In Washington the delegation had a brief interview with President McKinley, but Quanah's plea that the opening of their reservation be postponed another five years and the individual Indian allotments be increased to 320 acres was cut short.[1] Congress had spoken and the Indians must conform.

The principal chiefs of the three tribes, Quanah, Apiatan, and Apache John, and most of their followers appeared resigned to their fate. The Kiowa faction headed by Lone Wolf, with Delos by his side, was not ready to submit and it soon secured the support of some Comanches who followed the lead of Eschiti and his main henchman, William Tivis. The latter, like Delos, was Carlisle trained. These irreconcilables wanted to hire an attorney to continue the fight, and the name of John T. Hill, the shady character who had helped negotiate the Jerome Agreement eight years earlier, was bandied about. Then the Supreme Court in December 1900 quashed the Choctaw and Chickasaw claims to the $1.5 million Congress had authorized in 1900 for the purchase of the surplus land, and the Lone Wolf faction's bargaining position improved.

In the spring of 1901 the irreconcilables took action. On their own initiative Lone Wolf and Delos proceeded to Washington and retained an attorney, not Hill but William M. Springer. Springer was well known in the nation's capital. A member for twenty years of Illinois's delegation to the House of Representatives, when he was defeated for reelection in 1894, he had been consoled with a federal judgeship in Indian Territory. Springer left that position in 1900 to practice law in Washington. As Lone Wolf's attorney his first move was to seek an injunction from the Supreme Court of the District of Columbia blocking the opening of the reservation. Springer also drafted a memorial, which he sent back to Anadarko by Delos with instructions to secure enough signatures to give weight to Lone Wolf's request for an injunction.[2]

This set off a tug of war on the reservation between the Lone Wolf faction and the three principal chiefs backed by Agent Randlett. The agent had Delos fired from his government job and replaced him with William E. Pedrick, a Kiowa squaw man and the brother-in-law of Apiatan. Attorney W. C. Shelley, who had some ties with the Lone Wolf faction, responded by urging the removal of Apiatan from the Court of Indian Offenses for being a polygamist.

Complaints were also made against Laura Pedrick, Apiatan's sister and William's wife, that were designed to get her discharged from her position as field matron in the Indian Service. But unlike the days when he seemed responsive to any suggestion from Attorney Shelley at the expense of Agent Frank Baldwin, Indian Commissioner Jones supported Agent Randlett in this struggle.

The agent was able to hold the principal chiefs in line with his advice "to make the most of the good bargain" Congress had provided,[3] although Delos managed to secure numerous signatures on the memorial Springer had drafted. Lone Wolf led a group of Indians who presented it to President McKinley early in June 1901. Attorney Springer also added the name of Eschiti and seven other Indians to Lone Wolf's petition to the District of Columbia Supreme Court, but to no avail. The court denied the injunction, reasoning that it could not intervene, because the Indians were subject to the control of Congress.[4] Attorney Springer promptly announced that he would appeal and expressed confidence that he could obtain for the Indians at least twice the sum the United States had agreed to pay them for their land. In September, Springer requested the Oklahoma Territory Supreme Court to stay the opening of the reservation, and again was denied. By that time all the Indians had been allotted homesteads and the surplus land had been opened for settlement.

Allotment had begun in late July 1900 and was completed within a year. Throughout the 1890s agents had encouraged the Indians to select their homesteads and many had done so. These areas were now confirmed to them if they did not intrude upon the tracts reserved for the military reservation, the agency, or the religious groups functioning on the reservation. If an Indian already had established himself on section 16 or 36 of a township he could remain there; otherwise these tracts were reserved for the support of public schools. With few exceptions the Indians were able to select the land they wished and an effort was made to assist them in obtaining the best land available. Unfortunately, most of the reservation was suited only for grazing and some Indians ended up with allotments of this variety. The location of the Indian homesteads tended to follow previous residential patterns. The Comanches generally selected homesteads south of the Wichita Mountains, while the Kiowas and Kiowa-Apaches clustered to the north.

When the Indians had first learned of the additional 480,000 acres available to them, they hoped that this meant an additional 160 acres per capita, making a total of 320.[5] They were speedily disabused of this since Congress had not intended that they should retain so much good land. The 480,000 acres would be selected from the inferior lands left after the round of 160-acre allotments and would be held in common.

Although the Indians were disappointed in their hopes for 320-acre homesteads, seventeen squaw men were able to pull it off in a patently unfair fashion. The Treaty of Medicine Lodge had provided that heads of families prepared to undertake careers as farmers could have up to 320 acres set aside for them. Joseph Chandler had applied as early as 1871, acting in the name of his Comanche wife Tomasa, who after Chandler's death married George W. Conover. Other squaw men recognized this as a possible loophole that would enable them to double the size of allotments permitted under the Jerome Agreement. In 1898 three squaw men applied for 320-acre allotments, and two of them, William Wyatt and John Nestell, retained William C. Shelley to represent them. Fourteen others, including Quanah's son-in-law Emmett Cox, also filed for 320 acres. Despite Agent Randlett's protest that the Indians would be upset "and the world will decide with them, that there is no justice in making such allowance,"[6] the squaw men retained their double allotments. It was yet another illustration of the white man's ability—and drive—to exploit the system to satisfy his lust for land.

The Indian not only lacked the knowledge to manipulate the system, he lacked the white man's powerful urge to do so.

The 480,000 acres Congress assigned to the Comanches and associated tribes to hold in common sparked a last battle among the white ranchers seeking to exploit the Indians. But whereas they once had been using two-thirds of the reservation, they now were reduced to quarreling about one-seventh of it. The bone of contention was referred to as the Big Pasture, a tract of about 400,000 acres fronting on Red River. The other 80,000 acres was in three tracts, two of them convenient to the Comanches, who had more cattle than the other two tribes.

Agent Randlett subdivided the Big Pasture into four units, which were then leased at ten cents an acre to four ranchers who had been on the reservation for years, E. C. Sugg, Samuel B. Burnett, Daniel Waggoner's son Tom, and Asher Silberstein. With the possible exception of Silberstein, no one was happy with the arrangement. Each could point to corrals, tanks, fences, and bunkhouses that he had constructed and maintained but was now forced to give up. In the confusion surrounding the opening of the reservation other ranchers pushed herds across Red River and intruded on pastures that Sugg, Burnett, and Waggoner had been leasing. Tom Waggoner damned them as "little cattle men that has no right whatever there." His piteous "I have no chance to do any thing only starve to death"[7] would have inspired more compassion had the Waggoner family not been one of the wealthiest in Texas. The trouble was that the ranchers' nearly twenty years preferential status on the reservation had given them a sense of proprietorship which was outraged by the other whites seeking the same advantages.

It was inevitable that with the total amount of land available drastically reduced, the ranchers should fall to quarreling among themselves about the disposition of the Big Pasture. Sugg and Burnett took their frustrations out on each other. Since Sugg's new pasture had been carved largely from Burnett's old lease, Burnett did his best to prevent Sugg's men from constructing the necessary fences. The major battle was fought in Washington, where both enlisted help. Sugg was aided by Representative Charles Curtis of Kansas and by an attorney for the Rock Island Railroad. But Burnett brought up even heavier artillery in the person of Texas Senator Joseph Bailey, who accompanied him on a visit to the commissioner of Indian Affairs. Burnett also was helped by a congressman who interceded for him with the secretary of the interior. Agent Randlett, a stern old man used to having his own way, protested in vain when Burnett went over his head, and he expressed "sorrow and shame because of the degradation to which I have been subjected."[8]

Agent Randlett was not a man to trifle with. In an attempt to increase profits for the Indians, he further subdivided the Big Pasture so that more cattlemen could bid for leases, thus incidentally getting back at Burnett. He also was able to successfully oppose Senator Bailey's attempt, supported by eleven other members of the Texas delegation, to extend for five months the existing leases. The new leases, which ran for three years beginning July 1, 1902, required Burnett and Waggoner to pay an average of nearly thirty cents an acre. This they did, despite protestations of impending economic ruin, thereby suggesting what a fine bargain the reservation grass had been for them in the earlier years. For the Indians the new leases meant annual grass payments of over $130,000.

Of the other three pastures, no. 3, which included 22,500 acres and lay directly west of the railroad town of Duncan, also caused controversy. The Duncanites were appalled at the creation of the pasture where they had hoped to see hundreds of homesteads occupied by potential customers. They appealed to Randlett to save them from financial disaster, pointing out how the towns competing with them were advertising their plight.[9]

Pursuing tactics that whites had found successful in other situations, the Duncanites sought help from the

Indian factions. Quanah declined to become involved, but Eschiti permitted his name to be used in a statement deploring the location of pasture no. 3.[10] So desperate were Duncan's businessmen that they offered to lease the land for agricultural purposes at higher rates than cattlemen were able to pay. In the spring of 1902 the secretary of the interior approved a plan by which pasture no. 3 was leased in units of 640 acres at a minimum of forty cents an acre, the lessee to fence it and the fences to revert to the Indians on the expiration of the lease. The Duncan businessmen who comprised most of the lessees, promptly subdivided the land into 160-acre tracts and sublet them to actual farmers.

The deliberations on the disposition of the 480,000 acres had taken place over a period of eighteen months, during which sooners had invaded the reservation. Within three weeks after the passage of the amended Jerome Agreement in June 1900 Agent Randlett estimated that there were as many white intruders in the Wichita Mountains as there were Indians on the reservation, with more whites on the way.[11] Those posing as prospectors used the agreement's provision relating to mineral law as an excuse for their activities. Their real intention was to scout out the best land in anticipation of an opening by a "run" such as had been employed elsewhere in Oklahoma.

In the thirteen months before the actual opening, the Indians were constantly harassed by the sooners. The public roads through the reservation were open to them, and the troops at Fort Sill were too few to be of much assistance. The cavalrymen did help clear the Wichita Mountains on one occasion, but the sooners quickly returned when the troops retired to their barracks. On the eve of the opening Agent Randlett estimated that at least 50,000 intruders were on the reservation.[12] Included along with the honest homeseekers were a number of thieves who stole Indian cattle and ponies and bootleggers who dispensed to the Indians what Randlett referred to as "bottled consolation."

William Kinman, who had been one of the most persistent sooners, had set himself up in business as an agent for those seeking homesteads. Out on bond in a case involving sale of liquor to the Indians, Kinman was now operating from a post office of which his wife was postmistress. As a result of Randlett's complaints against the Kinmans' new activities, an investigation resulted in charges filed against them for mail fraud. Randlett was rewarded for his industry in trying to protect the Indians by a legal suit that produced an injunction restraining him temporarily from interference with the squatters.[13]

In December 1900, after six months of constant harassment from sooners, Agent Randlett suggested to the Indian commissioner, who forwarded his proposal through channels to the General Land Office, that the reservation be opened by a lottery instead of a run.[14] This would reduce the incentive for the sooners to infiltrate the reservation. Whether or not Randlett initiated the idea, the president's proclamation of July 4, 1901 adopted the lottery procedure for the Kiowa, Comanche, and Kiowa-Apache Reservation.

The proclamation divided the reservation into two land districts for filing purposes, with one office at El Reno and another at Lawton. Between July 10 and July 26 individuals could register for the approximately 13,000 homesteads and more than 165,000 did so. About 50,000 of them anxiously witnessed the drawings at El Reno from July 29 to August 1. Those whose names were selected in the drawings were entitled to choose allotments in the order in which their names were drawn. The first two selected, from the only available land adjacent to the Lawton town site, allotments valued in excess of $20,000.[15]

The next major scene of activity was the tent city of 10,000 adjacent to the site of Lawton, where an auction of town lots was held August 6. Within hours Lawton was a frantic scene of new owners pitching tents on their property while trying to fend off squatters. The Comanches must have been bemused by the hectic activity which

transformed the dusty prairie into a bustling frontier town
that within a week featured banks operating under canvas
and sported over fifty saloons, including one called The
Carrie Nation.[16]

The Carrie Nation may have provided solace for some of
those whites who did not draw one of the approximately
13,000 lucky numbers in the lottery or whose number
came up too late to claim one of the good tracts available.
A year later nearly 23,000 acres still had not been filed on,
most of it in the barren Wichita Mountains.[17] Meanwhile,
disappointed boomers were trying to stake out mineral
claims on Indian allotments or challenging the authenticity
of Indian title to valuable tracts.

The mineral claims stemmed from an ambiguity in the
June 6, 1900 law opening the reservation. It could be con-
strued to permit filing on Indian allotments under mineral
law and many whites did just that. Agent Randlett quickly
sought a ruling from Washington to squelch such efforts,
but it took over two weeks for the Interior Department to
rule that the whites were trespassers and should be removed. Even then, Randlett was directed that "it is not
deemed advisable . . . to resort to harsh force."[18] As usual
the government was more sensitive to white than Indian
needs and the trespassers were to be given time to withdraw after proper notification.

Such attitudes encouraged other whites to challenge
Indian allotments, particularly those that were held in the
names of the 163 Comanche victims of the smallpox epidemic in the winter of 1900–01. Squatters also camped on
some of the 320-acre allotments of adopted squaw men
and their children, as well as on the homesteads of Mexican captives of the Comanches and associated tribes. The
latter individuals were taken in their youth and now considered by the Indians as members of their tribes. Nevertheless, if the Mexicans had been allotted good land there
were unscrupulous whites who hoped to swindle them out
of it on a technicality. Even two deputy United States
marshals were among the squatters.[19] In October 1901

President Theodore Roosevelt authorized the use of troops to remove the squatters, but more than sixty legal challenges ultimately required rulings from the Department of the Interior. As late as December 1902 troops were still being called upon to evict trespassers from Indian allotments.

Some of these squatters could have been honestly mistaken about the legality of their claims. There were whites, however, who were common thieves and they made drastic inroads upon Indian cattle and horses. The livestock likewise suffered from the application of the territorial herd law, whose effect was accentuated by the failure of the Indians to properly care for their animals. The law was designed to protect farmers from stock running loose and provided that they could impound animals intruding on their land and force their owner to compensate them for their care. Because few Indians were content to constantly remain on their allotments and care for their cattle, they frequently lost them when confronted by white men with large bills for the maintenance of their stock. Some whites were suspected of permitting Indian cattle and horses to enter their fields and graze on poor crops, and then holding the animals and demanding damages from their owners.

The sharp decrease in Indian herds in the years immediately following the opening of the reservation was partially due to the diminishing level of support provided the Indians by the government. Hungry tribesmen were being fed from the herds of friends and relatives. Beginning in 1901, no Indians administered by the Kiowa, Comanche, and Wichita Agency received government rations unless they could be classified as dependent because of age or infirmity.[20] This was part of a general effort to force the Indians to become more self-reliant. However, the United States continued to assist the Indians on a modest scale. Funds previously used to purchase rations were now being assigned to the employment of Indians at $1.25 per day to do road work and other necessary chores for the agency. As of

1905 Congress was still appropriating about $25,000 a year for the support of the Comanches and associated tribes, most of it going into salaries and wages for agency employees, but a few sets of harness and some wagons and plows were being issued to the Indians.[21]

Despite the decline in the level of support provided by the government and the constant preaching of agency officials, few of the roughly 1,400 Comanches worked their land or cared for their livestock to the satisfaction of their supervisors. They continued to derive income from the 480,000 acres the Indians retained, a total of about $136,000 a year to be divided among 2,800 Comanches, Kiowas, and Kiowa-Apaches.[22] In addition, families collected rent varying from $0.25 to $3.00 per acre from the allotments of their children. Moreover, most adults chose to rent their own allotments rather than work them, retaining a few acres on which to reside. The hundreds of small frame houses constructed by the government in recent years were more often than not occupied by the families of the white renters. The Indian owners lived in camps as they had since time immemorial. In the five years following the opening, the Comanches also shared in the $500,000 that the 1900 law provided should be paid them, with the $1.5 million balance being held in the treasury to draw 4 percent interest.

The $500,000, plus the income from the 480,000 acres, was turned over to the Indians in a series of per capita payments. Coming at intervals of several months they ranged from $20 to $60. Each payment was a bonanza for the local merchants, the whiskey vendors, and the loan sharks. A Lawton paper reported the impact of one payment in 1904:

> Every store in the city has been full all day and the red men have bought everything from an ice cream soda to the finest vehicles offered for sale. The Indian has little conception of the value of a dollar and so long as it will last there is nothing too good.[23]

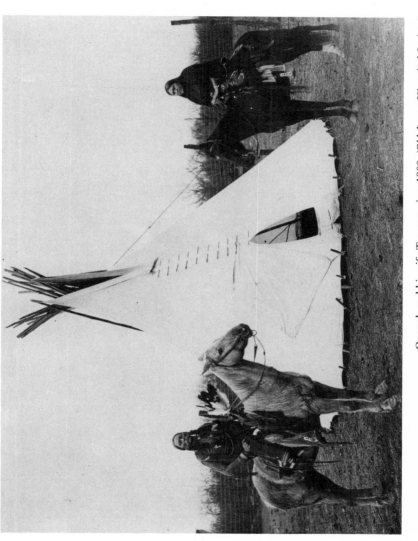

Quanah and his wife Tonarcy, circa 1900. (Oklahoma Historical Society)

Quanah's home, circa 1900. (Oklahoma Historical Society)

Fort Sill Indian School, circa 1900. (National Archives)

Indian Delegation on Peyote to the Oklahoma Constitutional Convention, 1907. *In the first row, from the left, Tennyson Berry, Codsy, Apache John, Otto Wells, Quanah, Little Bird, and Young Calf.* (Fort Sill Museum)

Unaccustomed to handling cash and bolstered by the knowledge that their allotments were held in trust for them by the United States, the Indians indulged their desires during the payments. In the long intervals between payments they lived on credit extended by the local merchants, turned to the loan sharks, or depended upon more fortunate friends and relatives. Although their homesteads could not be seized for debt, other property could, and it was not unusual for a merchant to secure a court order requiring the seizure and sale of an Indian's property to satisfy indebtedness. The Indian's ignorance of the language and the law made him easy prey to such actions.

The loan shark problem was particularly bad, with local bankers active in the role. The Indian would borrow at usurious rates of interest, signing a chattel mortgage on his stock and farm equipment. Agent Randlett was especially incensed at the operations of one Anadarko banker:

> This man has been of more damage to the moral character and well being of the Indians of this Agency than all the barrooms, gambling houses and houses of female prostitution that ever have been established in Caddo County. As a usurer he . . . equals the atrocious attributes of Shylock in his cold-blooded, inhuman methods of making collections . . . I will not permit him to come upon the reserves of this Agency to do any kind of business with the Indians.[24]

This white man was one of several charged by Randlett with trying to slip into the reservation disguised by blankets and shawls as Indian women. The agent was pleased to report in 1905 that one banker in Kiowa County had been found guilty and fined $1,000 for charging Indians interest rates of 150 to 3,360 percent.[25] But the practice persisted. An Indian desperate to feed his family, or as was too often the case anxious to get in a card game or buy a bottle of whiskey, was an easy victim for the pawnbroker or banker.

Gambling always had been a popular pastime with the Comanches, but alcohol was a new vice. Agent Randlett inveighed against the bootleggers who circulated among the Indian camps with their "bottled consolation." He was even more indignant that the town officials of Lawton and Anadarko made no effort to reduce the temptations for the Indians and denounced them publicly. The situation at Anadarko Randlett found particularly revolting:

> Any day at almost any hour Indians are seen drunk . . . and without any apparent effort to drag the drunken Indians to jail and police court for fine. Several of the boys of the Riverside School have become thoroughly demoralized and are able at any time they go into town to procure whiskey. . . . They have to be sought for and brought home in a wagon.[26]

Quanah had not developed a drinking problem, although the opening of the reservation had produced changes in his life-style. No longer did he have access to almost unlimited range for his cattle. Now, like other Comanches, Quanah had to pay $1 an acre to graze more than the few head his allotment would support. Furthermore, the chief was not the recipient of income from Texas cattlemen on the scale that he had once enjoyed, and his standard of living fell proportionately.

The Comanche chief did continue to play the role of the progressive leader and his agent was grateful. Quanah set a good example by sending his children to Carlisle and Chilocco and cooperated with agency employees in settling domestic quarrels and property disputes. As a member of the seven-man Business Council through which Agent Randlett tried to administer the affairs of the three tribes, Quanah followed the progressive line and backed Randlett against the Lone Wolf–Eschiti faction among the Kiowas and Comanches.

There were compensations for Quanah. The agent strengthened his hand by having the chief's warrant of Quanah's rival Eschiti recalled. When Quanah wanted his daughter Wanada returned from Carlisle before her term was up, this was arranged, and two years later the chief was able to secure for her a position as assistant matron at the Fort Sill School. In 1904 Quanah himself went on the government payroll as an assistant farmer at $240 per year.[27] Randlett justified this in terms of both the services he called upon Quanah to perform and the Comanche's diminished fortunes.

Quanah had his share of the penalties as well as the rewards of leadership. A missionary charged him with being prominent in the peyote cult and the polygamy issue again was raised against him. Agent Randlett denied Quanah was a leader of the peyote cult while tacitly admitting that the chief was a participant. An investigator from Washington confirmed that Quanah was living with three wives but concluded this was a reduction from seven. The white man went on to explain Quanah's leadership role as a result of sheer ability rather than government favoritism:

> If ever Nature stamped a man with the seal of headship she did it in his case. Quanah would have been a leader and a governor in any circle where fate may have cast him—it is in his blood.[28]

The investigator also pointed out that the chief's much criticized pigtails were just "double the number affected by George Washington."[29] On another occasion Randlett cited Quanah to defend the Indian practice of wearing their hair in braids, which violated the government's mandate against long hair. He said he had chided the chief about it, only to have Quanah remind him that the agent's own Chinese servant wore his hair in a pigtail.[30]

As one of the most publicized Indians in the United States, Quanah was a logical choice to be included among the five tribesmen to ride in Theodore Roosevelt's inaugural parade in 1905. And when Roosevelt came to Oklahoma a few weeks later to hunt wolves and coyotes in the Big Pasture, Quanah was singled out again for special attention. Arriving at Anadarko the president saw Quanah in the crowd and summoned him to his side. The Comanche later brought members of his family to meet

Roosevelt at his hunting camp and took the opportunity to discuss some of his people's problems. The president was sufficiently impressed to urge the commissioner of Indian Affairs himself to visit Anadarko. "My sympathies have been much excited and I have been aroused by what I have seen down here," wrote Roosevelt, "and I am concerned at the condition of these Indians and the seeming helplessness of their future."[31]

Quanah could secure an audience with the president of the United States; however, he was discovering that allotment and the opening of the reservation had not brought him all the privileges of citizenship. When his son Harold died in 1902, Quanah had inherited his allotment. When he chose to sell it he learned to his discomfiture that he could draw on the income only in amounts and at times acceptable to the Indian Office. The Indian would have the protection afforded by wardship, but only at the cost of his economic freedom.

The decision of the United States Supreme Court in *Lone Wolf* v. *Hitchcock* in January 1903 vitiated the efforts of the Lone Wolf–Eschiti faction to overturn the Jerome Agreement and clearly established the wardship status of the Indian by reaffirming Congress's "plenary authority over the tribal relations of the Indians." The court dismissed the complaint that the Jerome Agreement had been altered by Congress by holding that Congress had the power "to abrogate the provisions of an Indian treaty."[32] The Indian Rights Association recognized the significance of the Lone Wolf decision: "It is now distinctly understood that Congress has a right to do as it pleases; that it is under no obligation to respect any treaty, for the Indians have no rights which command respect."[33]

The association had involved itself with the case in its last stage and in the process antagonized Agent Randlett. The association had decided to act after the original decision by the Supreme Court of the District of Columbia was upheld by the Court of Appeals and employed a Philadelphia lawyer to assist William Springer in presenting the case to the United States Supreme Court.

As Agent Randlett saw it, Attorney Springer and the Indian Rights Association were sniping at him from the flanks while he was absorbed in trying to defend the Comanches and associated tribes from the squatters, usurers, and bootleggers. Randlett also resented a reference made at the 1901 Lake Mohonk Conference to the drunken Indians in Anadarko. Although he had been as critical as anyone of the conditions at Anadarko, reference to them at Lake Mohonk was taken by him as implied criticism of his administration. In his next annual report the agent denounced the Indian Rights Association for having become "the allies of grafting attorneys" and suggested that the time had come, "when the righteous should, in praying for the interests of his agency, plead, 'God, save them from their friends.'"[34]

Even then Agent Randlett's superiors were pondering charges of improper conduct brought against him by Senator Matthew S. Quay at the suggestion of the Indian Rights Association. The senator proposed that an investigator be dispatched to Anadarko and that he specifically be instructed to include Lone Wolf, Big Tree, and Eschiti among those whom he interviewed.

In 1903 Agent Randlett and his agency were subjected to two thorough investigations as a result of charges brought by dissident Indians and Senator Quay. In January and February, Inspector James McLaughlin, who had been to Anadarko on a comparable mission in 1898, carried out a thorough probe of the agency. McLaughlin's report was a ringing vindication of Agent Randlett:

> I am convinced that it has been of vast benefit to the Government and fortunate for the Indians . . . that a strong, fearless and just man, such as Col. Randlett, was agent here during the opening of this reservation to settlement.[35]

Nevertheless, President Roosevelt felt impelled by accu-

sations that Agent Randlett had taken bribes in the course
of allotting the reservation to dispatch yet another investigator to Anadarko. Roosevelt's choice was Francis E.
Leupp, a personal acquaintance and a New York journalist
who had once served the Indian Rights Association as its
Washington-based lobbyist. Later he would be the president's choice as commissioner of Indian Affairs. Leupp
also gave Randlett a clean bill of health, defending him in a
statement that graphically portrayed an agent's problems:

> When an Agent has sat in one swivel chair for four
> consecutive years, practically every day from eight in
> the morning 'til five in the evening, hearing complaints,
> issuing orders, writing letters, opening bids, signing
> leases, supervising accounts, drawing checks, settling
> domestic disputes, exercising the functions of a guardi-
> an for orphan children, unravelling the intricacies of
> heirship . . . adjusting debts and credits between indi-
> vidual Indians, preparing cases for the prosecution of
> dram sellers or the ejection of intruders, devising forms
> for legal instruments which will save some remnant for
> the Indian after the white man gets through stripping
> him—performing these and a hundred other kindred
> duties day in and day out—who will cast the first stone
> at him if his spirit revolts now and then. . . . How
> many men in private life could endure such an unre-
> mitting grind as this, and meet with a smile a daily
> accusation of fraud, conspiracy, and misappropriation
> of funds, often from the very persons whose poor little
> possessions he is trying to save for them?[36]

What apparently shocked Leupp the most at Anadarko
was something that had bothered Inspector McLaughlin in
1898: the casualness with which sworn statements had
been made. "Among a certain class of citizens affidavits
are to be had on any side of any subject, and in quantities
as wanted," Leupp said.[37] After a strenuous six weeks at
Anadarko, the investigator concluded:

I must be content with the satisfaction of adding one more testimonial to the worth of an admirable but much maligned public servant, and with instituting certain criminal proceedings through the United States court which may make perjury a little less profitable as a trade hereafter in the neighborhood of the Kiowa Agency.[38]

James F. Randlett had less than two years to serve as agent for the Comanche and associated tribes at the time Leupp composed his final report. In his last months at Anadarko Randlett was trying to salvage for the Indians as much as he could of the 480,000 acres held in common by them under the 1900 act. The white man's campaign against the 480,000 acres had commenced before the ink was dry on the legislation setting it aside for the benefit of the Indians. Several bills were introduced into Congress in the period 1902 to 1905 to open the land for settlement. Texas congressman John H. Stephens was one of the leaders in this effort. His hometown Vernon was just across Red River from the Big Pasture and definitely would profit from the opening. Speaking in behalf of his bill in 1903, Stephens stressed the theme popular in Congress that if the Indians were able to sell their land, "no appropriations will have to be made for them in the future."[39]

Randlett vigorously opposed the legislation. He argued that under the terms of the proposed legislation the Indians would be selling for $600,000 land bringing them an annual lease income of $136,295. The $600,000, the agent emphasized, held in the Treasury at 5 percent would yield them only $30,000 a year. Randlett also pointed out that the Indians would be losing the use of more than 50,000 acres of pasture that they had reserved for their own cattle, thus reducing them to complete dependence on the inadequate 160-acre homesteads.[40]

The agent's counterproposal was that all children of the Comanche and associated tribes born since the 1900 opening be allotted 160-acre homesteads and that the remaining land continue to be leased to white farmers and ranchers. Also, Randlett reminded his superiors that the Lone Wolf decision clearly established the Indians as "the wards of the nation":

> Congress, the guardian, may deal with the lands of the Indian wards of the nation precisely as an individual legal guardian would deal with and dispose of the lands of an infant or other incompetent person, being careful at all times that no injustice was visited upon the ward.[41]

However, congressmen took their role as representatives of their white constituents more seriously than their role as guardians of the Indians.

Randlett retired in 1905 due to age and infirmity; he was over seventy and had been in ill health for some time. His handpicked successor, his chief clerk John P. Blackman kept plugging for Randlett's proposal of allotments to Indian children, but he discouraged Eschiti from circulating a petition against another opening. Like his predecessor, Blackman believed he could represent the Indians better than they could represent themselves. Quanah accepted Blackman as he had Randlett and became an advocate of the plan to allot the children. As usual, however, the decisions were to be made in Washington.

Early in 1906 a Stephens bill to open the 480,000-acre Indian tract, plus 25,000 acres that had been set aside as a wood reserve for Fort Sill, began to move in Congress. It passed the House and received a favorable report from a Senate committee. Despite a protest from Agent Blackman that the $1.50-an-acre minimum price set by the bill was far too small compensation for the Indians, the Stephens proposal was approved by Congress and sent to the president on March 20.

The Indians' interests finally found an effective advocate in President Roosevelt. On the recommendation of the commissioner of Indian Affairs, Roosevelt threatened to veto the bill unless it were recalled for further consideration.[42] This Congress did and rewrote the bill to provide for allotments for the 517 Indian children born since the 1900 opening and for a minimum price for the remaining land of not $1.50 per acre, but a substantial $5. In this form it was signed into law by Roosevelt on June 5, 1906.[43]

Even this victory for the Indian was not unalloyed. Agent Blackman wished to select the 160-acre allotments for the children from the relatively fertile pasture no. 3 adjacent to Duncan. However, the white farmers who had been leasing this land were given preference over the Indians who had owned it. On June 18, 1906 Roosevelt approved a law permitting the white lessees to purchase their farms at a price established by an evaluation board, only one of whose three members would be an appointee of the agent representing the Indians.[44]

By September 1906 Agent Blackman had selected allotments for the Indian children, and the remaining 2,531 tracts were opened for sale to the public. The Indians had $4,015,785.25 added to their account in the United States Treasury as a result of the sales.[45] The Comanches and associated tribes had finally entered an era in which they would own land solely as individuals. Only in that respect was it the situation anticipated by the government officials who had drafted the Treaty of Medicine Lodge. The Indians were still far from the 1867 vision of independent farmers ready for assimilation into the mainstream of American society.

Epilogue

In the several years after the opening of the 480,000-acre tract in 1906, the Comanches came no nearer escaping their dependence on the government. Practically all the Indians still owned land for which the United States acted as trustee. Notwithstanding the lip service paid to the concept of assimilation, Comanche children continued to attend government schools, they and their parents were treated by government doctors, and they patronized government-licensed traders. Instead of the Indian Office, or Bureau of Indian Affairs as it would come to be called, withering away with allotment in severalty, its responsibilities seemed to multiply. It now supervised all leasing arrangements and the disbursement of the income to the Comanches. Even if the Indian sold land, the bureau held the proceeds for him and doled it out as it judged the Indian needed it.

Still operating on the theory that the Indian need hold no more land then he personally could work, Congress added the Burke Act of 1906 and the Noncompetent Indian Act of 1907 to the Dead Indian Act of 1902. The Burke Act authorized the Indian who had been declared by the bureau to be competent to handle his business affairs to receive full title to his land. The 1907 legislation permitted even the noncompetent Indian to sell a portion of his allotment to finance improvements on the land remaining to him, and the Dead Indian Act allowed him to sell land he had inherited. There is little evidence that the Indians profited from such legislation. In 1910 the official in charge of the Comanches and associated tribes estimated that 90 percent of the land of his agency for which the Indian received full title was promptly sold and 50 percent of the proceeds was squandered.[1]

Perhaps of even greater long-range significance than its provision for "competent" Indians were the Burke Act's clauses relating to trusteeship and citizenship. They made possible trusteeship beyond the usual twenty-five-year period specified in the Dawes Act of 1887 and other severalty legislation. In addition, the law withheld citizenship in subsequent allotments until the expiration of the trusteeship period. The door was now open for Indians to remain indefinitely wards of the United States.

The Comanches were settling into a way of life that would change little in the next quarter-century. Most leased their allotments, retaining only enough land for a house and garden. By 1910 few held any cattle, although most retained a horse or two. The Comanches received from the interest on tribal funds held in the United States Treasury annual per capita payments that seldom exceeded $100. Some Indians also worked part-time as farmhands, chopping and picking cotton or working in the grain harvest. From these varied sources the Comanche family would receive an income of $400 or $500 a year. Living in their own houses and cultivating small gardens on tax-free land, attending government schools, and using government medical facilties, the Indians were able to eke out an existence. Not driven by the white man's compulsion to acquire material possessions or spurred by his work ethic, the Comanche was secure in the knowledge that if emergencies occurred he could turn to the government or to friends and relatives who would not deny a fellow Comanche help. The result was—by the white man's standards—a rather aimless existence spent largely in lounging around the traders' stores, haunting the streets of Lawton and other neighboring towns, and visiting friends and relatives.

In this way of life a revival meeting, a funeral, or a Fourth of July celebration could provide the pretext for leaving home for days or weeks. Their agents complained that the Comanches' endless peregrinations made it impossible for them to adequately care for what little livestock they retained. Typical of what disturbed the agents was a

Baptist camp meeting in the summer of 1909 that drew 2,000 Indians to a site near Anadarko. Almost half of them were from neighboring reservations, and at the conclusion of the camp meeting many visited with the Comanches and Kiowas, were honored by gift-dances, and departed laden with presents. A few weeks later some of the Comanches and Kiowas returned the visits by calling on the Cheyennes and Arapahos, who entertained them and showered them with gifts. Meanwhile, their crops and livestock suffered.

Such an Indian life-style helped white men justify schemes to further reduce Indian landholdings. Less than two years after the opening of the 480,000 acres a bill was introduced into Congress to reduce the allotments of the members of the Comanche and associated tribes to 80 acres. The sponsor argued for his bill in a fashion reminiscent of the rationale for earlier reductions of Indian landholdings. He said that by selling 80 acres a Comanche would be able to properly equip the remaining half of his allotment for successful farming.[2] The bill was no idle threat, because Oklahoma had achieved statehood in 1907 and now had a voting delegation in Congress to push such legislation. Indian opposition to such action was indicated by their agent, who also forwarded a letter by Quanah. The agent urged resistance to the bill "as Indian lands are selling fast enough under present rules and regulations."[3]

Not only was the reduction to 80 acres blocked, but the Comanche and associated tribes were able to get legislation they did desire. This was a bill that became law May 29, 1908, and provided, as amended June 25, 1910, that homesteads of 120 acres each should be granted to the children born after the 1906 allotments.[4] The land was of very poor quality since it was all that remained in the public domain from the opening of the reservation; nevertheless it did provide 169 Indian children with a homestead of sorts.[5]

Quanah had had a hand in this last allotment, having been involved in other Comanche activities until his death in 1911. In many respects his career with its frustrations and triumphs was that of the average Comanche writ large.

In tribal affairs Quanah continued to cooperate loyally with the Indian agents, or superintendents as they were called after 1906, while remaining a leader in the peyote cult. On Agent John P. Blackman's death in 1907 he was succeeded by Ernest Stecker, who owed his appointment to the influence of Hugh L. Scott, under whom Stecker had served as first sergeant of the Indian troop at Fort Sill in the 1890s.

Stecker and Blackman were as high in their praise of Quanah as had been any of their predecessors. On the agency payroll as a farmer, the Comanche's principal function was as a liaison man between the government and his tribe. In this capacity Quanah was called upon to go to Anadarko frequently and he began drawing per diem like any bureaucrat. The Indian who as a young man had followed the buffalo herds and raided the Texas frontier now collected $1.76 for a rail round trip to Anadarko, $1 for lunch and dinner, and $0.25 for lodging. The chief also had a telephone installed in his home at government expense, justified on the grounds that he was "necessarily consulted frequently with reference to Agency matters."[6] Always alert to perquisites of office, Quanah used his influence to secure a place on the agency payroll for Aubra Birdsong, his white son-in-law.

As a member of the Business Council for the Kiowas, Comanches, and Kiowa-Apaches, Quanah still was allied with Apiatan and Apache John and supported by Comanche headman Arushe. Otto Wells, who generally was found opposing Quanah and supporting Eschiti, was removed from the Business Council in 1908 on the insistence of Superintendent Stecker and replaced by Mamsookawat.

One of the few subjects on which Quanah and the other tribal leaders seemed to be in agreement was opposition to the red card system, which was inaugurated in 1907 and lasted two years. Each Indian was issued a card authorizing him credit from a specified licensed trader up to a total of

75 percent of the next anticipated per capita payment. John P. Blackman had conceived the system in an effort to help the Indians escape the clutches of the usurers and merchants. However, the tribesmen disliked being restricted to a single trader, and because merchants in the nearby towns continued to accept notes and mortgages, the cards failed to achieve their purpose. The Indians constantly were being sued and much of the agent's time was consumed in consulting with his charges about their legal problems and accompanying them to court.

Once in a great while the situation was reversed. Quanah was in court in 1908 trying to collect from a white man. The case grew out of Comanche participation in a street fair in Lawton. The Indians had been promised compensation, but those contracting for the exhibition had failed to deliver and Quanah had sued.

No parade or other community celebration in the area was complete without its contingent of Indians in warbonnets and buckskin. Quanah was one of Oklahoma's most celebrated Indians, and promoters were eager to have him for their events. In August 1908 Cache capitalized on its famous neighbor by advertising a "Quanah Parker Celebration" featuring camping, burro rides, rodeo events, Indian dances, a stagecoach robbery (featuring Quanah's coach), and orators, including Quanah.

For a few years Samuel B. Burnett, one of the Texas cattlemen with whom the Comanche chief long had been associated, arranged for him to lead delegations to the Fort Worth Fat Stock Shows. The Texan provided palominos and Appaloosas for the Indian parade through the streets of Fort Worth, and the Comanches came equipped with tepees, which they pitched in the show grounds. For the 1909 show Quanah agreed to bring with him a Kiowa chief and Geronimo. Burnett reciprocated by arranging for Quanah and friends to hunt on a ranch in west Texas and entertaining them on Burnett property near Vernon. However, Quanah had to purchase a license to hunt, a requirement that distressed him enough to write the governor of Texas, whom he assured, "I am Texas man myself."[7]

In 1910 Quanah was a featured attraction at the Texas State Fair in Dallas. One of the townsites on the reservation had been named Quanah, and it was the terminus of a railroad, the Quanah, Acme and Pacific, that its proprietor hoped to build to El Paso. The proprietor was able to have one of the days of the 1910 state fair designated "Quanah Route Day." The railroad's sole passenger train was parked on a siding in the fairgrounds and provided quarters for the chief and a party of Comanches who helped publicize the new road.

No longer the recipient of grass money or of the monetary favors of ranchers leasing reservation lands, the Comanche chief was finding it more and more difficult to live on the scale he previously had enjoyed. Nevertheless, the visitors continued to show up at the sprawling ranch house with its two-story porch and star-emblazoned roof. Quanah could not deny his Indian friends and relatives his hospitality, and whites, total strangers, also sought him out. Some did not get past the tall picket fence that surrounded the house, but others were too important to turn away. Among the celebrities whom Quanah found himself entertaining was Lord Bryce, the English ambassador, whom the Comanche met at the Cache station and personally escorted out to his home.

The same year that Lord Bryce visited Oklahoma, buffalo returned to Comanche country. In 1901 Agent Randlett had informed Quanah of the government's decision to create the Wichita Mountains Wild Life Refuge from some of the land remaining unsold from the opening of the reservation. The agent presented this to the chief as in Quanah's interest because it would safeguard him from the possibility of undesirable neighbors.[8] It also meant that when the New York Zoological Society donated fifteen buffalo to start a herd in the refuge the Parker family had a ringside seat for the return of the great animals.[9] When the buffalo were loosed from pens in which they had been held the first winter, Quanah was present with other Comanches to see the miniature herd gallop free over grasslands that had once supported buffalo too numerous to count.

Quanah also was present at the inauguration of the state of Oklahoma's first governor, and he lobbied at the constitutional convention in behalf of peyote. The convention did not impose a ban on peyote, and when a bill for that purpose was introduced into the legislature in 1909 Quanah's testimony helped defeat it. However, the federal government also was attempting to curtail peyote use. Quanah and his associates obtained some of their supply from Laredo merchants, who mailed it to Oklahoma. A special agent of the Bureau of Indian Affairs visited the border town in 1909 and bought up and destroyed the available buttons, although a new supply was soon on hand. Superintendent Stecker, whose long acquaintance with the Comanches had familiarized him with the problem, played down the danger of peyote and reminded his superiors of the ineffectuality of laws prohibiting the manufacture and consumption of alcoholic beverages. Stecker tried to restrict the use of peyote rather than ban it. Commissioner of Indian Affairs Robert G. Valentine came to this position after visiting Anadarko, but confiscations continued to take place. Early in 1910 Quanah asked his old acquaintance Hugh L. Scott to intercede with Commissioner Valentine, and he himself wrote Valentine on the subject. By his unabashed support of peyote the chief had been able to get it condoned by a succession of government officials who had needed his backing on more significant agency issues.

Education was just one of the areas where Quanah's cooperation had been appreciated. He had not been one of the first Comanche leaders to send his children to school. Nevertheless, once he had done so the chief continued to send them, not only to the Fort Sill School but also to Carlisle and Chilocco. Together with Mamsookawat and a few other Comanches, Quanah now decided to try the public school system. In 1906 he enrolled a son in the Cache school only to have the child's readmission denied the following year. The explanation offered was that Quanah lived outside the school district. It also was suggested that there was some reluctance by the school board to mix Indian and white children.[10] The Comanches were encountering a type of discrimination that had been manifested elsewhere in the West since the government began in the 1890s to try to integrate Indian children into public schools. Quanah's response was to devise with the school superintendent of Comanche County plans for a new school district to encompass his home. In September 1908 the school opened for twenty-five children, thirteen of them white.

Quanah showed the same initiative in having his mother's body moved to Oklahoma. In 1908 he located the site of her grave by advertising in Texas newspapers and thus contacting some of his white relatives. Having done this he persuaded Texas congressman John Stephens to sponsor a bill by which Congress appropriated $800 to finance the reburial of Cynthia Ann. Late in 1910 her body was transported to Post Oak Mission cemetery, near Quanah's homestead, and reinterred. Local ministers presided over the ceremony and the chief made a brief talk stressing the common origin and destiny of whites and Indians.

In less than three months Quanah himself would be buried there. In January 1911 he wrote his Oklahoma congressman, Scott Ferris, a rather confused letter reciting some of his services to the United States and asking help.[11] In passing the letter on to the commissioner of Indian Affairs, Ferris suggested that some sinecure be made available to the old chief, who was in ill health. Despite his condition, Quanah attended a medicine dance—some said it was a peyote ceremony—among the Cheyennes in late January. Returning by train he became quite ill and he died February 23, 1911. Over 1,000 people attended his funeral at Post Oak Mission, where he was laid to rest beside Cynthia Ann.

Quanah was the last Comanche chief. On Superintendent

Stecker's suggestion, the government did not recognize a successor. The Business Council would continue to be the agency through which the United States would manage the Comanches and associated tribes.

The chief's life had spanned a long period of Comanche history. In his childhood they had been a powerful force on the south plains and the scourge of the Texas settlements, as was reflected in the circumstances of his own birth. From his surrender in 1875 Quanah had exemplified the progressive Indian and had been the Comanche mainstay of agents and superintendents. But like other Indians, Quanah had not become thoroughly acculturated. When the reservation was opened in 1900, he was ill prepared to manage his finances, and his braids, multiple wives, and adherence to the peyote cult were manifestations of his links with his Comanche culture.

In 1867 the United States had imposed the Treaty of Medicine Lodge on the Comanches as a means of locating the Indians on reservations, hopefully not only to free land for white settlement but to avert the extermination of the Indians by the invading whites. The treaty had also provided a framework of services and supervision that it was expected, in thirty years would prepare the Comanches for assimilation by the greater society.

What actually had been accomplished was to strip the Comanches of virtually all their land and much of the basis of their culture. Some individuals, usually mixed-bloods, had for all practical purposes relinquished their Indian identity. Most, however, had been pauperized by the system and had developed a painful dependence on the Bureau of Indian Affairs. Resentful of the control exercised by the government over even the smallest details of their lives, yet believing that only by continued association with it could they maintain their status as Comanches, they found themselves in the dilemma that still confronts them today.

Abbreviations Used in the Notes

AAG	assistant adjutant general
AR	Annual Report
CIA	commissioner of Indian Affairs
IALS	Indian Affairs—Letters Sent
IF	Inspectors Files
IMLS	Indian Miscellaneous, Letters Sent
IOLB	Indian Office Letter Book
IOLR	Indian Office—Letters Received
IORB	Indian Office Report Book
IRAP	Indian Rights Association Papers
K	Kiowa Agency Letter Book
M	Microcopy
NA	National Archives
OHS	Oklahoma Historical Society
R	Roll

Notes

CHAPTER 1

1. *Senate Executive Documents,* no. 13, 40th Cong., 1st sess., 1867, p. 35.

2. Senate *Congressional Globe,* 50th Cong., 1st sess., p. 705.

3. Ibid., p. 673.

4. Ibid., p. 667.

5. *Senate Reports* no. 156, 39th Cong., 2d sess., 1867, p. 10.

6. Ibid., pp. 5-6.

7. Ibid., p. 10.

8. *Senate Exec. Doc.,* no. 13, 40th Cong., 1st sess. 1867, p. 57.

9. Ibid., p. 20.

10. Taylor to secy. of the interior, July 12, 1867, IOLB (see Abbreviations) 16:387.

11. Senate, *Congressional Globe,* 40th Cong., 1st sess., 1867, p. 670.

12. Ibid., p. 667.

13. For example, see Secy. James Harlan to Gen. Pope, July 6, 1865, IALS 5:278; AR of Secy. O. H. Browning, 1867 (ser. 1326, p. 8).

14. For the best description of the Comanche society before the people became reservation Indians, see Ernest Wallace and E. Adamson Hoebel, *The Comanches.*

15. Rupert Norvall Richardson, *The Comanche Barrier to South Plains Settlement,* p. 66.

16. Charles J. Kappler, *Indian Treaties 1778-1883,* p. 435.

17. Colonel Wilbur Sturtevant Nye, *Carbine and Lance,* p. 17.

18. An excellent account of the Comanchero trade is to be found in Charles L. Kenner, *A History of New Mexican Plains Indian Relations.*

19. Kappler, *Treaties,* p. 554.

20. Neighbors to Gen. D. E. Twiggs, July 17, 1857, in AR of the secy. of the interior, 1857 (ser. 919, pp. 553-54).

21. AR of Mitchell, 1852 (ser. 658, p. 357).

22. AR of Fitzpatrick, 1853 (ser. 690, p. 360).

23. Ibid., p. 364.

24. Ibid., p. 363.

25. AR of J. W. Whitfield, 1854 (ser. 746, p. 297).

26. For example, see AR of George W. Manypenny, 1855 (ser. 810, p. 338).

27. Rupert Norvall Richardson, *The Frontier of Northwest Texas 1846 to 1876*, p. 193.

28. Quoted in Raymond Estep, *The Removal of the Texas Indians and the Founding of Fort Cobb*, p. 7.

29. AR of Thompson, 1859 (ser. 1023, pp. 6-7).

30. *The War of the Rebellion, Official Records of the Union and Confederate Armies* (Washington, D.C.: Government Printing Office, 1880-1901), ser. IV, 1:542 ff.

31. Boone to CIA, Oct. 19, 1861, in IOLR, M 234, R 878:524.

32. AR of W. P. Dole, 1861 (ser. 1117, p. 715).

33. Agreement at Fort Wise, IOLR, M234, R878:521.

34. Boone to CIA, Dec. 30, 1861, IOLR, M234, R878:615.

35. *New York Times*, March 28, 1863, p. 4, and April 10, 1863, p. 5; Colley to CIA, IOLR, M234, R878:805.

36. Robert M. Utley, *Frontiersmen in Blue*, pp. 298-99.

37. AR of CIA, 1865 (ser. 1248, pp. 574-75).

38. Ibid. pp. 711-12.

39. Ibid., p. 719.

40. Leavenworth to the CIA, Nov. 9, 1865, IOLR, M234, R375:34.

41. AR of Cooley, 1866 (ser. 1284, p. 3).

42. Gov. J. W. Throckmorton to CIA, Nov. 5, 1866, in Winfrey and Day, eds., *Indian Papers of Texas*, 4:124.

43. Maj. J. W. Barry to Gov. Throckmorton, March 16, 1867, in Winfrey and Day, eds., *Indian Papers of Texas*, 4:176.

44. Kenner, *New Mexican—Plains Indian Relations*, p. 174.

45. AR of A. B. Norton, 1867 (ser. 1326, p. 194).

46. Leavenworth to CIA, June 5, 1866, in IOLR, M234, R234:250, and Feb. 26, 1867, in IOLR, M234, R375:505.

47. CIA to Leavenworth, April 20, 1867, in IOLB 83:7.

48. Copy of report of Lt. G. A. Hesselberger, in IOLR, M234, R375:88.

49. Endorsement by Sherman on report of Lt. Mark Walker, May 14, 1867, in IOLR, M234, R375:714.

50. Leavenworth to CIA, June 18, 1867, in IOLR, M234, R375:604.

CHAPTER 2

1. The best description of the setting for the negotiations is to be found in Douglas C. Jones, *The Treaty of Medicine Lodge*, pp. 110 ff.

2. Leavenworth to the CIA, Sept. 2, 1867, in IOLR, M234, R375:628.

3. AR of CIA, 1868 (ser. 1366, p. 459).

4. Proceedings of Council, IOLR, M234, R60:1525 ff.; Henry M. Stanley's eyewitness account, "A British Journalist Reports the Medicine Lodge Peace Councils of 1867," *Kansas Historical Quarterly* 33 (Autumn 1967): 249-320.

5. Stanley, "British Journalist," p. 282.

6. Ibid., p. 283.

7. Proceedings of Council, IOLR, M234, R60:1525 ff.

8. Ibid.

9. Ibid.

10. For the text of the treaty see Kappler, *Treaties*, pp. 977-82.

11. Thomas Murphy to CIA, IOLR, M234, R375:717.

12. Jones, *Treaty of Medicine Lodge*, pp. 51, 144.

13. Kappler, *Treaties*, pp. 982-84.

14. AR of CIA, 1868 (ser. 1366, p. 463).

15. Ibid., p. 465.

16. Ibid.

17. Ibid., p. 462.

CHAPTER 3

1. Acting CIA to secy. of the interior, IOLB 16:47.

2. Leavenworth to CIA, Dec. 14, 1867, IOLR, M234, R375:689.

3. Leavenworth to CIA, May 21, 1868, IOLR, M234, R375:859.

4. Copy of McCusker to Gen. William B. Hazen, Dec. 21, 1868, IOLR, M234, R346:519.

5. Supt. Murphy to CIA, Sept. 19, 1868, IOLR, M234, R59:352.

6. Todd to CIA, July 22, 1868, IOLR, M234, R375:992.

7. Leavenworth to CIA, May 21, 1868, IOLR, M234, R375:859.

8. Hazen to Gen. Sherman, June 30, 1869, in AR of CIA, 1869 (ser. 1414, p. 835); A. G. Boone to CIA, March 8, 1869, IOLR, M234, R376:211.

9. Leavenworth to CIA, July 30, 1878, IOLR, M234, R375:893.

10. Leavenworth to CIA, Aug. 1, 1868, IOLR, M234, R59:106.

11. Leavenworth to CIA, May 21, 1868, IOLR, M234, R375:859.

12. CIA to secy. of the interior, June 5, 1868, IOLR, M234, R375: 873.

13. Leavenworth to CIA, April 22, 1868, IOLR, M234, R375:848.

14. Palmer to CIA, June 10, 1868, IOLR, M234, R375:967.

15. Taylor to secy. of the interior, April 6, 1868, IORB, 17:240.

16. Hazen to Sen. John B. Henderson, June 10, 1867, in *New York Times*, July 5, 1867, p. 3.

17. Walkley to Hazen, Dec. 28, 1868, IOLR, M234, R376:525.

18. Marvin Kroeker, "Colonel W. B. Hazen In the Indian Territory," *Chronicles of Oklahoma*, Spring 1964, p. 60.

19. Murphy to CIA, Nov. 15, 1868, IOLR, M234, R59:376.

20. Kenner, *New Mexican—Plains Indian Relations*, p. 182.

21. Hazen to Sheridan, Feb. 13, 1869, IOLR, M234, R376:532.

22. Hazen to Gen. Sherman, June 30, 1869, in AR of CIA, 1869 (ser. 1414, p. 835).

23. Boone to Murphy, April 27, 1869, IOLR, M234, R376:466.

CHAPTER 4

1. Lawrie Tatum, *Our Red Brothers*, p. 24.

2. Special Estimate, July 10, 1869, IOLR, M234, R376:286.

3. Tatum to Hoag, Aug. 21, 1869, IOLR, M234, R376:307.

4. Acting CIA to Hoag, Sept. 14, 1869, IOLB, 91:418.

5. AR of Tatum, 1869 (ser. 1414, p. 827).

6. AR of Walker, 1872 (ser. 1560, p. 394).

7. AR of CIA, 1869 (ser. 1414, p. 898).

8. AR of Walker, 1872 (ser. 1560, p. 396).

9. Tatum to CIA, July 24, 1869, IOLR, M234, R376:291.

10. CIA to Hoag, Aug. 12, 1869, IOLB 91:268.

11. Tatum to Hoag, Oct. 21, 1871, K2:21, OHS.

12. Tatum to Hoag, Nov. 11, 1871, IOLB, M234, R377:392.

13. Thomas Murphy to CIA, Aug. 16, 1871, IOLR, M234, R60:1029.

14. AR of Tatum, 1869 (ser. 1414, p. 828).

15. CIA to secy. of interior, April 29, 1869, IOLB 18:321.

16. Tatum to Hoag, March 31, 1873, IOLR, M234, R378:234.

17. Tatum to Hoag, Aug. 17, 1869, IOLR, M234, R376:315.

18. AR of CIA, 1869 (ser. 1414, p. 504).

19. Ibid., p. 507.

20. Robert C. Carriker, *Fort Supply, Indian Territory*, p. 42.

21. Tatum to Hoag, Feb. 11, 1870, IOLR, M234, R376:798.

22. Copy of Col. Grierson to AAG, Dept. of the Mo., June 14, 1870, IOLR, M234, R376:590; Horace T. Jones to Tatum, Dec. 6, 1870, IOLR, M234, R377:179.

23. Tatum, *Our Red Brothers*, p. 35.

24. Newspaper clipping, IOLR, M234, R59:1038.

25. Report on council, July 14, 1870, IOLR, M234, R376:727.

26. Robert G. Athearn, *William Tecumseh Sherman and the Settlement of the West*, p. 289.

27. Tatum, *Our Red Brothers*, pp. 44-45; Tatum to Hoag, Aug. 19, 1870, IOLR, M234, R376:995.

28. Tatum to Hoag, Sept. 6, 1870, IOLR, M234, R376:1013.

29. Tatum to Hoag, Oct. 27, 1870, IOLR, M234, R376:1043.

30. Tatum to Hoag, Sept. 1, 1870, IOLR, M234, R376:1005; Tatum to Hoag, Sept. 26, 1870, IOLR, M234, R376:1023.

31. William Nicholson, "A Tour of Indian Agencies in Kansas and the Indian Territory in 1870," p. 354.

32. Walter L. Burr to CIA, IOLR, M234, R377:137.

33. AR of Butler, 1871 (ser. 1505, pp. 891-92); Josiah Butler, "Pioneer School Teaching at the Comanche-Kiowa Agency School 1870-3," p. 502.

34. Statements by Jack County citizens, May 2, 1871, IOLR, M234, R469:490.

35. This account of the confrontation is based on Sherman to Col. Ranald Mackenzie, May 19, 1871, IOLR, M234, R377:13; Sherman to Gen. E. D. Townshend, May 28, 1871, IOLR, M234, R377:25; Tatum to Sherman, May 29, 1871, IOLR, M234, R377:54; Sherman to Tommy Sherman, May 29, 1871, in James M. Merrill, "General Sherman's Letter to His Son," pp. 126-31; Nye, *Carbine and Lance*, pp. 132-43.

36. Secy. Delano to CIA, June 20, 1871, IOLR, M234, R377:401.

37. Hoag to Tatum, June 26, 1871, IOLR, M234, R377:286.

38. AR of Tatum, 1871 (ser. 1505, p. 919).

39. Thomas Wistar to Tatum, July 31, 1871, in Kiowa Agency Files: Agents and Agency, OHS.

40. L. Butler to Tatum, Sept. 9, 1871, in ibid.

41. James D. Richardson, ed., *Messages and Papers of the Presidents* (Washington, D.C.: Bureau of National Literature, 1897), 6:4106.

42. AR of Tatum, 1872 (ser. 1560, p. 631).

43. William Curtis Nunn, "Texas During the Administration of E. J. Davis," pp. 245-46.

44. Kenner, *New Mexico-Plains Indian Relations*, p. 193.

45. AR of Tatum, 1872 (ser. 1560, p. 632).

46. Ernest Wallace, ed., *Ranald S. Mackenzie's Official Correspondence Relating to Texas, 1871-1873*, p. 89.

47. Beede to Hoag, June 21, 1872, IOLR, M234, R61:619.

48. Hoag to CIA, Jan. 13, 1872, IOLR, M234, R62:499.

49. AR of Hoag, 1872 (ser. 1560, p. 612).

50. Hoag to CIA, March 6, 1872, IOLR, M234, R377:617.

51. Secy. Delano to Gov. Davis, June 14, 1872, IMLS, 12:55.

52. Beede to Hoag, Aug. 13, 1872, IOLR, M234, R61:789.

53. Ibid., R61:759.

54. Alvord to CIA, Aug. 26, 1872 IOLR, M234, R60:1414.

55. CIA to Indian delegation, IOLR, M234, R377:963.

56. Mackenzie to AAG, Dept. of Texas, Oct. 12, 1872, IOLR, M234, R62:110.

57. Lt. M. Leeper to post adjutant, April 3, 1873, IOLR, M234, R378:592.

58. Tatum, *Our Red Brothers*, pp. 145-48.

59. Tatum to Hoag, Dec. 9, 1872, Appointment Files, National Archives.

CHAPTER 5

1. Capt. G. K. Sanderson to AAG, Dept. of Texas, April 4, 1873, IOLR, M234, R378:786; Beede to Hoag, April 4, 1873, IOLR, M234, R378:204.

2. *Friends Review* 38 (1885): 570.

3. Haworth to Hoag, June 12, 1873, IOLR, M234, R378:316.

4. Acting CIA to Hoag, Aug. 12, 1873, IOLB 114:67.

5. CIA to Secy. Delano, May 22, 1873, IORB 23:16.

6. Haworth to Cyrus Beede, May 8, 1873, IOLR, M234, R378:289.

7. Thomas C. Battey, *The Life and Adventures Of A Quaker Among the Indians*, pp. 163-64.

8. Secy. Delano to Gov. Davis, March 22, 1873, IOLR, M234, R378:573.

9. Gov. Davis to Secy. Delano, May 12, 1873, in *New York Times*, May 26, 1873, p. 1.

10. Beede to CIA, May 14, 1873, IOLR, R378:287.

11. Sherman's endorsement of letter of Lt. Col. Brook, IOLR, M234, R63:425.

12. Haworth to Hoag, Aug. 21, 1873, IOLR, M234, R378:435.

13. Hoag to CIA, July 31, 1873, IOLR, M234, R378:386.

14. Winfrey and Day, eds., *Indian Papers of Texas*, 4:344.

15. Ibid., p355.

16. Ibid., pp. 357-58.

17. Ibid., p. 356.

18. Ibid., p. 358.

19. Ibid.

20. CIA to Gov. Davis, Oct. 7, 1873, IOLR, M234, R378:51.

21. Battey, *Life and Adventures Of A Quaker*, pp. 202-03.

22. *New York Times*, Oct. 14, 1873, p. 1; CIA to Col. J. W. Davidson, Oct. 9, 1873, IOLR, M234, R378:59.

23. Sherman's endorsement on order of Col. Davidson, Nov. 3, 1873, IOLR, M234, R378:853.

24. Enclosed in Gov. Davis to CIA, Dec. 29, 1873, IOLR, M234, R63:850.

25. Haworth to CIA, Nov. 20, 1873, IOLR, M234, R378:490.

26. AR of CIA, 1873 (ser. 1601, p. 375).

27. CIA to Haworth, Nov. 24, 1873, IOLB, 114:474.

28. Hoag to CIA, Nov. 24, 1873, IOLR, M234, R378:511.

29. Hoag letter quoted by Representative William Lougbridge, House, *Congressional Record*, 43d Cong., 1st sess., 1874, p. 3468.

30. Hoag to CIA, Dec. 1, 1873, IOLR, M234, R378:510.

31. Brunot to Secy. Delano, Nov. 25, 1873, IOLR, M234, R378:22.

32. Beede to CIA, Oct. 30, 1873, IOLR, M234, R62:827.

33. Beede to CIA, March 10, 1874, IOLR, M234, R63:1110.

34. Beede to Hoag, March 30, 1874, IOLR, M234, R379:162.

35. Frank M. Temple, "Colonel Grierson In the Southwest," p. 39.

36. Eschiti is the present family spelling. There are at least fifteen variations on this, the most common being Isatai. He also shows up in the records as White Eagle, and Coyote Droppings has been translated as Rear-end-of-a-wolf.

37. Haworth to Hoag, May 6, 1874, IOLR, M234, R379:218.

38. Col. Davidson to AAG, Dept. of Texas, July 20, 1874, IOLR, M234, R64:1083.

39. Haworth to Hoag, June 8, 1874, IOLR, M234, R379:297.

40. Haworth to Hoag, June 6, 1874, IOLR, M234, R379:291.

41. Battey, *Life and Adventures Of A Quaker*, p. 277.

42. Haworth to Hoag, May 25, 1874, IOLR, M234, R379:257.

43. Haworth to Beede, June 29, 1874, IOLR, M234, R64:4.

44. Haworth to Hoag, June 22, 1874, IOLR, M234, R379:309.

45. Capt. Sanderson to post adjutant, Aug. 8, 1874, IOLR, M234, R379:870.

46. Capt. Sanderson to Haworth, Aug. 10, 1874, IOLR, M234, R379:417.

47. Col. Davidson to AAG, Dept. of Texas, IOLR, M234, R379:37.

48. Haworth to Hoag, May 18, 1875. IOLR, M234, R380:241.

49. Joe F. Taylor, ed., "The Indian Campaign on the Staked Plains, 1874-1875, Part 1," *Panhandle-Plains Historical Review* 34 (1961): 179.

50. Taylor, "The Indian Campaign, Part 2," *Panhandle-Plains Historical Review* 35 (1962): 280.

51. AR of Hoag, 1874 (ser. 1639), p. 522).

52. "A Day Among the Kiowas and Comanches," *Catholic World* (Sept. 1876): 840-41.

53. AR of Haworth, 1875 (ser. 1680, p. 775); Nye, *Carbine and Lance*, p. 230.

54. Mackenzie to Gen. Sheridan, April 17, 1875, *American Scene*, 8, no. 2.

55. Ibid.

56. Sturm's journal is to be found in Dept. of the Missouri—Letters Received (221-5-1875), Record Group 98, NA.

57. Ibid.

58. Ibid.

59. Ibid.

60. Sturm to Mackenzie, May 21, 1875, Dept. of the Missouri—Letters Received (248-5-1875), Record Group 98, NA.

CHAPTER 6

1. Mackenzie to ——, June 3, 1875, *American Scene*, 8, no. 2.

2. Smith to secy. of the interior, July 3, 1875, IORB, 26:339.

3. AR of CIA, 1875 (ser. 1680, p. 514).

4. J. P. C. Shanks to asst. secy. of the interior, April 19, 1875, IOLR, M234, R66:473.

5. Carriker, *Fort Supply*, p. 113.

6. J. R. Richards to Supt. Nicholson, Aug. 4, 1877, IOLR, M234, R382:117; Lt. Parker to post adjutant, Aug. 10, 1877, R382:195; CIA to secy. of the interior, Sept. 7, 1877, IORB, 29:289.

7. AR of Hunt, 1879 (ser. 1910, p. 170).

8. Mackenzie to AAG, Dept. of the Missouri, Aug. 31, 1875, IOLR, M234, R66:940.

9. Mackenzie to AAG, Dept. of the Missouri, June 6, 1876, Fort Sill Letter Book, Fort Sill Museum.

10. Report of William M. Leeds, Feb. 5, 1877, IOLR, M234, R68:972.

11. E. Fenlon to Haworth, Feb. 7, 1873, IOLR, M234, R383:218.

12. Delano to the president, Sept. 14, 1875, IMLS, 16:213.

13. CIA to secy. of the interior, Sept. 27, 1875, IORB, 26:556.

14. Agent Hunt to CIA, Feb. 12, 1879, IOLR, M234, R384:276; CIA to secy. of the interior, March 24, 1879, IORB, 32:475.

15. Agent Hunt to CIA, Nov. 23, 1878, IOLR, M234, R383:973.

16. AR of CIA, 1877 (ser. 1800, p. 399).

17. Haworth to CIA, Feb. 15, 1875, IOLR, M234, R380:154.

18. Cowgill to CIA, Aug. 8, 1875, IOLR, M234, R380:74.

19. *New York Times,* April 14, 1876, p. 3.

20. Report of William M. Leeds, Feb. 5, 1877, IOLR, M234, R68:972.

21. Clipping in IOLR, M234, R380:565.

22. April 7, 1876, p. 5.

23. Lt. Col. John P. Hatch to AAG, Dept. of the Missouri, March 31, 1877, IOLR, M234, R382:668.

24. Quoted in Secy. Schurz to secy. of war, IMLS, 20:88.

25. Haworth to E. C. Kemble, Dec. 29, 1874, IOLR, M234, R380:593.

26. Haworth to Agent Miles, Jan. 3, 1878, Cheyenne and Arapaho Files: Foreign Relations, OHS.

CHAPTER 7

1. Friends to President Hayes, April 11, 1878, IOLR, M234, R69:1285.

2. Hunt to CIA, Oct. 11, 1878, IOLR, M234, R383:892.

3. Response to questionnaire, March 22, 1878, Kiowa Agency Files: Reports of Agents, OHS.

4. George W. Hunt to CIA, May 28, 1878, IOLR, M234, R383:606.

5. Mills to secy. of the interior, March 21, 1878, IOLR, M234, R384:160.

6. Davidson to AAG, Dept. of the Missouri, April 18, 1878, IOLR, M234, R384:334.

7. H. P. N. Gammel, *The Laws of Texas 1822-1897,* p. 1489.

8. Cited in CIA to Hunt, Oct. 21, 1882, IOLB (Civilization) 37:96.

9. Kenner, *New Mexican-Plains Indian Relations,* p. 211.

10. CIA to Hunt, July 18, 1881, IOLB (Civilization) 32:388; Nye, *Carbine and Lance,* pp. 263 ff.

11. Hunt to CIA, Dec. 18, 1880, IOLR, M234, R386:556.

12. Response to questionnaire, March 22, 1878, Kiowa Agency Files: Reports of Agents, OHS.

13. AR of Hunt, 1885 (ser. 2379, p. 311).

14. Response to questionnaire, March 22, 1878, Kiowa Agency Files: Reports of Agents, OHS.

15. CIA to Hunt, May 5, 1879, IOLB (Civilization) 25:2; AR of Hunt, 1879 (ser. 1910, p. 176).

16. AR of Hunt, 1882 (ser. 2100, p. 129).

17. Secy. of the interior to CIA, March 1, 1883, Indian Division, Letters Sent 31:252.

18. AR of Hunt, 1885 (ser. 2379, p. 311).

19. Davis to post adjutant, June 13, 1879, Kiowa Agency Files: Cattle Grazing, OHS.

20. CIA to secy. of the interior, Jan. 18, 1881, IORB 38:236.

21. CIA to secy. of the interior, April 2, 1881, IORB 39:1; AR of CIA, 1881 (ser. 2018, p. 11); AR of secy. of the interior, 1881 (ser. 2017, p. xi).

22. CIA to Hunt, March 15, 1882, IOLB (Finance) 183:393.

23. Hunt to CIA, April 26, 1882, K 10:237, OHS.

24. Senate, *Congressional Record*, 47th Cong., 1st sess., 1882, pp. 2638-39.

25. Circular no. 10, March 1, 1878, *Circulars*, Book no. 1, NA.

26. Circular no. 23, Aug. 22, 1878, *Circulars*, Book no. 2, NA.

27. Circular no. 102, Sept. 27, 1882, *Circulars*, Book no. 3, NA.

28. Circular no. 112, May 31, 1883, *Circulars*, Book no. 3, NA.

29. For a more complete discussion of this, see William T. Hagan, *Indian Police and Judges.*

30. Haworth to CIA, Jan. 26, 1878, IOLR, M234, R383:115.

31. William T. Hagan, "Kiowas, Comanches, and Cattlemen, 1867-1906."

32. Secy. of the interior to secy. of war, Aug. 5, 1882 (ser. 2165, p. 75).

33. H. P. Jones to Hunt, June 21, 1883, Kiowa Agency Files: Quanah Parker, OHS; Geo. W. Fox, Jr. to Hunt, Oct. 13, 1884, Kiowa Agency Files: Cattle Grazing, OHS.

34. Lester Fields Sheffy, *The Francklyn Land and Cattle Company*, pp. 109 ff.

35. Council of May 23, 1884, K 17:46, OHS.

36. Folsom to CIA, Dec. 16, 1884 (ser. 2362, p. 672).

37. *New York Times*, Aug. 2, 1885, p. 7.

38. Annuity Issue, Nov. 27, 1878, IOLR, M234, R384:472.

39. Hunt to CIA, Nov. 24, 1880, IOLR, M234, R386:496.

40. Annuity Issue, Nov. 27, 1878, IOLR, M234, R384:472.

41. Dallas *Weekly Herald*, June 5, 1875, p. 1.

42. Mackenzie to Isaac Parker, Sept. 5, 1877, Fort Sill Letter Book, Fort Sill Museum.

43. Goodnight to Hunt, Sept. 25, 1880, Kiowa Agency Files: Quanah Parker, OHS.

44. Davidson to AAG, Dept. of the Missouri, Oct. 29, 1878, IOLR, M234, R384:444.

45. Council of June 10, 1881, IOLR (10933-1881).

46. Quanah to Hunt, July 9, 1885, Kiowa Agency Files: Quanah Parker, OHS.

47. Council on Leasing, Feb. 5, 1885 (ser. 2362, p. 764).

48. Thomas F. Woodward to Hunt, Feb. 5, 1884 (ser. 2362, p. 654).

49. Quoted in James T. DeShields, *Cynthia Ann Parker*, p. 62.

50. *Dallas Morning News*, Dec. 21, 1885, copy in Fort Sill Museum. A detailed discussion of the episode is to be found in Ronnie Tyler, "Quanah Parker's Narrow Escape."

51. Quanah to secy. of the interior, March 25, 1885, Kiowa Agency Appointments File, NA.

52. For a discussion of their role, see William T. Hagan, "Squaw Men on the Kiowa, Comanche and Apache Reservation."

53. Clark to Agent Hall, Jan. 27, 1886, Kiowa Agency Files: Medicine Men, OHS.

54. Conover to Agent Myers, Oct. 4, 1889, Kiowa Agency Files: Cattle Grazing, OHS.

55. AR of Hunt, 1884 (ser. 2287, p. 124).

56. AR of CIA, 1882 (ser. 2100, p. 34).

57. AR of secy. of the interior, 1883 (ser. 2190, p. ix).

58. CIA to Hunt, April 18, 1884, IOLB (Civilization) 44:338.

59. Report of Indian School superintendent, 1885 (ser. 2379, p. 114).

60. Ibid., 108.

61. CIA to Hunt, July 19, 1882, Kiowa Agency Files: Carlisle, OHS.

62. Pratt to Hunt, May 3, 1884, Kiowa Agency Files: Carlisle, OHS.

63. List dated Dec. 19, 1900, Kiowa Agency Files: Carlisle, OHS.

64. CIA to Agent Hall, Sept. 17, 1885, IOLB (Education) 1:27.

65. William J. Pollock to CIA, Feb. 20, 1880, IF, no. 1274, NA.

66. CIA to Hunt, Nov. 11, 1884, IOLB (Civilization) 47:264.

67. Paris H. Folsom to CIA, Dec. 16, 1884 (ser. 2362, p. 670).

68. Beck to secy. of the interior, Jan. 24, 1885, Kiowa Agency Appointments File, NA.

69. Price to secy. of the interior, Dec. 27, 1884, Kiowa Agency Appointments File, NA.

CHAPTER 8

1. AR of CIA, 1889 (ser. 2725, p. 3).

2. AR of secy. of the interior, 1890 (ser. 2840, p. xxiv).

3. CIA to Agent Day, June 14, 1892, IOLB (Land) 120:91.

4. Quoted in Dora Neill Raymond, *Captain Lee Hall of Texas,* p. 203.

5. J. J. Methvin, *In the Limelight,* p. 50.

6. C. C. Painter, *The Condition of Affairs In Indian Territory and California,* p. 44.

7. E. E. White, *Experiences of a Special Indian Agent.*

8. L. F. Pearson to Myers, March 22, 1889, Kiowa Agency Files: Agents and Agency, OHS.

9. Kiowa Agency Appointments File, NA.

10. James A. Gary to secy. of the interior, Oct. 30, 1891, Kiowa Agency Appointments File, NA.

11. CIA to secy. of the interior, IORB, 29:381.

12. *Senate Reports,* no. 2707, "Report of the Senate Select Committee on Indian Traders," 50th Cong., 2d sess. (ser. 2623, p. vi).

13. CIA to Indian Agents, Aug. 28, 1890, Kiowa Agency Files: Vices, OHS.

14. Circular no. 67, May 10, 1881, *Circulars,* Book no. 2.

15. Circular no. 157, Oct. 5, 1885, *Circulars,* Book no. 3.

16. Hunt to CIA, June 1, 1880, IOLR, M234, R386:347.

17. Hunt to CIA, July 7, 1885, K20:89, OHS.

18. W. H. Cleveland, March 30, 1891, IOLR (15879-1891); J. A. Leonard to CIA, IOLR (22565-1891).

19. George W. Conover, *Sixty Years In Southwest Oklahoma,* p. 71.

20. Flipper to post adjutant, May 2, 1880, IOLR, M234, R386:973.

21. Hall to CIA, June 28, 1886, K 24:6, OHS.

22. Council Resolution, May 26, 1890, IOLR (17186-1890).

23. CIA to secy. of the interior, Oct. 24, 1890, IOLB (Land) 206:102.

24. Arthur W. Tinker to secy. of the interior, June 30, 1891, IOLR (26273-1891).

25. Petition, June 7, 1892, Special Cases, no. 191, NA; CIA to secy. of the interior, June 15, 1892, IOLB (Land) 120:112.

26. CIA to Agent Adams, Dec. 18, 1890, Kiowa Agency Files: Indian Houses, OHS.

27. AR of CIA, 1885 (ser. 2379, p. xii).

28. Grantham to Agent [Oct. 25, 1890], Kiowa Agency Files: Quanah Parker, OHS.

29. Circular of Agent Hall, enclosed in Hall to CIA, Oct. 29, 1885, IOLR (7421-1886).

30. AR of Adams, 1890 (ser. 2841, p. 186).

31. CIA to Agent White, May 7, 1888, IOLB (Land) 173:217.

32. Clark to Agent, Feb. 29, 1892, Kiowa Agency Files: Estates, OHS.

33. Report of Inspector Tinker, May 23, 1891, IF 9:460, NA.

34. CIA to agents, July 21, 1890, AR of CIA, 1890 (ser. 2841, p. cxlvi).

35. Copy of CIA to secy. of the interior, Dec. 8, 1890, IRAP, R17.

36. CIA to Agent Adams, Dec. 13, 1890, IOLB (Accounts) 117:30.

37. *Marlow Magnet*, June 15, 1893, p. 1.

38. Ibid., July 4, 1893, p. 1.

39. CIA to Agent Adams, July 26, 1890, Kiowa Agency Files: Marriages, OHS.

40. Adams to CIA, July 17, 1890, K 33:219, OHS.

41. Adams to CIA, Aug. 12, 1890, K 33:266, OHS.

42. Adams to CIA, Nov. 3, 1890, K 35:109, OHS.

43. AR of Teller, 1883 (ser. 2190, p. xi).

44. Quanah to Hall, April 7, 1887, Kiowa Agency Files: Quanah Parker, OHS.

45. Goodnight to Agent White, July 3, 1888, Kiowa Agency Files: Celebrations, OHS.

46. Adams to Goodnight, July 5, 1890, K 33:195, OHS.

47. Quanah to Adams, May 13, 1890, Kiowa Agency Files: Quanah Parker, OHS.

48. Hugh L. Scott, "The Messiah Dance In the Indian Territory," in Scott Papers, Box no. 75, Library of Congress.

49. CIA to Adams, Dec. 5, 1890, IOLB (Accounts) 117:267.

50. Davis to AAG, Dept. of the Missouri, Dec. 23, 1890, Special Cases, no. 188, NA.

51. Scott to post adjutant, Dec. 16, 1890, Special Cases, no. 188, NA.

52. Scott to post adjutant, Feb. 10, 1891, Special Cases, no. 188, NA.

53. Adams to CIA, Feb. 4, 1891, Special Cases, no. 188, NA.

54. Quanah to editor of Fort Worth *Gazette,* enclosed in Wirt Davis to AAG, Dept. of the Missouri, Special Cases, no. 188, NA.

55. Clark to Colonel ——, Aug. 11, 1883, Kiowa Agency Files: Medicine Men, OHS.

56. AR of Hall, 1886 (ser. 2467, p. 348).

57. AR of White, 1888 (ser. 2637, pp. 98–99).

58. White's order of June 6, 1888, Kiowa Agency Files: Vices, OHS.

59. AR of Myers, 1889 (ser. 2725, p. 191).

60. AR of White, 1888 (ser. 2637, p. 97).

61. Atkins to secy. of the interior, Dec. 28, 1887, IOLB (Education) 11:74.

62. AR of CIA, 1890 (ser. 2841, p. cli).

63. CIA Morgan to agents and superintendents, Dec. 10, 1889, AR of CIA, 1890 (ser. 2841, p. clxvii).

64. CIA Morgan to agents and superintendents, Jan. 28, 1890, AR of CIA, 1890 (ser. 2841, p. clxviii).

65. Report of Inspector Armstrong, Sept. 7, 1885, IF 2:284, NA.

66. Painter to Herbert Welsh, June 6, 1887, IRAP, R12.

67. CIA to Agent Myers, July 26, 1889, IOLB (Education) 18:301.

68. Painter to Herbert Welsh, June 6, 1887, IRA, R12.

69. Myers to CIA, Sept. 7, 1889, K 31:327.

70. AR of Hall, 1887 (ser. 2542, p. 165); Report of Inspector Thomas, June 30, 1888, Inspectors Files 6:206, NA; AR of Agent Myers, 1889 (ser. 2725, p. 189).

71. Report of Inspector Mallet, Sept. 7, 1889, IF 7:450, NA.

72. CIA to Day, July 13, 1892, IOLB (Education) 41:418.

73. Report of Inspector Tinker, June 18, 1891, IF 9:471, NA.

74. Report of Inspector Gardner, Nov. 16, 1892, IF 11:1, NA.

CHAPTER 9

1. Morgan to agents, Jan. 24, 1890, AR of CIA, 1890 (ser. 2841, p. clxvii).

2. Ibid.

3. C. C. Painter to Herbert Welsh, Feb. 15, 1887, IRAP, R12; CIA to Lone Wolf, Feb. 16, 1887, IOLB (Land) 78:253.

4. CIA to Hall, March 24, 1887, IOLB (Land) 79:412.

5. Acting secy. of the interior to CIA, June 10, 1887, IDLS 50:466.

6. Agent Myers to CIA, Sept. 7, 1889, K 31:325, OHS.

7. Clipping from *Iowa Park Texan*, enclosed in J. S. Works to secy. of the interior [March 1892], Special Cases, no. 191.

8. "Commissioner's Journal," *Senate Doc.*, no. 77, 55th Cong., 3d sess., 1899, pp. 8-58.

9. Ibid., p. 9.

10. Ibid., p. 10.

11. Ibid., p. 11.

12. CIA to secy. of the interior, Nov. 17, 1892, IOLB (Land) 248:21.

13. "Journal," pp. 29-30.

14. Ibid., p. 33.

15. Ibid.

16. Ibid., p. 32.

17. *Twelfth Annual Report of the Executive Committee of the Indian Rights Association* (Philadelphia, 1895), pp. 18-19, 45.

18. "Journal," p. 36.

19. Ibid., p. 37.

20. Ibid., p. 39.

21. Ibid., pp. 30-31.

22. Ibid., p. 42.

23. Ibid., p. 44.

24. Ibid., pp. 51-52.

25. Ibid., p. 15.

26. Ibid., p. 30.

27. CIA to secy. of the interior, Nov. 17, 1892, IOLB (Land) 248:21.

28. CIA to Prindle, Nov. 10, 1892, IOLB (Land) 247:361.

CHAPTER 10

1. CIA to Agent Baldwin, March 13, 1895, IOLB (Land) 300:301.

2. *Minco Minstrel*, July 14, 1893, p. 5.

3. W. H. Able to CIA [n.d.], IOLR (25353-1894).

4. Methvin, *In the Limelight*, p. 96.

5. AR of CIA, 1900 (ser. 4101, p. 10).

6. All population statistics are from the annual reports of the agents.

7. Agent Myers to CIA, May 28, 1889, K 31:15, OHS.

8. W. H. Able to CIA, Nov. 24, 1894, IOLR (3712-1894).

9. Copy of CIA to secy. of the interior, Dec. 8, 1890, IRAP, R17.

10. CIA to Agent Baldwin, April 7, 1896, IOLB (Education) 75:39.

11. AR of Agent Adams, 1890 (ser. 2841, p. 186).

12. AR of Baldwin, 1897 (ser. 3641, p. 233).

13. G. B. Pray to CIA, Sept. 15, 1898, IOLR (42609–1898).

14. Baldwin to CIA, May 23, 1896, K 51:149, OHS.

15. Cyrus Beede to secy. of the interior, Sept. 5, 1898, Interior Dept.–Letters Received (41159–1898); AR of J. W. Haddon, Aug. 27, 1899 (ser. 3915: p. 290).

16. 28 St. 313.

17. Baldwin to secy. of the interior, May 26, 1898, Special Cases, no. 191, NA.

18. AR of Agent Randlett, 1900 (ser. 4101, p. 333).

19. *The Sixteenth Annual Report of the Executive Committee of the Indian Rights Association* (Philadelphia, 1899), p. 44.

20. CIA to Baldwin, Oct. 13, 1897, IOLB (Land) 366:24.

21. CIA to Methvin, June 3, 1893, IOLB (Land) 260:1.

22. Charles Reed McBurney, "Cache Creek Indian Mission" (M.A. thesis, University of Kansas, 1948), p. 107.

23. *Marlow Magnet*, April 12, 1894, p. 4.

24. Ibid., June 14, 1894, p. 4.

25. *Minco Minstrel*, July 14, 1893, p. 5.

26. *Marlow Magnet*, March 22, 1894, p. 1.

27. Ibid., March 1, 1894, p. 1.

28. *Guthrie Daily Leader*, Nov. 2, 1893, p. 2.

29. *Minco Minstrel*, Oct. 13, 1893, p. 1.

30. R. E. Montgomery to President Cleveland, Jan. 29, 1894, Special Cases, no. 199, NA.

31. CIA to J. McCarthy, Oct. 25, 1893, IOLB (Land) 267:272.

32. *Chickasha Express*, Nov. 10, 1893, p. 1.

33. *Minco Minstrel*, Oct. 21, 1893, p. 2.

34. *Marlow Magnet*, April 26, 1894, p. 1.

35. J. C. Terrell, Jr. to S. W. T. Lanham, March 22, 1897, Special Cases, no. 191, NA.

36. CIA to James Hall, May 31, 1892, IOLB (Land) 238:232.

37. Baldwin to CIA, Jan. 22, 1895, K 44:83.

38. Report to Baldwin [Jan. 1895], K 44:86.

39. CIA to Baldwin, Feb. 27, 1895, IOLB (Land) 299:104; Baldwin to CIA, Aug. 26, 1895, K 46:96, OHS.

40. Baldwin to CIA, Feb. 9, 1898, K 58:289.

41. Wilson and Silberstein to Baldwin, June 25, 1896, Kiowa Agency Files: Cattle Grazing, OHS.

42. Examination of James N. Jones, April 28, 1899, Kiowa Agency Files: Cattle Grazing, OHS.

43. Council with CIA, March 17, 1898, IOLR (12521½-1898).

44. Beede to secy. of the interior, Sept. 16, 1898, IOLR (43348-1898).

45. Baldwin to CIA, May 13, 1896, IOLR (18973-1896).

46. Baldwin to CIA, Dec. 28, 1896, Special Cases, no. 191, NA.

47. Pray to CIA, Aug. 30, 1898, Special Cases, no. 191, NA.

48. Baldwin to Burnett, Jan. 20, 1896, K 49:161; Baldwin to secy. of the interior, Jan. 28, 1896, Special Cases, no. 191, NA.

49. Copies of Quanah's letters, Feb. 1, 1898, Kiowa Agency Files: Federal Relations, OHS.

50. Baldwin to CIA, Aug. 3, 1897, IOLR (32253-1897).

51. AR of Baldwin, 1895 (ser. 3382, p. 250).

52. Gilbert B. Pray to CIA, Sept. 29, 1898, K63:68, OHS.

53. Baldwin to CIA, May 17, 1895, K 44:388, OHS.

54. Baldwin to CIA, July 24, 1895, K 46:19, OHS.

55. Baldwin's endorsement on charges brought against him in his personnel file, Record Group 94, NA.

56. Baldwin to William C. Shelley, Jan. 17, 1896, K 49:151.

57. Baldwin to George Wright, May 31, 1897, Interior Dept.—Letters Received (2261-1894).

58. Baldwin to S. B. Burnett, March 22, 1897, K 56:38.

59. Baldwin to CIA, Nov. 5, 1897, K 58:100.

60. Baldwin to CIA, Jan. 8, 1898, K 58:212.

61. George Madera to agent, Aug. 14, 1894, Kiowa Agency Files: Quanah Parker, OHS.

62. Martha Leota Buntin, "History of the Kiowa, Comanche, and Wichita Indian Agency," p. 137.

63. CIA to Baldwin, Aug. 22, 1896, IOLB (Land) 338:147.

64. Secy. of the interior to secy. of war, April 16, 1897, Indian Division, Letters Sent 91:310.

65. Baldwin to CIA, Jan. 11, 1898, K 58:21, OHS.

66. Report of Francis E. Leupp, March 31, 1897, in Welsh Collection, Historical Society of Pennsylvania.

67. Francis E. Leupp to Herbert Welsh, March 19, 1898, IRAP, R24.

68. Pray to CIA, May 25, 1898, IOLR (24520-1898).

69. S. M. Brosius to Herbert Welsh, Oct. 21, 1898, IRAP, R24.

70. McLaughlin to secy. of the interior, Nov. 19, 1898, McLaughlin Papers, R23:408.

71. Randlett to CIA, Aug. 18, 1899, K72:101, OHS.

72. Randlett to CIA, April 5, 1900, Special Cases, no. 191, NA.

CHAPTER 11

1. Morgan to secy. of the interior, Nov. 17, 1892, IOLB (Land) 248:21.

2. Noble to the president, Dec. 23, 1892, Indian Division, Letters Sent 77:372.

3. CIA to secy. of the interior, Jan. 19, 1900, IOLB (Land) 418:208.

4. Copy of the memorial from National Anthropological Archives, Smithsonian Institution; the endorsements and a version of Scott's accompanying letter may be found in *Senate Doc.*, no. 77, 55th Cong., 3d sess., 1899, pp. 4-5.

5. Ibid., p. 6.

6. Ibid., p. 7.

7. Ibid.

8. *Marlow Magnet*, Feb. 1, 1894, p. 1.

9. Informal talk of Jan. 30, 1896, Kiowa Agency Files: Councils, OHS.

10. Baldwin to House Committee on Indian Affairs, March 29, 1897, IOLR (11978-1897).

11. Conference, April 29, 1897, IOLR (20253-1897).

12. AR of Baldwin, 1897 (ser. 3641, p. 233).

13. Baldwin to CIA, Aug. 3, 1897, IOLR (35253-1897).

14. S. M. Brosius to Herbert Welsh, June 8, 1898, IRAP, R24.

15. S. M. Brosius to Herbert Welsh, Feb. 12 and Feb. 13, 1899, IRAP, R25.

16. *An Appeal in Behalf of the Comanches, Kiowas, and Apaches* (Philadelphia: Indian Rights Association, 1899), p. 5.

17. Abbott to Herbert Welsh, Feb. 20, 1899, IRAP, R25.

18. Council, Oct. 9-11, 1899, IOLR (70550-1901).

19. CIA to secy. of the interior, Dec. 23, 1899, IOLB (Land) 425:87.

20. CIA to secy. of the interior, Jan. 5, 1900, IOLB (Land) 426:444.

21. Oklahoma City *Daily Oklahoman*, Feb. 15, 1900, p. 1.

22. Herbert Welsh to George F. Hoar, March 14, 1900, IRAP, R10.

23. For the final version of the Jerome Agreement, see *Statutes at Large*, 31 St. 676.

24. Brosius to M. K. Sniffen, March 9, 1900, IRAP, R26.

CHAPTER 12

1. *Woodward News*, Aug. 10, 1900, p. 2.

2. *El Reno News,* June 27, 1901, p. 10; Randlett to CIA, June 1, 1901, K 87:329, OHS.

3. Randlett to Quanah, June 3, 1901, K 88:111, OHS.

4. *New York Times,* June 21, 1901, p. 2.

5. Indians to CIA, Sept. 17, 1900, IOLR (46605-1900).

6. Randlett to CIA, Dec. 10, 1900, K 81:197, OHS.

7. Waggoner to Randlett, Sept. 11, 1901, Special Cases, no. 191, NA.

8. Randlett to Sugg, Nov. 2, 1901, K 92:318, OHS.

9. Alexander Gullet and W. I. Gilbert to Randlett, June 6, 1901, Kiowa Agency Files: Cattle Grazing, OHS.

10. Randlett to CIA, June 12, 1901, K 89:157, OHS.

11. Oklahoma City, *Daily Oklahoman,* June 28, 1900, p. 2.

12. Randlett to secy. of the interior, July 25, 1901, K 90:165, OHS.

13. CIA to secy. of the interior, Oct. 19, 1900, IOLB (Land) 228:261.

14. CIA to commissioner of the General Land Office, Dec. 31, 1900, IOLB (Land) 464:83.

15. "Drawing Homesteads In Oklahoma," *The Independent,* Aug. 8, 1901, p. 1826.

16. For the opening, see "Drawing Homesteads In Oklahoma," *The Independent,* Aug. 8, 1901, p. 1826; William Hymen Murphy, "A History of the Opening of the Wichita-Caddo-Kiowa-Comanche-Apache Reservation"; John Curry Haley, "The Opening of the Kiowa and Comanche Country"; Berlin B. Chapman, "Land Office Business at Lawton and El Reno."

17. Chapman, "Land Office Business," p. 19.

18. CIA to Randlett, Sept. 9, 1901, IOLB (Land) 499:429.

19. Randlett to CIA, Oct. 7, 1901, K 92:160, OHS.

20. Randlett to CIA, Oct. 2, 1901, K 89:426.

21. CIA to Agent, June 28, 1905, Kiowa Agency Files: Finance; Randlett to CIA, Jan. 21, 1906, K 119:80, OHS.

22. AR of Randlett, 1904 (ser. 4798, p. 294).

23. Lawton *Daily News Republican,* Aug. 25, 1904, p. 1.

24. Randlett to CIA, Oct. 21, 1904, K 118:102.

25. AR of Randlett, 1905 (ser. 4959, p. 300).

26. Randlett to Horace Speed, Dec. 30, 1902, K 101:412.

27. Randlett to CIA, Feb. 1, 1904, IOLR (8733-1904).

28. *Senate Doc.,* no. 26, 58th Cong., 2d sess. 1903 (serial 4646, p. 468).

29. Ibid., p. 469.

30. Randlett to CIA, July 30, 1902, K 101:95, OHS.

31. Roosevelt to CIA, April 14, 1905, IOLR (37866-1905).

32. 187 U.S. Supreme Court 553.

33. *Twenty-first Annual Report of the Executive Committee of the Indian Rights Association* (Philadelphia, 1904), p. 24.

34. AR of Randlett, 1902 (ser. 4458, p. 289).

35. McLaughlin to secy. of the interior, Feb. 11, 1903, McLaughlin Papers, R25:263.

36. *Senate Doc.*, no. 26, 58th Cong., 2d sess., 1903 (ser. 4646, p. 473).

37. Ibid., p. 495.

38. Ibid., p. 497.

39. *Congressional Record*, 57th Cong., 2d sess., 1903, p. 2291.

40. AR of Randlett, 1904 (ser. 4798, p. 294); Randlett to CIA, April 5, 1904, K 110:369, OHS.

41. AR of Randlett, 1904 (ser. 4798, p. 294).

42. *Congressional Record*, 59th Cong., 1st sess., 1906, p. 4739; Blackman to CIA, April 2, 1906, K 129:304.

43. *Statutes at Large*, 34 St. 213.

44. Ibid., 34 St. 550.

45. AR of CIA, 1907 (ser. 5296, p. 113).

EPILOGUE

1. Kiowa Agency Narrative Report, 1910, Narrative Report Files, NA.

2. Oklahoma City *Daily Oklahoman*, Nov. 29, 1908, p. 8.

3. Agent Stecker to CIA, Dec. 29, 1908, Special Cases, no. 306, NA.

4. *Statutes at Large*, 35 St. 456; 36 St. 861.

5. Kiowa Agency Narrative Report, 1911, Narrative Report Files, NA.

6. Charles H. Dickson to CIA, Dec. 24, 1907, IOLR (45761-1907).

7. James M. Day, "Two Quanah Parker Letters," p. 317.

8. Agent Randlett to Quanah, May 29, 1901, K 87:297, OHS.

9. For the establishment of the park and the arrival of the buffalo, see Jack D. Haley, "The Wichita Mountains: The Struggle to Preserve A Wilderness."

10. Oklahoma City *Daily Oklahoman*, Aug. 24, 1907, p. 1.

11. Ferris to CIA, Jan. 24, 1911, Special Cases, no. 150, NA.

Bibliography

MANUSCRIPTS

National Archives
Record Group 75
Letters Received by the Office of Indian Affairs (both manuscript and microfilm)
Letter Books of the Office of Indian Affairs
Inspector Reports, 1873–1880
Abstracts of Inspectors Reports, 1873–1880
Circulars, 1854–1885
Special Cases
Indian Claims Commission, Docket no. 32
Record Group 48
Letter Books of the Indian Division, Office of the Secretary of the Interior
Letters Received by the Indian Division, Office of the Secretary of the Interior
Record Group 94
Personnel Files of Frank D. Baldwin, Hugh G. Brown, Maury Nichols, and James F. Randlett
Oklahoma Historical Society
Kiowa Agency Files: includes 519 volumes, about 160 of them letterpress copy books, and nearly 750,000 pages of manuscript
Cheyenne and Arapaho Agency Files: Foreign Relations
Library of Congress
Hugh L. Scott Papers
Fort Worth Federal Records Center
Kiowa Agency Files
Fort Sill Museum
Picture Collections
Fort Sill Letter Books

317

Library of the University of Oklahoma
   Doris Duke Collection
Historical Society of Pennsylvania
   Indian Rights Association Papers (microfilm edition
      by Scholarly Resources, Incorporated, Philadelphia)
   Herbert Welsh Papers
Haverford College
   Quaker Collection
Reed Library, State University College, Fredonia, micro-
   film rolls 23, 25, and 30 of Major James McLaughlin
   Papers (originals in Assumption College Archives)

BOOKS, ARTICLES, AND THESES

Agnew, Brad. "The 1858 War Against the Comanches."
   Chronicles of Oklahoma (Summer 1971), pp. 211-29.
American Scene 8 (1967), no. 2.
Athearn, Robert G. *William Tecumseh Sherman and the
   Settlement of the West.* Norman: University of Okla-
   homa Press, 1956.
Baldwin, Alice Blackwood. *Memories of the Late Frank D.
   Baldwin, Major General, U.S.A.* Los Angeles: Wetzel,
   1929.
Battey, Thomas C. *The Life and Adventures of a Quaker
   Among the Indians.* Introduction by Alice Marriott.
   Norman: University of Oklahoma Press, 1968.
Berthrong, Donald J. *The Southern Cheyennes.* Norman:
   University of Oklahoma Press, 1963.
———. "White Neighbors Come Among the Southern
   Cheyenne and Arapaho." *Kansas Quarterly* (Fall 1971),
   pp. 105-15.
"A British Journalist Reports the Medicine Lodge Peace
   Councils of 1867." *Kansas Historical Quarterly* (Autumn
   1967), pp. 249-320.
Buntin, Martha Leota. "Beginning of the Leasing of the
   Surplus Lands on the Kiowa and Comanche Reservation."
   Chronicles of Oklahoma (September 1932), pp. 369-82.
———. "History of the Kiowa, Comanche, and Wichita Indi-
   an Agency." M.A. thesis, University of Oklahoma, 1931.

Butler, Josiah. "Pioneer School Teaching at the Comanche-Kiowa Agency School 1870-3," *Chronicles of Oklahoma* (December 1928), pp. 482-528.

Carriker, Robert C. *Fort Supply, Indian Territory*. Norman: University of Oklahoma Press, 1970.

Chapman, Berlin B. "The Day in Court For the Kiowa, Comanche and Apache Tribes." *Great Plains Journal* (Fall 1962), pp. 1-21.

——. "Land Office Business at Lawton and El Reno." *Great Plains Journal* (Fall 1967), pp. 1-25.

Conover, George W. *Sixty Years in Southwest Oklahoma*. Anadarko: N. T. Plummer, n.d.

Corwin, Hugh D. "Delos K. Lonewolf, Kiowa." *Chronicles of Oklahoma* (Winter 1961-62), pp. 433-36.

——. "Protestant Missionary Work Among the Comanches and Kiowas." *Chronicles of Oklahoma* (Spring 1968), pp. 41-57.

Cox, James D. *Historical and Biographical Record of the Cattle Industry and the Gentlemen of Texas and Adjacent Territory*. 2 vols. New York: Antiquarian Press, 1959.

Cutler, Lee. "Lawrie Tatum and the Kiowa Agency 1869-1873." *Arizona and the West* (Autumn 1971), pp. 221-44.

Day, James M. "Two Quanah Parker Letters." *Chronicles of Oklahoma* (Autumn 1966), pp. 313-18.

"A Day Among the Kiowas and Comanches." *Catholic World* (September 1876), pp. 837-48.

DeShields, James T., *Cynthia Ann Parker*. San Antonio: Naylor, 1934.

Douglas, C. L. *Cattle Kings of Texas*. Dallas: Cecil Baugh, 1939.

"Drawing Homesteads in Oklahoma." *The Independent*, Aug. 8, 1901, p. 1826.

Ellis, Richard N. *General Pope and U.S. Indian Policy*. Albuquerque: University of New Mexico Press, 1970.

Estep, Raymond. *The Removal of the Texas Indians and the Founding of Fort Cobb*. Oklahoma City: Oklahoma Historical Society, 1961.

Fritz, Henry E. *The Movement for Indian Assimilation,*

1860-1890, Philadelphia: University of Pennsylvania Press, 1963.

Gammel, H. P. N. *The Laws of Texas 1822-1897.* Austin: Gammel, 1898.

Gibson, A. M. "Confederates on the Plains." *Great Plains Journal* (Fall 1964), pp. 7-16.

Hagan, William T. *Indian Police and Judges.* New Haven: Yale University Press, 1966.

———. "Kiowas, Comanches, and Cattlemen, 1867-1906." *Pacific Historical Review* (August 1971), pp. 333-55.

———. "Squaw Men on the Kiowa, Comanche, and Apache Reservation." In *The Frontier Challenge,* edited by John G. Clark, pp. 171-202. Lawrence: University Press of Kansas, 1971.

Haley, Jack D. "The Wichita Mountains: The Struggle to Preserve A Wilderness." *Chronicles of Oklahoma* (Fall 1973), pp. 71-99, and (Spring 1974), pp. 149-83.

Haley, John Curry. "The Opening of the Kiowa and Comanche Country." M.A. thesis, University of Oklahoma, 1940.

Hiatt, Burritt M. "James M. Haworth, Quaker Indian Agent." *Bulletin of the Friends Historical Association* (Autumn 1958), pp. 80-93.

Indian Rights Association Executive Committee Annual Reports. Philadelphia, 1886-1907.

Jackson, Clyde L., and Jackson, Grace. *Quanah Parker.* San Antonio: Naylor, 1959.

Jones, Douglas C. *The Treaty of Medicine Lodge.* Norman: University of Oklahoma Press, 1966.

Kappler, Charles J. *Indian Treaties 1778-1883.* New York, Interland, 1972.

Kelsey, Rayner W. *Friends and the Indians, 1655-1917.* Philadelphia: Associated Executive Committee of Friends On Indian Affairs, 1917.

Kenner, Charles N. *A History of New Mexican-Plains Indian Relations.* Norman: University of Oklahoma Press, 1969.

Kiowa-Comanche Indians: Transcript of Hearing of the

Kiowa, Comanche, and Apache Tribes of Indians vs. The United States of America. 2 vols. New York: Garland, 1974.

Kroeker, Marvin. "Colonel W. B. Hazen In the Indian Territory." *Chronicles of Oklahoma* (Spring 1964), pp. 53-73.

Mayhall, Mildred P. *The Kiowas.* Norman: University of Oklahoma Press, 1962.

Merrill, James M. "General Sherman's Letter to His Son: A Visit to Fort Sill." *Chronicles of Oklahoma* (Summer 1969), pp. 126-31.

Methvin, J. J. *In the Limelight.* Anadarko: Plummer, 1928.

Monahan, Forrest D., Jr. "The Kiowa–Comanche Reservation In the 1890's." *Chronicles of Oklahoma* (Winter 1967-1968). pp. 451-63.

Mooney, James. *The Ghost-Dance Religion and the Sioux Outbreak of 1890.* Glorieta, N. M.: Rio Grande Press, 1973.

Murphy, William Hymen. "A History of the Opening of the Wichita–Caddo–Kiowa–Comanche–Apache Reservation." M.A. thesis, Oklahoma Agricultural and Mechanical University, 1932.

Nicholson, William. "A Tour of Indian Agencies in Kansas and the Indian Territory in 1870." *Kansas Historical Quarterly* 3 (Nov. 1934): 289-326, 343-84.

Nunn, William Curtis. "Texas During the Administration of E. J. Davis." Ph.D. dissertation, University of Texas, 1938.

Nye, Wilbur Sturtevant. *Bad Medicine and Good.* Norman: University of Oklahoma Press, 1962.

———. *Carbine and Lance.* Norman: University of Oklahoma Press, 1962.

Painter, C. C. *The Condition of Indian Affairs In Indian Territory and California.* Philadelphia: Indian Rights Association, 1888.

Priest, Loring Benson. *Uncle Sam's Stepchildren.* New York: Octagon Press, 1969.

Raymond, Dora Neill. *Captain Lee Hall of Texas*. Norman: University of Oklahoma Press, 1940.

Richardson, Rupert Norvall. *The Comanche Barrier to South Plains Settlement*. Glendale, Calif.: Arthur H. Clark 1933.

———. *The Frontier of Northwest Texas 1846 to 1876*. Glendale, Calif.: Arthur H. Clark, 1963.

———, ed. "The Death of Nacona and the Recovery of Cynthia Ann Parker." *Southwestern Quarterly* (July 1942), pp. 15-21.

Roosevelt, Theodore. "A Wolf Hunt in Oklahoma." *Scribners* (November 1905), pp. 513-32.

Scott, Hugh Lenox. *Some Memoirs of a Soldier*. New York: Century, 1928.

Sheffy, Lester Fields. *The Francklyn Land and Cattle Company*. Austin: University of Texas Press, 1963.

Steele, Aubrey Leroy. "The Beginning of Quaker Administration of Indian Affairs in Oklahoma." *Chronicles of Oklahoma* (December 1939), pp. 364-92.

———. "Quaker Control of the Kiowa–Comanche Agency." M.A. thesis, University of Oklahoma, 1938.

———. "Lawrie Tatum's Indian Policy." *Chronicles of Oklahoma* (Spring 1944), pp. 83-98.

Tatum, Lawrie. *Our Red Brothers*. Foreword by Richard N. Ellis. Lincoln: University of Nebraska Press, 1970.

Taylor, Joe F., ed. "The Indian Campaign on the Staked Plains, 1874-1875." *Panhandle-Plains Historical Review* 34 (1961), 35 (1962).

Temple, Frank M. "Colonel Grierson in the Southwest." *Panhandle-Plains Historical Review* 30 (1957): 27-54.

Tilghman, Zoe A. *Quanah, The Eagle of the Comanches*. Oklahoma City: Harlow, 1938.

Tyler, Ronnie. "Quanah Parker's Narrow Escape." *Chronicles of Oklahoma* (Summer 1968), pp. 182-88.

Unrau, William E. "Indian Agent vs. the Army: Some Background Notes on the Kiowa-Comanche Treaty of 1865." *Kansas Historical Quarterly* (Summer 1964), pp. 129-52.

———. "Investigation or Probity? Investigations Into the Affairs of the Kiowa-Comanche Indian Agency, 1867." *Chronicles of Oklahoma* (Autumn 1964), pp. 300-19.

Utley, Robert M. *Frontiersmen in Blue.* New York, Macmillan, 1967.

Wallace, Ernest. "The Comanches On the White Man's Road." *West Texas Historical Association Yearbook* (October 1953), pp. 3-32.

———. *Ranald S. Mackenzie on the Texas Frontier.* Lubbock: West Texas Museum Association, 1967.

———, ed. *Ranald S. Mackenzie's Official Correspondence Relating to Texas, 1871-1873.* Lubbock: West Texas Museum Association, 1967.

———, and Hoebel, E. Adamson. *The Comanches.* Norman: University of Oklahoma Press, 1952.

White, E. E. *Experiences of a Special Indian Agent.* Introduction by Edward Everett Dale. Norman: University of Oklahoma Press, 1965.

Winfrey, Dorman H., and Day, James M., eds. *The Indian Papers of Texas and the Southwest.* 5 vols. Austin: Pemberton Press, 1966.

Zimmerman, Jean L. "Colonel Ranald S. Mackenzie at Fort Sill." *Chronicles of Oklahoma* (Spring 1966), pp. 12-21.

Index

Abbott, Lyman, 257
Abilene, 150, 174
Adams, A. M., 67
Adams, Charles E., 169-70, 173-74, 184, 187-92, 199, 210, 245
Adams, Zonee, 210
Addington, J. P., 181
Adobe Walls, Battle of: (*1864*), 20, 108; (*1874*), 107-08, 110
Agents: appointment of, 167-70; army officers as, 216-18; regulation of, 157-58
Aitson, Lucius, 163, 224
Allotment of land, 166, 170, 200, 201; Cherokee Commission negotiations, 203-15; children's allotments, 272, 283-85; Indian attitude toward, 201-04; after Jerome Agreement, 264-65; by lottery, 269-70; mineral claims on Indian allotments, 270; sale or lease of allotments by Indians, 286-87; size of allotments reduced, 288
Alvord, Henry E., 53, 86, 87, 89
Anadarko. *See* Kiowa, Comanche, and Wichita Agency
Annuity goods, 66-67, 75, 103, 154, 161, 195, 219
Apache John, 240, 254, 263, 289
Apaches, 9, 155, 255
Apiatan, 213, 240, 243-48, 289; and Jerome Agreement, 253-55, 260; as judge, 244-46; and opening of reservation for settlement, 262, 263
Arapahos, 12, 29, 39, 53, 54, 58, 66, 106, 107, 120, 288; cattle for, 143, 152; and Ghost Dance, 189-90; land sold to government, 204, 207,

215; at Medicine Lodge conference, 27, 29
Arkansas River, 20
Army, U.S., 2, 6, 7, 19-20, 25, 80, 108-09, 120, 121; attacks on Indians, 17, 88, 90, 104-05, 112; black troops, 141; cavalry escorts for Indians to Texas, 141-42; rations used for Indians, 125, 146; squatters evicted by, 271; and transfer of Fort Sill agency, 135-37. *See also* Campaigns against Indians
Arushe, 289
Asatoyet (Gray Leggings), 87, 98, 102, 133
Asp (lawyer), 208
Atkins, J. D. C., 194, 201
Atoka, 87
Augur, General C. C., 28, 93, 103, 109

Bailey, Joseph W., 233, 253-54, 267
Baldwin, Frank D., 218, 222-24, 230, 235, 261, 264; and Jerome Agreement, 254, 255; and land leasing, 236, 238, 240-42; traders' feud with, 242-47
Baldwin's Springs, 174
Bankers, 277
Bannocks, 145
Baptists, 230, 288
Barnum, P. T., Museum, 19
Beck, J. R., 165
Beede, Cyrus, 91, 104, 107, 109, 110, 113, 247; conferences with Indians, 86, 89, 91, 92, 95; and leasing of land to cattlemen, 238; and Quaker policy with Indians, 80, 85, 97
Big Bow, 152

325

Wichitas, 52, 58, 66, 68-69, 106, 191;
land sold to government, 204, 209
Wild Horse, 107, 116, 117, 119
Wild West Shows, Indians in, 166-67,
186
Wilson, Alfred M., 203
Woodward, Thomas, 151, 213
Works, J. S. (Buckskin Joe), 233-34

Wovoka (Jack Wilson), 189, 191, 192
Wyandots, 255
Wyatt, William, 265

Yamparikas, 14, 19, 26, 27, 44-46,
49, 51, 52, 55, 71, 78, 86, 89, 109,
127, 133